*The Scarlet*

A Journey to Encounter Jesus
in the Old Testament


(with Bible Study Guides)


Eleanor P. Hamilton

# The Scarlet Thread

Cover design: Christopher J. Pennington

Unless otherwise noted, all scripture quotations are from *New American Standard Bible*, © 1960, 1962, 1963, 1968, 1971, 1972, 1973,1975, 1977, 1995 by The Lockman Foundation, and are used by permission. (www.Lockman.org)

*The Scarlet Thread*
Copyright © 2017 by Eleanor P. Hamilton
Autumn Light Publications, www.autumnlight.net
Columbia, MD 21044
978-0-9849797-9-0

*Like the contents of* The Scarlet Thread, *its completion and publication was a journey. I am particularly grateful to a small group of cherished sisters-in-Christ for urging me to finish my own journey and for allowing me the opportunity to share it with them. To Debbie, Linda, Connie, Lisa, Hannah, Wilma, and Marilyn— Thank you!*

# The Scarlet Thread

# Table of Contents

# Beginning the Journey

## *Background*

Long, long ago I remember reading through the Old Testament and encountering stories, circumstances, or even just familiar phrases that would suddenly bring Jesus to my mind, even though the words I read were written a thousand years before Jesus was born in Bethlehem. At some point I recall an opinion forming in my mind that every book of the Old Testament provides something in it that points to Jesus. I came to believe that if I looked closely I could find *Jesus* in every book of the Bible—not just figuratively because, after all, the purpose of the Bible is to show us Jesus. Rather, I came to believe that Jesus, physically or conceptually, frequently stepped directly into the pages of the Old Testament. I told myself that *someday* I would test my theory.

I came to think of this idea as *The Scarlet Thread*, referring of course to the blood of Jesus that purchased redemption for all of mankind, a redemption that was conceived before the foundations of the earth were established and continued as a plan throughout the generations of mankind. Whenever I thought or spoke of it, I would visualize a single red thread weaving itself through the massive tapestry of mankind's existence.

Years passed—even decades. Many times I remembered my promise to myself, but continued to delay. Then several years ago I began to feel the prompting of the Spirit to follow through on my promise. I don't believe the prompting came because there was need for proof of my theory, for over the years many writers of religious resources have touched on this very idea. Instead, I believe the call to begin was more an invitation from Jesus to journey through the Scriptures with Him—a journey He began to prepare for me all those years ago.

So the question for this study is: Can we find Jesus in every book of the Bible. More particularly, can we find Him in every book of the Old Testament, for of course there is no doubt that Jesus and His teachings appear in the twenty-seven books of the New

1

Testament? So, I began reading Old Testament books in simple narrative until I encountered *something* that brought the name or image of Jesus to my mind.

To a great extent, beyond the search for specific written evidence of the foreshadowing of the Christ, *The Scarlet Thread* is a personal journey, a walk through the pages of the Old Testament, prayerfully seeking occasions to stop and meet with Jesus along the way.

## *Understanding why I believe in my theory*

As I began this project, I reconsidered just why I instinctively believe that God wove an image of Jesus into the fabric of the Old Testament, and the following picture came to mind. I looked back, beyond when Jesus walked the earth, beyond when Jehovah set His mark upon Israel, even beyond the first "In the beginning." Though time did not exist before the world was created, for eternity had no need for a concept of time, I tried to imagine that period of existence before *the beginning*.

In those *moments* (for lack of a better word)—in those *moments* before God spoke the world into existence, the unchangeable God was there—God, who would later for our benefit describe Himself in ways that man would try to quantify and describe through the term *trinity*. Though our finite minds struggle with the concept of the trinity, we cannot escape the reality that Jehovah God chose to use a "we "in creation. Jesus, by His own declaration, participated in that divine act, not as a helper or a piece of God, but as God.

I imagined God, on the brink of creation, knowing that the creatures He would name *man* would only be in fellowship with Him for a short time, knowing they would either have to be given a divine Savior or else they would be forever separated from Him because of sin. God *knew* and still He created mankind. In that instant before He breathed life into man, He was already fully aware that one day He would have to set aside the glories of heaven to become one of them—fully human, even while He was still fully God.

2

As I look at this image in my mind, I cannot think otherwise than to believe that while He planned the path to salvation He would also provide the means for mankind to recognize Him when He came. That is why my heart tells me that every book of the Old Testament would have a part in the whole Bible's purpose—to point the way to the Messiah.

## *Purpose of* The Scarlet Thread

The initial purpose of *The Scarlet Thread* was simply to verify, for my own satisfaction, that Jesus can indeed be found in every book of the Old Testament.

As I approached the journey, I immediately realized that hindsight (the fact that I have experienced a relationship with Jesus for many more than 50 years) could easily highlight words, phrases, passages, circumstances, or concepts for me. Thus in those treasured pages I fully expected to find two intertwining paths, one that would show me how God wove into the fabric of the Written Word a picture of the one who would one day come to save the world and one that would use those same pictures to speak personal messages to those who would one day call Him Lord.

Thus the purpose of *The Scarlet Thread* is more than just verifying His presence in the Old Testament. It is a reminder that Jesus truly does delight in encountering His followers in the pages of Scripture. My prayer is that all who choose to read this text will also choose to take a similar journey to simply encounter Jesus through the pages of the Old Testament.

## *Unraveling the Scarlet Thread*

As I began my search for the *scarlet thread* that weaves itself through the Bible, I attempted to set aside any pre-conceived notions of what I would find. I simply read the books, chapter by chapter, verse by verse, marking each verse or passage that brought *Jesus* into my mind. Sometimes, I would pause and contemplate what it was that caused my heart and mind to see

# The Scarlet Thread

Jesus there but mostly, for the first part of my journey, I merely set markers to identify those places to which I would return at a time when I could visit with my Lord and allow His Spirit to fill my heart with greater understanding.

After all the verses were collected, I reviewed them and analyzed my findings. First, I verified that every book of the Old Testament was indeed represented. Second, I attempted to organize the verses into categories, creating groupings of similar terms or concepts that, taken together, seemed to build a multitude of welcoming retreats that each promised to wait for my return.

Third, I returned to each of those precious retreats. I wandered through the passages of Scripture, pausing for a few moments at some of the verses that called to me, pausing to be deeply absorbed by others. At each stop, I waited patiently to meet with Jesus. Sometimes His Spirit directed me to other Scriptures, sometimes to some outside resources, sometimes to memories of lessons I had learned in the past. And sometimes—sometimes, He drew me deep inside Himself to experience a relationship with Him too sweet to describe.

As I look back on the task that I had set forth for myself, I reflect on the original premise—I have proven that premise to my satisfaction; but, more than that, I shared an incredible journey with Jesus—one that, if you will forgive the ramblings of a heart filled with the wonder of such an experience, I would be honored to share with you now.

# I.     Pre-incarnate Christ

## *Defining the category*

By definition, *pre-incarnate* refers to having existence before incarnation; it asserts that Jesus existed before His conception and further suggests that in that time before He came to the earth as a baby, He interacted with the world He created.

Bible scholars and theologians frequently refer to *theophany.* From the Greek word *phaino* (meaning *appear)* taken in conjunction with *theos* (meaning God), theophany literally means *appearances of God.* More commonly, such appearances refer to the pre-incarnate Christ—the presence of Jesus in the world before He physically became Jesus.

Before using references to the pre-incarnate Christ as evidence of the presence of Jesus in the Old Testament, it must first be determined if Scripture does indeed record such evidence. As I conducted my personal (certainly not exhaustive) study of this matter, I discovered the following:

1. Many writers convincingly argue that there is an abundance of instances in the Old Testament where God *came down* to walk upon the earth in physical form. (The idea of equating *the angel of the Lord* in many Old Testament passages with the pre-incarnate Christ dates all the way back to the writings of some of the early church fathers, such as Justin Martyr and Tertullian. Since the Hebrew word used in these references means *messenger* and the Greek word for angel also meant *messenger,* it was easy to see *the angel of the Lord,* the *messenger of the Lord,* as God Himself.)

2. Other writers argue that those instances that appear to refer to the bodily appearance of God are as easily explained in a different way. (It appears that the first efforts to counter the idea put forth by some of the early church fathers evolved from use of Latin text, where the

---

Greek word that meant messenger became *angel* or *angelic being*, which would imply a lower being. Thus some church leaders of that era feared that to equate the *angel of the Lord* with the pre-incarnate Christ would lead to an Arian view (founded by Arius, 250-336 AD), which believed that Jesus was a subordinate entity to God the Father.)

3. While writers that argue the case for pre-incarnate appearances would produce lists that are mostly the same, there is not always agreement as to whether some specific occurrences are, or are not, a pre-incarnate appearance of the Son of God.

I considered these facts:

1. Though the record of the physical person we call *Jesus* began in Bethlehem a little more than two thousand years ago, Scripture tells us that Jesus, the Son of God, *is, was, and always will be*. In John 8:58 Jesus spelled out this fact when He said, "Before Abraham was born, I am." The Jews of that day immediately understood that Jesus was claiming not only to have existed before Abraham, but to actually *be* God. This pre-existence naturally presumes at least the possibility that Jesus, the second *person* of God, could at some point, or points, have chosen to interact with mankind in a physical manner.

2. The most common description of the pre-incarnate Christ is *the angel of the LORD*. Just as Jesus repeatedly remarks that He was "sent by God" or "sent by the Father," references to the *angel of the Lord* in the Old Testament generally specify, or at least allude to, the fact that this *angel* was sent by God—sent for a specific purpose. The similarity in the purposes for which *the angel of the LORD* and *Jesus* were sent also suggests the possibility that they could be one and the same. Purposes include intercession, revealing truth, comforting the weak or down-trodden, delivering from bondage, judging sin, etc.

3.  After Jesus is born, becoming God incarnate, references to *the angel of the LORD* cease. There are references to angels in the New Testament, but never to *the angel of the LORD*.

For the purposes of this study, I have chosen to include this category because I am convinced by the Biblical studies surrounding that point of view and because I personally *see* Jesus in these instances. However, while I accept most of the references generally labeled as a pre-incarnate appearance of Christ as accurate interpretations of Bible passages, I believe the concept has sometimes been stretched to include more incidents than it should.

## *Overview of pre-incarnate passages*

Usually, but not always, passages describing the pre-incarnate Christ refer to *the angel of the Lord*, not to be confused with *an angel of the Lord*. (*My angel, the angel of God*, and *the angel of His presence* are also used.) *The angel of the Lord* appeared to Hagar (Genesis 16:7-14), to Abraham (Genesis 22:11-13) to Balaam (Numbers 22:22-35), to Gideon (Judges 6:11-27), and to Manoah and his wife (Judges 13:3-23).

It is the characteristics that are attributed to *the angel of the Lord* that suggests that Scripture is indeed referring to Christ—the second *person* of God. In Exodus 3:6, the *angel of the Lord* claimed to be God. Judges 6:16 and Zechariah 12:8-9 specifically identify *the angel* as God. Gideon (Judges 6:22) and Manoah (Judges 13:22) both thought that they would die because they had seen him (the angel) face to face. The angel is called *wonderful* in Judges 13:18 and in other references accepted the worship of men (something an angel would never do). *The angel* is also attributed with prophesying and doing great miracles and in several instances promised to accomplish what only God could do (Genesis 21:18, 22:17; Exodus 3:8).

Other occurrences of the pre-incarnate Christ, when He is not referred to as *the angel of the Lord*, include Genesis 32:24-32 when He wrestled with Jacob and Joshua 5:13-15 when He met

Joshua near Jericho. Though often omitted from list of incidences of the pre-incarnate Christ, references to times that "God came down to earth" could also refer to a pre-incarnate appearance of Christ—as in Genesis 11:5 and Exodus 19:20. Some scholars have suggested that perhaps the first such encounter is related in Genesis 3:8, when Adam and Eve heard the sound of the Lord God walking in the garden.

As a point of caution, I would suggest that we must always be careful that we don't attribute the status of pre-incarnate Christ too quickly as we read the Scriptures, for certainly not every angel and not every miracle-worker was God in the form of man. One notable example is Melchizedek, Priest and King of Salem. Little is known of this person and, perhaps because of the mystery surrounding him, many people who study the Scriptures have provided convincing evidence that Melchizedek was another incidence of the pre-incarnate Christ. On the other hand, other notable scholars provide equally convincing evidence that Melchizedek was not the pre-incarnate Christ. Some rabbinic literature suggests that Melchizedek was actually Shem, son of Noah, who lived to be at least 602 years old according to Genesis 11:10-11. (For the record, *The Scarlet Thread* considers Melchizedek as a *type* of Christ, rather than the pre-incarnate Christ. *Types* of Christ are the subject later chapters.)

## *Specific Examples—Stops along my journey*

### *"The LORD came down...."*
Genesis 11:5—The Lord came down to see the city and the tower. Exodus 19:20—The Lord came down on Mt. Sinai and then called Moses to meet Him there.

If, as some Bible scholars teach, Genesis 11:5 and Exodus 19:20 are literal examples of the pre-incarnate Christ coming down from heaven to walk among His people, then we have to wonder what would prompt the appearance.

In Genesis 11:5 we read that mankind, not long after the flood, was already beginning to try to stretch beyond their need for their creator. In verse 4 we read that they wanted to "make a name for themselves," as though they needed an identity beyond the name God had given them, beyond the relationship they had with their creator. So, why did the Lord *come down?* He could see what was happening from heaven. He did not need to get closer to be sure of what they were doing. Perhaps this incident was like moments when we see our children making wrong choices and we want to believe it's not really as bad as it looks. Perhaps our loving Father came down to see the mess mankind was making of the world and was *hoping* that it wasn't as bad as it seemed. But it was and He made a decision to "confuse their language."

Exodus 19:20 is not really difficult to understand. God had selected the tribe, and even the family, among the race of man, through which He would eventually restore His creation. He had watched the people of Israel fall from their high place in the lands where He had sent them to become slaves in the foreign land of Egypt. He had heard the cries of the Israelites, and He had chosen Moses to lead them out of bondage. As Exodus 19 opens, God is getting ready to establish a special relationship with Israel. Exodus 19:18 describes the picture that those at the bottom of the mountain saw; it gives us a vivid image of the awesome power of God, as He tells Moses that he must warn the people that they cannot come any closer. Then, *the Lord came down to Mt. Sinai.* Jehovah God, perhaps in the pre-incarnate form of Christ, stepped out of heaven to stand upon Mt. Sinai—to have a conversation with one of His people.

As I read these two passages, two things struck me. First, what a glorious image is seen in those words! I instantly recalled the words to a chorus we used to sing in church, "heaven came down and glory filled my soul, when at the cross the Savior made me whole," (*Heaven Came Down And Glory Filled My Soul*, John W. Peterson, 1961). *Heaven came down*—God, the creator of the universe, came down to walk upon the earth He created! To visualize Jehovah God stepping down from heaven to check on His people fills me with wonder. I am amazed by His tenderness and genuine concern for mankind. Then, to make the image even more splendid, I was struck with another image as well—two really—one of Jesus *coming down to earth* to be born of a virgin and another of a glorious moment when He will come down again!

### *"the angel of the LORD..."*
Genesis 16:7-14, 22:11-18; Exodus 3:2-6; Numbers 22:22-35; Judges 2:1-5, 5:23, 6:11-27, 13:2-23; II Samuel 24:15-17 (and I Chronicles 21:15-17); I Kings 19:1-8; II Kings 1:1-16; Psalm 34:7; Isaiah 37:36; Hosea 12:4-5 (explaining Genesis 32:24-32); Exodus 23:23, 32:34; Zechariah 1:7-14; Zechariah 3:1-7, 12:8

As recorded earlier in this text, most of the appearances that are considered to be examples of the pre-incarnate Christ mention *the* angel of the Lord; they also mostly refer to a physical presence that is seen. In each appearance, the angel interacts with mankind to comfort or heal, to prophesy or bless, to judge or even to curse the people. Scripture sometimes, but not always, specifically names the angel of the Lord as *the Lord*.

Whether because I recognize the angel of the Lord as the pre-incarnate Christ or I merely see in the description the same characteristics I find attributed to Jesus later, I found that most of these passages brought very clear pictures of Jesus to my mind. Below, I have chosen to comment on some of the appearances that poignantly caused me to pause in my journey through the Old Testament. Though I have not elaborated on every reference in the list above, I encourage you to study all of them.

### Hagar
Genesis 16: 7-14, 21:17

Verse 7 says that the angel of the Lord found her (Hagar). How like our Lord! (Luke 19:10 records that the Son of Man came to seek and to save that which was lost.)

The angel of the Lord found Hagar because He was looking for her. There is no suggestion that Hagar was looking for Him; she was just running away. Even though she must have been aware of the God of Abraham, until this incident Hagar did not consider the possibility that He would care about her, too. But God did not wait for her to seek Him; He went in search of her. He does the same for us—He does not require that we lift ourselves up to some higher level to reach him, but rather He comes to us and lifts us up to meet Him.

The verse goes on to say that the angel promised to make a great people of her descendants (a promise only God could keep). In verse 13 Hagar called the angel "a God who sees" and is amazed that she is still alive after seeing Him.

The angel of God spoke to Hagar again later, when Hagar's son was a young man and Sarah had finally had a son of her own. Sarah insisted that Abraham send Hagar and Ishmael away. The two headed out into the wilderness of Beersheba and were soon out of water and out of hope. Hagar settled her son in a clump of bushes and then waited to die, apparently forgetting that the angel of the Lord had promised to make a great nation from her son. But He did not forget. Thus the angel of God, hearing the cries of the child, called down to Hagar. Again, He calmed her fears and repeated His promise.

**Abraham and Isaac**
Genesis 22:11-18

In this passage the pre-incarnate Christ did not actually come down to earth. Abraham did not see Him, but he definitely heard Him, and because he immediately understood that God was speaking to him, he stopped before harming Isaac.

We know that *the angel* was God because in verse 16 He says, "By Myself I have sworn declares the LORD," and in verses 17-18, He went on to bless Abraham and to promise that Abraham's descendants would be as numerous as the stars of the heavens and the sands of the seas.

This passage is particularly interesting if we take a moment to contemplate the picture that is unfolding. Scripture says that *the angel of the Lord* spoke to Abraham. The pre-incarnate Christ, looked down upon Abraham, who is about to sacrifice his only son. I can't help but wonder if, in that moment, He thought about the day that would come, far in the future of mankind, when *He* would be the *only Son* that was about to be sacrificed—and the sacrifice would not, could not, be stopped.

**Moses**
Exodus 3:2-6

The second chapter of Exodus provides us a dynamic picture of *the angel of the Lord*. Verse 2 records, "The angel of the LORD appeared to him [Moses] in a blazing fire from the midst of a bush" and verse 6 relates that the angel spoke and said, "I am the God of your father." With such wording, there is no doubt in my mind that this angel *is* the Lord God, Almighty Yahweh. What we are not given in this text is a description of the appearance of the angel; we don't know if Moses saw the physical form of a man or some wisp-like composition of light and fire. We know only that the angel appeared through the burning bush and that His image was such that Moses hid his face because he was afraid to look at God. As I think on this passage, the story of the Hebrew children in the fiery furnace comes to mind. When I recall the fourth person in the furnace (Daniel 3:24-25) it is not difficult to believe that Moses did indeed see the form of a man standing within the raging fires of that mountain bush.

What an awesome moment that must have been! There is something about a blazing fire that commands instant attention and respect. Coupled with the supernatural failure of the bush (or the angel of the Lord) to be consumed, it would truly have etched a mark upon the heart and mind of Moses.

Before leaving this stop on my journey another thought came to mind as well, one of a dimly lit room full of timid followers of a recently-resurrected Messiah. When I recall that the Holy Spirit came upon the disciples on the Day of Pentecost as tongues of fire (Acts 2:3), I immediately make the connection between the burning bush that did not burn and the tongues of fire that rested upon the disciples, but did not burn or consume them. In a moment of amusement, I wonder if Jehovah God deliberately began both the first steps of releasing His chosen people from bondage to Egypt and the first steps of releasing the church to spread the message of redemption to the world by coming to His servants in the guise of fire.

## Balaam
Numbers 22:22-35

The familiar story of the talking donkey brings back memories of childhood Sunday School classes. It always had the makings for a very dramatic lesson—the villain (selfish oppressor if not actually an evil villain), the weak victim (not exactly a "damsel in distress" but at least a creature oppressed and mistreated for no good reason), and of course, the avenging hero (even if He couldn't be seen). Somehow, as I remember the story, I think it was always the donkey that stood out—after all, it's not every day that you meet a talking donkey.

Balaam was a sorcerer of some sort, who apparently hired himself out for profit. He had a reputation for success, for Balak said that he knew that those whom Balaam blessed would be blessed and those whom he cursed would be cursed. He was not an Israelite, but he was evidently aware of the power of Yahweh and, on the surface at least, claimed to answer to Him. Little is actually recorded about him in the Scripture beyond this particular story, but we are told that he was later involved in some way with attempts to turn the Israelites to idolatry. Peter, in II Peter 2:15, refers to those who had gone astray as "having followed the way of Balaam, the son of Beor, who loved the wages of unrighteousness."

As I look closely at the story, I am struck by the fact that God was angry because he (Balaam) was going to Moab to meet with Balak. Initially, I am confused for God had after all given Balaam permission to go (Numbers 22:20). Then I recall that the messengers, offering great bounty, were turned away the first time—because God told Balaam not to go. Then, when Balak sent a second group (more numerous and more influential) to ask him to come and curse the Israelites, instead of sending them away immediately, Balaam let them stay the night, saying he would find out if God would tell him more—as if he expected the Lord to change His mind. Perhaps at that point, knowing Balaam's heart,

God gave him over to his low character and told him to go—with the warning that he was to say *only* what God told him to say.

Just how trustworthy Balaam's intentions were, I wonder. Would he, once standing there beside Balak and his army, truly deliver the blessing of God, instead of the curses he was being paid to pronounce? Perhaps that is why the *angel of the Lord* stepped down to earth to block his path. In fact, verse 32 records the words of the *angel of the Lord*: "Behold, I have come out as an adversary, because your way was contrary to me." He even tells Balaam in verse 33, "If she [the donkey] had not turned aside from me, I would surely have killed you just now, and let her live."

God knew that once he got to Moab, Balaam was likely to follow his own plan rather than God's; so, He dramatically confronted Balaam and would have killed him if the episode had not ended as it did.

Another thought occurred to me as I read this passage. Buried within the words of the *angel of the Lord*, I noticed that Balaam struck the donkey three times—that simple number that seems to litter the pages of the Scriptures and makes one stop to ask if there is some significance. In this instance, the donkey was struck three times because it turned off the path to avoid the angel of the Lord three times. There is probably no particular significance; still, the striking of the one that was saving his life somehow seems to whisper some kind of underlying foreshadowing to me. I also find it very interesting that the Lord in essence was asking Balaam three times if he would obey the instructions he had been given, just as many centuries later He asked Peter three times if he loved Him enough to obey His command to *tend His sheep* (John 21: 15-17).

**Gideon**
Judges 6:11-27

The story of Gideon begins at a turn in the road of history. The Israelites have been under the thumb of the Midianites for seven years because they had been disobedient to God—not for the first time. Then, God hears the cries of His people and once again walks into the scene. Verse 11 says, "the angel of the LORD came and sat under the oak." Without fanfare or advance notice, God (the pre-incarnate Christ) comes and sits under a tree to talk to Gideon. He allows Gideon to complain that God has abandoned them, and even allows Gideon to test Him. At last Gideon follows the directions of *the angel of the LORD* and Israel is freed from the Midianites.

This appearance is so characteristic of God. *The angel of the Lord* was (and is) the creator of the world, the One who brought the Israelites through the wilderness and gave them the Promised Land, but He chose to appear as a simple traveler. There is an interesting change in the Scripture between verse 13 and verse 15. In verse 13 Gideon says, "O my lord, if the LORD," suggesting that he does not recognize that the person to whom he is speaking is actually *the Lord*. Then in verse 15 he says, "O Lord, how shall I deliver Israel." What happened? The answer, I think, lies in verse 14: "The LORD looked at him and said, 'Have I not sent you,'" Was it the look or the words? It could have been both, but I wonder if that moment when the Lord looked at Gideon, his eyes were opened and he just knew that this was the God of Moses, who had led the people out of Egypt.

I think there is a lot communicated by just a look and I think that particular look told Gideon that his Lord understood that he was weary, discouraged, and scared. I think it told Gideon that all of that could change, because He was there.

For a moment, I find myself thinking of another story of a stranger who stepped into the path of a couple of weary, discouraged men. After the disappointing death of one they thought would redeem Israel, two men traveled home to Emmaus, only to be joined in their journey by the very one that they mourned (Luke 24:13-31). As He had done with Gideon, the Lord allowed the men to pour out their hurt and confusion; He allowed them to question why God would allow such a thing to happen. Only then were their eyes opened and they understood who it was that traveled with them.

# The Scarlet Thread

## Manoah and his wife (Samson's parents)
Judges 13:2-23

Samson is one of the larger than life characters that we find in the pages of the Bible. Even those who have read little of its words generally know the story of Samson and Delilah. His name carries with it both a brilliant image of power and strength and the shadow of defeat and failure. In the epic tale that chronicled his wondrous deeds of great strength, his foolishness in trusting Delilah, and his final moment of triumph that literally brought the house down, we often lose sight of the story of his birth.

Israel was being oppressed by the Philistines, not for the first time—or the last, and God stepped into the scene to set the stage for a new judge that would deliver Israel. He appeared to Manoah and his wife to give them specific instruction about how to raise the miracle baby they would be given.

Three things strike me as I read of the appearance of the *angel of the Lord* to Manoah and his wife. First, I see the compassion of the Lord, using one who was barren to bring about the deliverance of Israel. Taking the disgrace that a childless woman in that culture suffered and turning it into a blessing for the whole nation seems to be a recurring theme in the Scriptures, one that reminds me of God's limitless power and His equally unmatched compassion for His people.

The second thing I notice in this reference to the *angel of the Lord* is the name He gives Himself. Verse 18 records the angel's words: "Why do you ask my name, seeing it is wonderful?" (NASB) and my thoughts immediately turn to Isaiah 9:6, as I learned it as a child. The King James Bible records, "and his name shall be called Wonderful, Counselor, The mighty God, The everlasting Father, The Prince of Peace." In other translations, the comma between Wonderful and Counselor has been dropped, but I frequently wonder if, in such translations, we have lost one of the awesome names that Isaiah recorded for us. (It is interesting to note as well that in the King James Version, Judges 13:18 reads:" And the angel of the LORD said unto him, Why askest thou thus after my name, seeing it is secret?".)

Lastly, the words of this historic occasion captured my imagination and held me spellbound for many moments. Manoah, who had not been present when the angel first came to his wife, prayed for the *angel of the Lord* to come back. My first thought was *what audacity!* But then I refocused and instead saw the love and the trust in that simple man who yearned for the Lord to give him greater understanding of the task that he and his wife were being given. The awesome beauty of the picture is that God smiled down upon Manoah and answered; God, in the form of a man, came back to visit with Manoah and his wife.

In those few verses I am reminded that God does indeed delight in visiting with His children. I realize that when I study His Word—when I intensely yearn to sink deeper into His presence—He smiles down upon me and His Spirit settles in so close to me that I seem to feel the physical presence of Christ. In those moments I want to freeze time so I can hold onto the precious time with Him.

## Angel encamps around us
Psalms 34:7

"The angel of the LORD encamps around those who fear Him and rescues them." What a wonderful promise, very much like Jesus' promise in Matthew, "I am with you always!"

As I read those precious words, I get a mental image of a small campsite pitched in a valley, with darkness closing in around it. The scene appears peaceful, but in my heart I know that dangers wait just beyond the hills. As I look more closely, I become aware that the vast armies of the enemy encircle the small camp, preparing to strike. Apprehension begins to rise in me, as I consider the fate of that small band of wanderers. Into such a circumstance the words of Psalms 34:7 echoes and I see the presence of *the angel of Lord* revealed. There, standing between the enemy and the small band of wanderers, I see God with His mighty arms wrapped around *those who fear Him.*

*"Those who fear Him"* refers to all those who stand in awe of His great power—those, like me, who recognize Him as the Mighty God, the All-powerful One, and claim His protection. In all the

fearful circumstances I encounter, it is very comforting to know that the pre-incarnate Christ whispered through the psalmist the same promise He later spoke through the gospels—"I am present with you."

### "*my angel ...*"
Exodus 23:23, 32:34

Both of these verses use the phrase "my angel will go before you." *My angel* is interpreted in the same manner as *the angel of the Lord*. In both verses Israel is heading off into the wilderness. They are being told that the angel of the Lord will go before them—He will show the way, He will protect them from harm, and He will successfully take them all the way through their journey.

In these passages, I hear the Father telling me that His Son, my Lord and Savior, will go before me. There is no place that I can go that He is not already there. I hear the words of Jesus echoing, "I go to prepare a place for you." (John 14:3) and I know that He will be present to lead me all the way through this life and He will be there at the end to meet me.

### "the man"
Hosea 12:4-5 (Genesis 32:24-32)

In the Genesis passage listed above, Jacob wrestles with *a man*, but through various clues we realize that it is not a man, but the Lord, the pre-incarnate Christ. Writing about Jacob's encounter with *a man*, Hosea tells us, "The LORD is His name."

# II.   Pictures of Christ in the Lives of Bible People

## *Defining the category*

*Typology*, or rather my particular modification of the study of typology, has, for more than fifty years, been a source of great pleasure. Even before I embarked on this special journey through the Scriptures, I would rejoice in moments when I would mentally see the image of Jesus overlaid on things, events, and people I encountered in the Old Testament.

Pictorial representations accounts for a large portion of the references to Jesus described in this book. It is, therefore, appropriate that some background should be laid to define what typology is and how my approach to it may fail to stay in the boundary of that definition.

Basically, typology is a study that assumes that people, objects, or circumstances in one era demonstrate a preordained, foreshadowing, or connection to later people, objects, or circumstances. As applied to the Scriptures, typology is a Bible study method that identifies specific people, objects, or circumstances in the Old Testament as being *preordained models of Jesus and/or certain characteristics about Him*. In its purest definition, the following facts must be true to consider any element (person/object/circumstance) to be a *type* of Christ:

1.  The Old Testament element must be a clearly defined representative of something that is to come. For instance, the sacrificial system of Israel clearly symbolizes the sacrifice of Jesus and His atoning work in providing redemption for man.

2.  The connection seen between the Old Testament element and the New Testament equivalent must be divinely designed. (Often, proponents of the study of typology seem to use whether or not the connection is mentioned in the New Testament as the determining factor. For

instance, though there may be common characteristics between Joseph and Jesus, Joseph would not truly be considered a type of Christ because that connection is not mentioned in the New Testament.)

3. There must be an element of prediction; the element is there for the purpose of being identified with something that is to come—again, as in the sacrificial system God gave the Israelites.

In its purest form, of course, the study of typology would seem to be quite limited. God designed certain key elements that would point to their future equivalent and the Holy Spirit revealed those types to the writers of the New Testament, who in turn provided the connection for us to find. Of course, typology is not always approached from its purest definition. Historically, perspectives have been varied.

During the Reformation period three different positions developed:

1. Some scholars continued to hold to the purer definition described previously.

2. Some scholars included any Old Testament event or person that resembled something or someone in the New Testament as being a *type*. (Some elements included by these scholars would probably be more accurately labeled as simple illustrations, or perhaps even as coincidences.)

3. Some scholars chose the middle ground, assuming more examples than considered by the purists, but attempting to avoid being too extreme in their application of types.

By the 19th century, many scholars were beginning to suggest that typology was an inferior way of studying the Scripture altogether.

Though I sometimes refer to typology when looking at the connections between an Old Testament element and its application to Jesus or His ministry, I am actually using the broader description. To me, the determining factor of whether an element in the Old Testament is a type (illustration, analogy, or picture) of Christ lies in whether I, through the prompting of the Holy Spirit, recognize Jesus in that text.

*The Scarlet Thread* simply examines specific people, objects, or circumstances, some part of which provide a picture or example of Jesus, without attempting to determine if the identification was (or was not) predetermined by the Spirit to be a type of Christ. Most, but not all, of the examples are in some manner referred to in the New Testament, though that is not the reason they are included here.

## *Overview of the selection of examples*

As I consider passages that in some way provide a picture of the coming Messiah, they generally fall into three categories. Sometimes, the passage (or verse) refers in some way to a person or group of people. In other examples, the reference may be to an object or event. In still other pictures, Christ is seen through the application of a specific title. Each of these three categories is looked at in separate chapters of this text, though it should be noted that often a passage crosses over into two, or even three, of the categories. In general, Chapter II of *The Scarlet Thread* describes pictures of Christ that are seen in people, or more specifically through certain parts of a person's life. Chapter III looks at objects in the Old Testament that project an image of Jesus and Chapter IV covers titles that, though rooted in the Old Testament, can accurately be applied to Jesus.

In identifying genuine accounts of Old Testament people who in some way illustrated or pointed to the coming Messiah, it is important to realize that casting a very broad net could produce a multitude of examples that seem to satisfy the conditions merely because they held the title of king or priest, or because some small part of their lives matched up to a detail in the life of Jesus when He walked upon the earth.

For examples in Chapter II, I have generally limited my references to people whose lives could serve as pictures of Jesus to those which prompted such an image for me. Some examples were selected because I encountered a verse that brought such an image to my mind and then worked backward to identify the specific person that had been connected to the reference. In addition, some examples were added to my list because the similarity to something in the life of Jesus had been pointed out or discovered in prior studies.

## Note: the list is not closed

It should be noted that as my journey continued through the Old Testament, I found that I encountered Jesus as I examined the lives of many of the characters mentioned in the Old Testament. However, this is certainly not an exhaustive list of such characters, for in other seasons of my life, the Holy Spirit may well reveal the image of my Lord in other Bible figures, as well.

## Note: one similarity, or a few, does not suggest the character is LIKE Christ!

Though it is obvious, or at least should be so, before looking at specific examples of individuals that showed me an Old Testament picture of Jesus, a small but very important disclaimer should be given: Just because one small glimpse into the lives of a certain individual provides a pre-birth image of the likeness of Jesus, this in no way suggests that the individual's whole life was exemplary. Indeed, if the full lifetime were examined we would find that most of the Bible characters fell far short of God's perfect plan for their lives, and the reason all such characters would fail to far short of God's perfect plan for their lives most likely lies in the fact that very little of their lives are recorded for us to study.

# Pictures of Christ in the Lives of Bible People
## *Specific Examples—Stops along my journey*

**Abel—Spilling of Innocent Blood**
Genesis 4; Matthew 23:35; Luke 11:51; Hebrews 11:4

Shepherd
Key verses: Genesis 4:2-4, 8
Abel was a keeper of flocks—a shepherd. He gave the Lord the first and the best of his flock. Genesis records that "the LORD had regard for Abel and for his offering." We are given to understand that Abel was *righteous* in that he sought always to please God. He was *innocent*, having done no wrong in the sight of God. But envy, anger, and hatred in the person of his brother Cain rose up and struck him down. In the short span of less than one man's lifetime, mankind had fallen from the perfection of creation to expulsion from the Garden of Eden, to the shedding of innocent blood.

Our Lord, too, was a shepherd who sacrificed His best—Himself. His innocent blood was also shed by men who were consumed with anger and hatred.

**Enoch—Loved by God**
Genesis 5:21-24; Hebrews 11:5; Jude 1:14

Walked with God
Key verse: Genesis 5:24

The greatest, perhaps only, fact other than genealogy that is known of Enoch is often seen first in the old trivia question about his son: *Who was the oldest man who ever lived, but died before his father?* The answer, of course, was Methuselah, who lived to be 969 years old. The explanation is found in Genesis 5:24, "Enoch walked with God; and he was not, for God took him."

The simple story of Enoch lives in at most 7 verses of Scripture. He was born. He had sons and daughters. *And he walked with God*. What a testimony! We cannot even comprehend what kind of man Enoch must have been—how different from all others that he must have been. Not since Adam had any Bible person had such a deep, personal relationship with Jehovah. Even in the scarcity of verses given to his story we are given a glimpse into the value that God places on relationship. Enoch walked with God; he shared time, he kept pace—step-by-step—walking side-by-side, day after day. The relationship between Enoch and God was so sweet that God spared Enoch the pain of physical death. Instead, He opened the doors to heaven and allowed His friend to enter into the glorious eternal dwelling.

It is not hard to see Jesus in the person of Enoch. He is an exceptional example of uprightness. The very fact that Enoch seemed to be perfectly (as much as is humanly possible) in step with God provides a small glimpse into the relationship we later see described between Jesus and the Father. Beyond that, we see the first Scriptural example of one born on earth ascending into the heavens. It can, of course, be argued that Enoch passed into heaven without dying a physical death and in that is unlike Christ, who died here on earth before ascending to return to heaven, but then we must remember that Jesus did not pass from death into heaven: He was alive when He ascended!

**Noah—Provided the Means of Salvation**
Genesis 6-9; Matthew 24:37-38; Luke 17:26-27; Hebrews 11:7; I Peter 3:20

Builder of the vehicle to save mankind
Key verses: Genesis 6:8-9; 22

The story of Noah building the ark is a familiar one. Genesis 6:8-9 gives us the first glimpse into why Noah would become great among the people of God—and why we begin early in his story to see the image of Jesus showing through. Verse 8 tells us that Noah "found favor in the eyes of the Lord," and verse 9 goes on to explain that, like Enoch, Noah "walked with God." Noah was a "righteous man, blameless in his time."

The descriptions in Genesis 6:8-9 alone cause me to pause in my journey to search for Jesus in the Old Testament, for it is rare that any among the race of man can be of such high integrity that they could be said to "walk with God," but my journey does not end there, but continues on to verse 22 where the Bible records that Noah "did according to all that God commanded him." In the next three chapters Noah's story unfolds to explain that he came to recognize his part in the plan that God designed to save a remnant of mankind. He accepted his part without objection— building the vehicle that God would use to save those who would enter into it.

Thus, in Noah I clearly see a *type* of Christ—a picture of the one who would accept without objection His role in Almighty God's plan to save all those who would choose to enter into the salvation of the Lord. In Christ I see not the one who would *build* the vehicle that would save the world, but the one who would *become* the instrument that would make salvation possible.

## Job—The Righteous Sufferer
The book of Job; James 5:11

<u>Blameless and upright</u>
Key verses: Job 1:1, 8

Little is known for sure regarding the timeframe in which the book of Job was written or who authored the book, but of the righteousness and integrity of the title character there is no doubt. Job 1:1 describes Job as "blameless, upright, fearing God and turning away from evil." Job was a righteous man, but in the entire 42 chapters of the book we witness the suffering that comes to him, merely because Satan wants to prove that God is mistaken about Job's love and devotion.

Knowing that God declares that Job is righteous and blameless shines a light on this person, bringing his suffering in sharp comparison to what our hearts tell us should be the case. The suffering of this righteous man brings a disturbing sense of wrong; it fills my mind with countless unexplainable questions.

Then, even as I struggle with the message of the book of Job, my heart brings me to a pause in my journey. And in that moment I leave the pages of the Job and remember that the Righteous

One—the Perfect One—also suffered. He was mocked and scorned; He was criticized and misunderstood.

## Melchizedek—Both King and Priest
Genesis 14:17-24; Hebrews 5:6, 10; 6:20; 7:1, 10, 17

Priest and King
Key verse: Genesis 14:18

Before Israel was a tribe, before Moses and Aaron brought the Israelites out of bondage to Egypt, before the priesthood of the Levites was established, and long before Israel cried out to have a king, there existed one man who was both king of what would one day be Jerusalem and priest of God Most High. That king/priest was called Melchizedek. Scripture does not give details about Melchizedek's territory, nor does it mention how he came to serve Jehovah God. All that we are told is that Abraham, after doing battle to rescue Lot, encountered Melchizedek, king of Salem.

As mentioned in the prior chapter, *The Pre-Incarnate Christ*, the mystery surrounding Melchizedek has caused many people who study the Scriptures to draw the conclusion that he was actually the pre-incarnate Christ. However, there is nothing in the verses surrounding the story of Melchizedek that suggests he is anything but a human being. In addition, New Testament references never so much as hint that Jesus is a priest of "the order of Melchizedek" (Hebrews 7:17) because he *was* Melchizedek. Thus, noting the unique dual role of priest and king, *The Scarlet Thread* considers Melchizedek as a type of Christ, rather than the pre-incarnate Christ.

Even before the sacrificial system was put in place and before Israel asked for a king, God identified that the Levites would be the line of priests and that Judah would become the line of kings for Israel. The two roles were distinctly separated, thus making prophesies ascribing both offices to the anointed one all the more impossible to be filled by a mere man. Thus, in this king/priest that appears so briefly in the Old Testament I clearly see the image of Jesus, a foreshadowing of the Messiah who would be both our High Priest and the King of Kings.

## Isaac—The Sacrifice
Genesis 17-28; Romans 9:7; Galatians 4:28; Hebrews 11:17

Foreshadowing of sacrifice
Key verses: Genesis 22:6-13

In the story detailing God's command to Abraham to sacrifice his son, it is generally Abraham who is the primary character: the one who loved God so much he was willing to do the unthinkable, the one who had to make the gut-wrenching decision to obey, the one whose absolute, unwavering trust in Jehovah earned him a place in the Hebrews Hall of Faith.

God called Abraham to go to the land of Moriah, to a particular mountain. There on the place where God directed, Abraham built an altar. He laid the wood upon the altar and he prepared to sacrifice his only son. We know the story: *the angel of the Lord*—the pre-incarnate Christ—stopped Abraham before he could carry out the sacrifice.

Yet as I look at the story of Abraham's faith, it is because of *Isaac* that I pause here in my journey, looking upon this primitive scene and gazing into the face of Jesus.

Isaac was the *only* son. Isaac was the *hope of Israel*, though Israel had not yet been established. Isaac was the *bearer* of the means of his own death, for he carried the wood for the sacrifice, just as Jesus many centuries later was told to do. Isaac was the willing sacrifice—old enough to fight his father when he realized Abraham's intent, perhaps strong enough to have been able to overpower him easily.

On that day, Isaac climbed the very hill in the land of Moriah that would one day become the center of all of Israel's sacrifices—the hill that would one day overlook another hill, called Golgotha—and he allowed himself to be bound and placed upon the altar. On that day Isaac painted a picture for generations of Bible readers to see—a picture of the price that would one day be required of God in order to redeem mankind.

As a side note: The religious world is filled with debates regarding the exact location of where Biblical stories may have occurred, especially those that involve key episodes in the life of Jesus. I find these debates fascinating, and sometimes attempt to sift through the chains of evidence that are given on both sides, while firmly reminding myself that beyond acknowledging the scriptural details that are given to us, I am under no compulsion to choose a side. One such debate I have encountered questions whether the place of Jesus' sacrifice and the place where Abraham almost sacrificed Isaac are one and the same.

Scripture tells us that Abraham went to a place on Mount Moriah and built an altar to sacrifice Isaac (Genesis 22). Scripture also tells us that David purchased a threshing field on Mount Moriah and built an altar (II Samuel 24). It was David's desire to build a temple to the Lord on that land, which was north of what had become known as the City of David; but it was Solomon who actually built the temple in that same location that David had chosen. Scripture also tells us that Zerubbabel's temple (also called Herod's temple) was built in that same location. If the temple was on Mount Moriah, where David had purchased the threshing floor and if this is the same location where Abraham's altar was built, it is not possible that Golgotha, where Jesus was crucified, could be the same location because the temple was standing there at the time.

Where then is the debate? As it happens, we must remember that not everything that happens *on Mount Moriah* has to happen at the same spot on the mountain. A look at the geography of Israel shows us that Mount Moriah is on three levels. As you approach it from the South, you first reach a lower ridge, which was the territory of Melchizedek in Abraham's time and later was conquered by David and became the City of David (Jerusalem). Above that level is another, where the threshing floor would have been in David's time. That became the Temple Mount, the place of Solomon's Temple. Farther to the north is a higher peak, one that in the time of Christ *may have been* the place called Golgotha.

Therein lies the debates concerning whether Jesus was crucified on the site of Abraham's altar (a detail we cannot possibly be sure of) or if, instead He was crucified at a place where He could look across to where that foreshadowing episode would have occurred. The entire area is referred to as Mount Moriah. The opposing views come down to whether Abraham prepared to sacrifice Isaac at the middle height—the place where the Temple later stood—or if he perhaps left his servants at that height and climbed higher and farther north to a different part of Mount Moriah that may, or may not, have been the place of the crucifixion.

For what it's worth, Jewish teachings have always held that the first and second temples were built on the spot where Abraham prepared to offer Isaac as a sacrifice to God. This is the location where God told Abraham to go and where He appeared to David in the threshing field; it is the place that God chose for Himself and thus is considered to be the holiest of all earthly places.

For the record, *The Scarlet Thread* assumes the position that the near-sacrifice of Isaac, the location of the temples, and the crucifixion all occurred on Mount Moriah, but not all in the same spot. I accept the position that Solomon built his temple on the place where Abraham obediently offered up his son to God, and thus the crucifixion occurred on a spot removed from that location.

# The Scarlet Thread

## Moses—Redeemer of the people, Mediator between God and man

Exodus 2-40, Leviticus, Numbers, Deuteronomy, multiple references in the New Testament, including Hebrews 11:23

<u>General parallels</u>

Moses is probably one of the two purest of examples of *types* of Christ found in the Old Testament. *Incidental* similarities between Moses and Jesus abound:

> • Moses left the wealth and riches of Pharaoh's palace to live among God's people; Jesus left the glories and riches of heaven to live among man, whom God sought to reclaim.
> • At birth, an edict from the highest authority of the respective lands threatened to end the lives of both Moses and Jesus.
> • Both Moses and Jesus were called *shepherds*.
> • Moses led the twelve tribes of Israel out of Egypt and prepared them to enter the Promised Land; Jesus led twelve disciples and prepared them to lead all of humanity to the One who could take them to the true Promised Land.

<u>Called to lead</u>
Key verses: Exodus 3:2-8

The role of Moses in which the image of Jesus is most clearly found spans a large portion of Moses' lifetime. In Exodus 3:2-8 we witness the point when God calls Moses to be His instrument in leading Israel out of the bondage of Egypt. Moses is commissioned to redeem God's chosen people, to bring about their release and to then lead them to the land God had prepared for them. In the mission itself we recognize the picture of Jesus, who was sent to earth to redeem all mankind and to bring them back into relationship with God.

# Pictures of Christ in the Lives of Bible People

<u>Judge of the people</u>
Key verses: Exodus 18:13-16

Early in their sojourn, Moses alone sat as judge for the people of Israel. In Chapter 18 we read that people would stand from morning to evening to have him hear their disputes. When Jethro, Moses' father-in-law, asked him about it, Moses answered, "the people come to me to inquire of God." In this we see not only the role of judge that pictures the coming Messiah, but the relationship between Moses and God, that he could speak to God and receive wisdom to settle the people's disputes—a relationship much like that between Jesus and the Father.

<u>Mediator between God and Man</u>
Key verse: Exodus 20:19

We looked earlier at Exodus 20:18-21, regarding God calling Moses up to Mt. Sinai to speak with him. Here we pause to make mention of verse 19. The people understood the *holiness* of Jehovah; they feared any direct contact with the thunder and lightning they saw upon the mountain. Instead, they chose to rely on Moses as their Mediator, saying, "Speak to us yourself and we will listen; but let not God speak to us." Thus we see that early in his leading of the tribes of Israel, Moses was established as the mediator, just as Jesus continues to be our Mediator.

In that role, Moses explained the law, setting the sacrificial system with all its regulations and practices in place. For that reason God's laws came to be known as the Law of Moses, and we see in him the picture of the time when *the Law* would find its fulfillment in the Anointed One, the Messiah.

## Boaz—Kinsman-Redeemer
Ruth; Matthew 1:5; Luke 3:32

<u>Right to redeem</u>
Key verses: Ruth 4:3-6

According to the laws of the Pentateuch, a kinsman—the closest male relative—was to help a fellow Israelite in poverty who was unable to redeem their inheritance or redeem that relative from a self-imposed slavery brought about by the need to pay a debt. In addition, that kinsman had the privilege (or the responsibility) of preserving the family line for a deceased male relative. That closest relative was called the *kinsman-redeemer* and he was the only person who had the right to perform those acts.

In the book of Ruth, we see this condition played out. Because a famine gripped the land of Judah, Naomi and her husband Elimelek left Bethlehem and lived for a while in Moab. Both sons grew to manhood and married Moabite women. Since Naomi's husband and both her sons had died during their years away, Naomi and Ruth (Mahlon's widow) returned to Bethlehem with no one to look after them. The land that Elimelek had before they left could be bought back by the kinsman-redeemer, but the transaction carried with it the responsibility to marry Ruth to preserve the line of Mahlon and Elimelek.

Though he was not Naomi's closest relative Boaz stands as the key example of that Israelite custom that God set in place long before he was born. In a shrewd move Boaz called upon the true kinsman-redeemer—the closest relative—to either do his duty or pass on that right to him. Boaz then redeemed Elimelek's land and family when he married Ruth.

The key concept to the custom of the kinsman-redeemer lies in the fact that the redeemer must be of that family line. It is a principle that we see ultimately played out when Jesus, a true son of *man*, is able to redeem the souls of all mankind because it is His physical birthright to do so.

### David—Shepherd King
I Samuel 16-30; II Samuel 1-24; I Kings 1-2; Matthew 1:6; Acts 7:46; Hebrews 11:32

General parallels

David is the second of the two purest of examples of *types* of Christ found in the Old Testament. Not only are there *incidental* similarities between David and Jesus, but Scripture repeatedly

Pictures of Christ in the Lives of Bible People

connects the two as it emphasizes God's promise that the throne of David would never end and identifies Jesus as the answer to that promise.

Some of the *incidental* similarities include:

- Both were born in Bethlehem.
- David was directly appointed by God—named to be the King of Israel, as Jesus was appointed by God to be the King of all kings.
- David was a shepherd before he was a king; Jesus came as our Good Shepherd and will come again to reign as King of Kings.
- Before he could accomplish the purpose God assigned him (to be king of Israel), the authorities (Saul and his supporters) repeatedly tried to kill him. Likewise, the religious leaders sought to destroy Jesus before He could accomplish the purpose for which He came to earth.
- Both David and Jesus were fully aware of the plots to kill them. David was betrayed by his counselor, Ahithophel (II Samuel 15-17); Jesus was betrayed by His friend, Judas.

The Biblical account of David spans the entire books of I and II Samuel, and finishes in the early part of I Kings, when he names his successor. Within those pages there could be many stops in our journey to see Jesus in this man who became the *heart* of Israel, but those that are described below are a few of the ones that most dearly touched the heart of this writer.

Between anointing and crowning of the King
Key verses: I Samuel 16: 12-13

In I Samuel 16 we read of the anointing of David, the act that officially began the preparation period that he would go through before he would actually claim the throne.  When Samuel anointed David, 'the Spirit of the LORD came mightily upon him. " To any who know much of the New Testament, this simple statement immediately calls to mind the baptism of Jesus, when the Spirit of the LORD descended upon Him like a dove (Matthew 3:16, John 1:32).

33

# The Scarlet Thread

## Desire to build a temple
Key verses: II Samuel 7:1-16

In II Samuel 7 we find that David has come to a time of rest in his reign and has developed a yearning to provide a house for the Lord. But in verses 12-13 he is told that it is his son who will build the temple. Verse 10 emphasizes that God will Himself choose the place where Israel will reside and where the temple will be built; verse 13 records that David's son (Solomon) will build the House of the Lord. (In I Chronicles 22:1-10 we are given the reason that David would not be permitted to build the temple. David was a warrior king who had "shed much blood on earth.") Yet, buried in the talk of the temple in II Samuel, David is given the greatest promise of all: "Your house and your kingdom shall endure before Me forever; your throne shall be established forever." David's yearning to build an earthly house is met with God's promise to allow him instead to establish the eternal house—the Messiah. Even the magnificent grandeur of Solomon's temple pales in comparison to God's gift to David in that moment.

## Extending forgiveness
Key verses: II Samuel 9:1-13

After all the plots and battles planned and executed by Saul in his attempts to kill David, there came a time that David's heart was softened. He wanted a healing of sorts, a peace, a forgiveness. Because of his deep friendship with Jonathan, Saul's son, David wanted to sweep aside the anger and bitterness and do some act of kindness for the family of Saul. Thus, in Chapter 9 of II Samuel we find him asking, "Is there yet anyone left of the house of Saul, that I may show him kindness for Jonathan's sake?" In the next several verses we find that he found Mephibosheth, a crippled son of Jonathan, and brought him into the king's house for the rest of his days.

As I ponder this simple act that reminds me of the human need to feel the solace of forgiving others, I am reminded of the greatest picture of forgiveness. I hear the words, "Father, forgive them," echo from the cross, as Jesus calls on Jehovah God to forgive these miserable examples of humanity *for His sake*.

## Pictures of Christ in the Lives of Bible People

<u>Facing Goliath</u>
Key verses: I Samuel 17:32-49

At one final stop in the life of David, we witness probably one of the most familiar stories of Scripture—the triumph of David over Goliath, as found in Chapter 17 of I Samuel. This encounter would not likely be counted among pictures that would point to the coming Christ by anyone reading the Old Testament for the first time, but rather might be noticed by one who has already met the Messiah. In I Samuel 17 we learn of the great Philistine champion who comes against David. Verse 45 records David's answer to Goliath's taunting, "You come to me with a sword, a spear, and a javelin, but I come to you in the name of the LORD of hosts, the God of the armies of Israel." As he stood his ground against this fearful giant, David was not alone, for by his side stood the God of heaven and His armies. And, of course, we know the outcome.

But, on this occasion, I would suggest that we pause to look a little deeper at this scene. As I Samuel leads into the story, a feeling of dread and fear emerges in the image of Goliath. We see a monolith of a man that hides the sun and makes mortal men tremble before him. We see fear so dark, so real, that the onlooker just knows that there is no chance of escape. We see the desperate condition of mankind embodied in a giant that laughs in the face of the feeble attempts to break through the evil that has taken root. We see sin, standing as a man, before the frail body of a young man. But if we readjust our vision, we realize that the young man who is facing down the evil of humanity, the sin that has taken root in God's perfect creation, is not David, but the Son of David, the Prince of Peace. He is not standing with a small sling and a few stones; He is hanging by nails upon a crude, wooden cross. But, like David before Him, this one, lone figure brings to bear the unquenchable power of Almighty God—and sin doesn't stand a chance!

## Jeremiah—the Weeping Prophet
II Chronicles 35-36; Jeremiah; Lamentations; Matthew 2:17-18, 27:9-10

Weeping for the sins of the people
Key verses: Jeremiah 20:2; 26:7-8; 32:2, 37:15-16, 38:6

When Pashhur the priest heard Jeremiah prophesying about what the future would hold for Judah, he was angered. He had Jeremiah beaten and put into the stocks. Such was not unusual treatment for Jeremiah, for his time of prophesying was filled with mocking, murder plots, beatings, imprisonment, and even being thrown into a cistern filled with mud. It is no wonder that Jeremiah is referred to as the *weeping prophet*, for he had much reason to weep—for himself and for Jerusalem. For this reason, Jeremiah is often seen as a picture of Christ, who mourned for Jerusalem even as its citizens plotted His end.

## Jonah—Three Days in the Fish
II Kings 14:25; Jonah; Matthew 12:39-41; Luke 11: 29-32

Jonah is most commonly seen as a *type* of Christ because of his three-day experience in the belly of the great fish. Both Matthew and Luke specifically name this example as the only *sign* that is given to the wicked generation. However, in Jonah's story, if we look closely, other encounters with the coming Messiah can be seen.

Storm on the sea
Key verses: Jonah 1:4-9, 12-16

After God called Jonah to go to Nineveh, He watched as this foolish prophet attempted to flee and even hide from Him. We see God's response in verse 4, "The LORD hurled a great wind on the sea and there was a great storm on the sea." And, where was Jonah? He had gone into the hold of the ship and gone to sleep. When the captain faced the raging storm and looked for solutions, he was ready to call upon any god who might be able to save them. So, he asked of Jonah, "How is it that you are sleeping? Get up, call on your god." (Jonah 1:6) Under very different circumstances, but with very similar results, Jesus' disciples once questioned Him, saying essentially, *this storm is about to kill us! How can you be sleeping? Do something!* (Matthew 8:24-6; Mark 4:38-39). As I stop in my journey to recognize pictures of Jesus in the Old Testament, I realize that both Jesus and Jonah knew who could calm that storm. They both knew that the storm had been placed in their path to teach a lesson.

As the story continues, I see yet another moment that prepares me for what is coming in the centuries ahead. In verse 12, Jonah realized the magnitude of his disobedience, but he also came to terms with his choice. In that moment Jonah could have kept quiet and perhaps he and all those on the ship would have been lost. Instead, he recognized that the salvation of this crew lay in his hands, for he knew that only by allowing the crew to throw him overboard could he be confident that the Lord would stop the storm. In that moment he had to choose sacrifice or rebellion. I can almost picture him standing on the ship, looking into the dark, turbulent waves; thinking, *is there any other way, Lord?* At the same time, I picture Jesus in the Garden of Gethsemane, asking the same question—and coming to the same conclusion, "Thy will be done." (Matthew 26:42)

Thrown into the sea
Key verses: Jonah 1:17, 2:10, 3:1

God prepared a fish to keep Jonah safe for three days and nights. God commanded his release from the fish. God gave Jonah a second chance. Beyond the obvious use of this experience as an illustration of the 3 days that Jesus would spend in the tomb, God used it to reveal His greater plan—Death would have the appearance of victory for three days, Death would be conquered by the power of God, Death would be forever lost in the shadow of His second chance. Jesus was held for three days in the tomb. Jesus, through the power of God, was raised from the dead, defeating Death once and for all. Jesus, through His sacrifice, offers all of us the second chance to be restored to our heavenly Father.

## Other Characters

Other key Old Testament characters that in some manner illustrate some part of Jesus' life or ministry here on earth includes:

### Adam—

He was the first of his kind and Jesus is even called the second Adam. (Genesis 2-5; Job 31:33; Hosea 6:7; Romans 5:14; I Corinthians 15:22, 45; I Timothy 2:13-14)

### Abraham (Abram)—

He left the riches of his homeland to follow the command of God, just as Jesus left the glories of heaven to come to earth to execute the plan that had been laid before the foundation of the earth. (Genesis 11-50; Exodus 32:13; Isaiah 41:8; Nehemiah 9:7; Matthew 8:11; John 8:56; Romans 4:2-3, 9; Galatians 3:6-8; Hebrews 11:17; James 2:21-23)

### Joseph—

He was a favored son, rejected by his own people and rose to sit on the right hand of Pharaoh, as Jesus, the *only* son of God, was rejected by His own people and now sits at the right hand of the Father. (Genesis 30:24-25; 35, 37, 39-50; Exodus 1; Psalm 81:5, 105:17; Acts 7:9, 13-18; Hebrews 11:22)

### Aaron—

He was the first high priest of Israel, and Jesus is called a high priest forever. (Exodus 4-40; Leviticus; Numbers; Deuteronomy; I Samuel 12:6-8; Psalm 77:20, 99:6, 105:26; Micah 6:4; Acts 7:40; Hebrews 9:4)

### Joshua—

He led Israel into the Promised Land, just as Jesus leads us to the glories of heaven. (Exodus 17:8-16, 32:17-18; Numbers 11:27-29, Numbers 14, 26-27, 32; Deuteronomy 1:38, 3:21-22, 3:28; 31:23-30, 34; Joshua; Judges 2:6-10; Acts 7:45; Hebrews 4:8)

### Esther—

She was willing to lay down her life to save her people, a choice that Jesus made as well. (Book of Esther)

# Pictures of Christ in the Lives of Bible People

**Elijah—**
Elijah called the people to repentance, as Jesus calls us all to come and follow Him. (I Kings 17-21; II Kings 1-2; II Chronicles 21:12; Malachi 4:5; Matthew 16:14; 17:3-4; 17:10-12; Mark 9:4-13; Luke 1:17, 4:25-26, 9:33; John 1:21, 25; Romans 11:2-5; James 5:17)

**Elisha—**
He is seen as being *greater* than the one who came before him, just as Jesus was *greater* than John the Baptist, the one who came before him. Elisha was chosen by Elijah and was given a double portion of Elijah's spirit when Elijah was taken into heaven. (I Kings 19:16-21; II Kings 2-25; Luke 4:27)

**Solomon—**
He was the first to fulfill the Davidic Covenant and to be called the *son of David*, a distinction that is used of Jesus, as well. (II Samuel 12:24; I Kings; II Kings 21:7-8, 23:13; I Chronicles 22:6-19, 28: 9-21, 29:29-27; II Chronicles; Nehemiah 13:26; Proverbs; Song of Solomon; Ecclesiastes; Jeremiah 52:20; Matthew 6:29, 12:42; Luke 11:31; 12:27; Acts 7:46-47)

**All the Judges—**
They were all deliverers who called Israel to return to the Lord and led Israel out of bondage when the people chose to follow them. (Book of Judges, later mentioned in the prophets)

**All the prophets—**
They called the covenant people to repentance. (Books of Isaiah, Jeremiah, Lamentations, Ezekiel, Daniel, Hosea, Joel, Amos, Obadiah, Jonah, Micah, Nahum, Habakkuk, Zephaniah, Haggai, Zachariah, Malachi, other mentions in the histories of Israel)

# The Scarlet Thread

# III.   Pictures of Christ in Specific Objects

## *Revisiting the definition of the category*

Looking for examples of *types* of Christ in the people of the Old Testament without some kind of limiting factor could produce a multitude of possibilities that seem to satisfy the conditions merely because the person held a specific title or shared a few details of life. Similarly, we must guard against attributing a connection to Jesus to objects or circumstances merely because, in a different scenario, such a connection would exist. Sometimes a rock is just a rock and a lamb is just a lamb.

For the verses and passages that are included in this chapter I have attempted to weed out such examples, except in situations where the text, even if it has no apparent connection to Jesus, causes me to think of Him.

## *Specific Examples—Stops along my journey*

Verses or passages have again been grouped together when they have brought to my mind similar thoughts or comments. Though I read and reflected on every reference, I did not necessarily comment on every verse.

### Ark (Noah's)
Genesis 6:18, 7:1, 16, Genesis Chapters 6-9

Throughout Chapters 6 to 9 of the book of Genesis, we find references to the ark—Noah's Ark it is called, though it is actually God's Ark. God designed it, and He commissioned Noah to build it. Then God used the vessel for the purpose it was created—as a vehicle to save the world.

Man needed to be saved, so God provided the way. The Ark was a vessel given by God—He opened it to receive those who were seen to be righteous (because of their choice to obey Him) and He was the one who closed it. To receive the salvation that was offered, Noah and his family made the choice to obey and enter into God's Ark. We cannot easily miss the image of Jesus in the story of Noah's Ark—sent by God, He too offers salvation to all who will choose to receive it.

Sin became entrenched in the world and God brought a temporary cleansing through the waters of the flood. (Notice that, dear traveler: *waters* in the Scriptures—even common references—often carry underlying images of deliverance or cleansing.)

Several thousand years later, when sin again filled the earth, Almighty God did not build another boat. Instead, God stepped down into the stream of human life and brought permanent cleansing through His own blood.

## Ark of the Covenant
Exodus 25:10-22; Exodus 37

The Old Testament tells of another ark, one that is mentioned about 170 times in those books. First introduced in Chapter 25 of Exodus, the ark was designed by God (no surprise there!). It is seen as a box, 2.5 cubits long, 1.5 cubits wide and 1.5 cubits high. A cubit was an ancient unit of measure using the length from the elbow to the tip of the middle finger, roughly 17-21 inches in length. Thus the ark was roughly 4 ft. x 2.5 ft. x 2.5 ft.—not particularly impressive until you recall that it was overlaid with pure gold, inside and out, and that the tablets of stone representing the covenant with God were placed inside. Added to the *box* that was referred to as the Ark of the Covenant was a cover called the *mercy seat*. Two gold cherubim were crafted on the cover—one on each end.

In Exodus 25:22, we begin to realize the true significance of this ark, for God told Moses, "There I will meet with you." The Ark of the Covenant represented the presence of God in the midst of the people of Israel. Centuries later God would stand in the midst of His people—not as a Spirit between two gold angels, but as a man, Emmanuel.

The Old Testament is filled with stories describing the movement of Israel. Masses of people trailed behind the Levites as they carried the Ark. The Ark went ahead of the people, leading them into the land God had prepared for them, just as God, by His Spirit, continues to lead us even today.

## Bread

According to my *Bible Gateway* search, about 215 references to *bread* are found in the Old Testament. Not all of them would necessarily prompt images of Jesus as I read the passages, of course, but it's interesting that in my 40 plus years of teaching children's lessons, *bread of life* is one of the most well-known descriptive names given to Jesus—perhaps because John 6:48 is such an easy verse for children to memorize.

At any rate, *Bread of Life* is a significant descriptive name for Jesus and it is deeply rooted in the pages of the Old Testament. As I wandered through those pages, I stopped often to encounter special moments with Him. Some of those moments, I have shared below.

Bread from Heaven
Exodus 16:4-32; Nehemiah 9:15; Psalm 105:40 (Numbers 11 and Deuteronomy 8 also include verses referencing *manna*.)

The opening verses of Exodus 16 says that the Israelites mumbled and grumbled and complained to Moses that God had brought them into the wilderness to die of hunger and thirst. In response, God told Moses, "I will rain bread from heaven." In verse 4, God went on to explain that the giving of the bread from heaven would serve as a test to see if they would walk in His instructions (about gathering only enough for one day, relying on Him day by day for the manna).

Recognizing manna as a representation of Jesus is quite easy, especially when it is called bread *from heaven*, but in this verse we see even greater similarities that enhance the connection between the two. God's provision—His gift of the bread of heaven—carried with it the requirement that it had to be physically accepted. The Israelites had to go out and gather it, making the conscious choice to take God at His word and accept

His gift. Beyond that, the gift carried with it a need to establish a day by day relationship; it had to be gathered one day at a time (with a special consideration given for the Sabbath). What a tremendous lesson for us! God's marvelous gift of salvation is given to us through the sacrifice of the *true bread of heaven*, but we must make the choice to accept it and once we do, we must continue in Him day by day for the rest of our time here on earth.

<u>Unleavened bread</u>
Exodus 12:8; Ezekiel 45:21 (Ezra 6:22 and multiple verses in Exodus 12, 13, 23, 29; Leviticus 8, 23; Numbers 9, 28; Deuteronomy 16; and II Chronicles 8, 30, 35 refer to *unleavened bread* in connection with the Feast of Unleavened Bread.)

In the opening verses of the 12$^{th}$ chapter of Exodus, we encounter the Israelites' preparation for the Lord's Passover. Though at this point they would not have comprehended the magnitude of the event, they were careful to follow the directions of Moses explicitly. As I came to Exodus 12:8, I read, "and they shall eat it [the lamb] with unleavened bread and bitter herbs." Logic tells me that the bread had to be prepared without leavening because there was no time to wait for the dough to rise. Still, *leavening* in the Scripture often represents sin, so I can't help but wonder if there was a greater, deeper, significance.

It was the Lord's Passover—it was to be a night like no other, when the Lord Himself went through the land of Egypt and struck down all the firstborn. As I read the description of the preparation, the Spirit allowed me to peek into this ancient scene. I saw fathers and sons rushing to select the purest of lambs. I saw mothers and daughters scurrying around the humble dwellings to prepare the herbs and the bread. I watched as they huddled together in the dim light, staffs in hand, as they hurriedly finished their meal—the lamb and the unleavened bread.

Unleavened—without leavening—without sin! For many years I have seen the Passover as a representation of God's redemption that ultimately was seen in Christ's sacrifice on the cross. I realized that the lamb that night looked ahead to the Lamb of God, and had even linked the unleavened bread with the absence of sin. Still, until these precious moments with Jesus in this journey the full image that both the unblemished lamb and the unleavened bread poignantly foreshadowed the sinless sacrifice of Jesus had somehow escaped my notice.

God's Word is so amazing! So many times I have read of the Passover, but on this journey the Lord showed me something new!

Showbread/Bread of the Presence
Exodus 25:30; I Kings 7:48; (Exodus 35, 39; Leviticus 24; Numbers 4; I Samuel 21; and II Chronicles 4 include verses regarding the *bread of the Presence* in the tabernacle or in the temple.)

One of the furnishings in the tabernacle, and later in the temple, was a gold table that sat just outside the Holy of Holies. Every Sabbath newly prepared *bread of the Presence* (showbread or shewbread in some translations) was placed on the table, set forth before the Lord. The continual presence of the bread represented the everlasting covenant between Israel and the Lord.

As with everything in the design of the tabernacle, and later the temple, the bread of the Presence is a beautiful picture of Jesus. The Hebrew word for this bread literally refers to the *face* or *presence* of God, suggesting that God was present in the bread, or in the tabernacle or temple, or in the midst of the people. It is easy to see how this concept is literally seen in the name Emmanuel—the name given by God. It can also be seen that though the physical bread had to be continually replaced, the constant presence of bread on the table conveyed the concept of an everlasting relationship, one that is only possible through Jesus Christ.

Bread from heaven (again)
Deuteronomy 8:3

We cannot leave our encounters with Jesus, as seen in the various references to bread in the Old Testament without looking at one more, a reminder that echoes directly from the mouth of Jesus. In Deuteronomy 8:3, Moses is speaking to the Israelites, reminding them of the manna—the *bread from heaven*—that had sustained them in the wilderness. Then, explaining why God had provided for them in the manner in which He did, Moses said, "He [God] humbled you and let you be hungry, and fed you with manna which you did not know, nor did your fathers know, that He might make you understand that man does not live by bread alone, but man lives by everything that proceeds out of the mouth of the LORD."

Do you hear the echo? "man does not live by bread alone, but man lives by everything that proceeds out of the mouth of the LORD." Can't you just hear Jesus saying those words to Satan? (Matthew 4:4)

## Bronze serpent
Numbers 21:8-9

I pause at Numbers 21:8-9 to wonder in amazement, both at the weak, fickle spirit of those long ago wanderers and at the inconceivable patience and forgiveness of our holy God. Over and over the Israelites came to their knees before the Lord and promised undying love and service, only to shortly thereafter again become griping, grumbling, ungrateful, disobedient servants.

Through the eyes of the Spirit, I look upon this scene: I picture a landscape of scrub brush and stone, darkened by the setting sun and by the blackness of sinful hearts. I see thousands and thousands of people, favored most among the nations of the earth by Jehovah, but groveling on the ground in pain and shame. I see Almighty God watching, broken-hearted again by the ingratitude and disobedience of His chosen people.

Then He speaks to Moses: "Make a snake. Lift it up." The Scripture doesn't include what I seem to hear: "Make a snake. Lift it up. Let them glimpse the unshakable, undeniable, consequence of their sin. Let them look upon the cross that will one day lift *my*

Son to hang between heaven and earth to pay the debt that mankind has already begun to build."

I pause in silence as I encounter the crucified Christ here in the wilderness. I wonder if even Moses recognized the significance of this simple gesture. He made a bronze snake—because it was snakes that plagued the land, or because God was saying that in the future fulfillment of this image, Satan, the serpent, would lose his battle at that cross?

Moses made the bronze snake and lifted it high. He then called on all the afflicted of Israel, "*Look up!*" How odd it seems, and yet not really odd at all, that even in offering healing, the Lord allowed each individual to choose whether to accept His offer. I wonder if any refused to do that simple task—*just look up*.

## City of Refuge/Refuge

Cities of Refuge: Numbers 35: 1-15, 22-28; Joshua 20:1-9; I Chronicles 6:57, 67

Refuge: Ruth 2:12; II Samuel 22:3, 31; Psalms 2:12, 5:11, 7:1, 11:1, 14:6, 16:1, 17:7, 18:2, 18:30, 25:20, 31:1, 31:19, 34:8; 34:22, 36:7, 37:40, 46:1, 52:7, 55:8, 57:1, 59:16, 61:3, 61:4, 62:7, 62:8, 64:10, 71:1, 71:7, 73:28, 91:2, 91:4, 91:9, 94:22, 118:8, 118:9, 141:8, 142:5, 143:9, 144:2; Proverbs 14:26, 32; 30:5; Isaiah 4:6, 10: 31-32, 17:10; Isaiah 14:32, 25:4, 32:2, 57:13; Jeremiah 16:19, 17:17; Joel 3:16; Nahum 1:7; Zephaniah 3:12

Reference to Refuge, relating to City of Refuge
God commanded that 48 cities be given to the Levites, for them to live in and use to support their families. Of the 48, six were to be cities of refuge, places of protection where a person who unintentionally killed another could find safety until he could stand trial.

Numbers 35:24-26 explains that the congregation would have the authority to judge between the one who sought refuge in one of the cities and the blood avenger of the family of the victim. The ordinance provided that, if found innocent, the person would be given asylum in the city of refuge to which he had fled until the death of the current high priest and would then be allowed to return to his homeland—free from any revenge by the victim's family. If the offender was found guilty, or if the person was found innocent but then left the city of refuge before the death of the high priest, the person who killed another unintentionally would have no protection from the blood avenger.

There is a great significance attached to these cities, as a practical means to protect a person who could potentially be killed out of revenge rather than justice and as a spiritual principle seen first in the concept of God's loving protection of His people and later in the person of Jesus Christ.

It is interesting to look at the fact that there are six cities of refuge. In the study of Biblical numerology, it could be noted that seven generally implies a divine perfection or completion, whereas six would then suggest that the idea or condition in question falls short of that. In such a study we could then realize that the six cities of refuge, while set in place to serve the practical needs of the people, also reminded them that their ultimate refuge is in Almighty God.

Still, as I consider the six cities of refuge and their purpose, I find myself looking at the spiritual model of their design. Jesus is *the city of refuge* to which we all run. In this age, before the coming reign of the King of Kings, Satan tries to lay claim to the souls of man, through the presence of *sin*. As sinners, we allow ourselves to fall prey to his claim and thus, as *self-appointed* blood avenger of the earth, he is able to hold us captive—*unless* we have claimed refuge in *the* city of refuge, Jesus Christ. Residing *in* Christ, we are protected from any harm the blood avenger would seek to do to us. We are allowed, through the Spirit, to see through the illusion of Satan's power over us. And since we reside in Christ until the High Priest dies (which of course can never occur since Jesus is forever our High Priest), we are assured of our protection.

To escape the blood avenger, a person would flee to a city of refuge—flee, run, race, move heaven and earth to get there! I can't help wonder why so many today fail to recognize the urgency to do the same.

## Reference to Refuge, not relating to City of Refuge

Not all mentions of refuge refer to the cities of refuge, but perhaps the others often come out of the Old Testament writers' realization that God provided cities of refuge to help them understand that He—God (Father, Son, and Spirit)—was (and is) indeed their (and our) personal refuge.

In the *refuge* verses, I see the image of a strong tower, a fortress that stands like a solitary giant in the wasteland of the earthly battles, calling out to me to rest within its walls. Such fortresses were built to display the might of the kingdom, warning enemies of the power they would be up against if they chose to engage the kingdom in battle. The structures provided protection and comfort and the one who is my refuge provides peace from the turmoil that is life and rest to regain strength for another battle. David, when he cried out to God in Psalm 16:1, "Preserve me, O God, for I take refuge in You," declared the simple truth of his reliance on God. Then, in Psalm 46:1, he again declared the certainty that God is always ready to be that fortress, that protection, for us, "God is our refuge and strength, a very present help in trouble." Nahum, in 1:7, carried the description further; not only is His stronghold present in our lives, but, as Nahum records, "He knows those who take refuge in Him." It is so very comforting to know that the King of the fortress is acutely aware of my presence within His walls and He stands ready to be *my* refuge.

Like his father, Solomon knew that the Lord was his refuge during his time in this physical world, but he also reminded us that God will be our refuge in the transition to the next world. He described God's promise to be our refuge in the end in Proverbs 14:32, "The wicked is thrust down by his wrongdoing, but the righteous has a refuge when he dies." Isaiah (14:32) also looked ahead to the Lord's unending promise, "How then will one answer the messengers of the nation? That the LORD has founded Zion, and the afflicted of His people will seek refuge in it."

The initial reading of the *refuge* verses first brings the reminder that God—Jehovah, the heavenly Father, is that refuge. His is the promise that the Scripture writers clung to; His is the promise that I cling to. But in the face of fear or anxiety, humanity tends to seek something more solid, a face to go with the promise. As I linger amid the *refuge* verses, I realize that Jesus *is* the refuge I hold to. When doubt and fear threatens to invade my mind, I mentally hold onto the physical person of Christ. In my heart and mind I see Him, and I feel His presence with me. Whether I subconsciously visualize some artist's representation of Jesus or I focus on an unclear face in the shadows, the result is the same. God is with me, Jesus, my friend and my Savior, is my refuge.

## Cornerstone/Stone
Psalm 118:22; Job 38:4-6; Isaiah 28:16

Chief Cornerstone
Psalm 118:22

In Psalm 118:22 the psalmist records that "the stone which the builders rejected has become the chief cornerstone." The cornerstone is the foundation stone, important to a masonry structure because it is set first and all other stones are positioned in reference to it. *Cornerstone* is a word that evokes images of power, of rigidity and unchangeable certainty, and of stability. It brings to mind the beginning, the first steps, but because it is used as the reference point, it also holds the promise that if subsequent stones are laid properly the finished project will perfectly fulfill its purpose. What a beautiful picture of our relationship with Jesus, as we faithfully lay the stones of our lives, always using our Cornerstone as our reference point.

The Foundation
Job 38:4-6; Isaiah 28:16

When God finally speaks to Job in Chapter 38 of that book, He says, "Where were you when I laid the foundation of the earth? Tell me who measures the earth, who laid its cornerstone." God was responding to the presumption of mankind. In the face of our audacity, He pointedly reminds us that He laid the foundation, He laid the cornerstone. As I read the words I am reminded of Peter's words (from I Peter 2:7), as he quoted from Isaiah 28:16, "Behold, I lay in Zion a chief cornerstone and he who believes on Him will by no means be put to shame."

I contemplate God's words in Job and I am taken back before time. Before God formed the earth, He first set in place His plan to save mankind. *He first laid the cornerstone of salvation, and then He created mankind.* To think of that moment before the earth was created, and see my Messiah already there, is more precious than I can truly put into words. The look that I seem to see in His eyes—sad, but victorious—cuts through to my heart when I consider that the plan was set in place for *me*!

**Feasts of Israel**
Leviticus 23, and other chapters, other books

Leviticus 23 provides a summary of the annual Feasts of Israel. Multiple references then exist throughout the Old Testament history.

Moses, at God's instruction, instituted seven specific feasts or holidays. Three of the seven occurred in the spring, one in the summer, and the remaining three in the fall. After contemplating the feasts for quite a while, I realized they all, in some manner, presented a picture of the Messiah or His coming kingdom.

*Hebrews for Christians*, (www.hebrew4christians.com), greatly helped me to understand the full picture shown through the cycle of the feasts. Below is a little of what I discovered.

Spring Feasts:

Passover (in Hebrew called *Pesach*) occurs on the $14^{th}$ day of the first month of the Jewish calendar (Nisan). Passover celebrates the Salvation of Israel. Their salvation from the bondage of Egypt symbolically shows us the salvation we find in the death and resurrection of Jesus. The image that comes to mind first is probably the *blood of the lamb*—the Passover lamb whose blood was placed on the doorposts and the Lamb of God whose blood stained the wooden cross. (*Lamb of God* is discussed later in this chapter.)

The Feast of Unleavened Bread (in Hebrew called *Chag HaMotzi*) occurs the day after Passover. This feast lasts for seven days, during which the Jews were to eat only bread that was made without leaven or yeast. This feast would be a reminder of the bread eaten on that Passover night, but it also reminded them to continue in their walk with the Lord. The symbolic reference to Christ is of course seen in the fact that He is the *bread of life* and that there is no sin (*leavening*) in Him. (*Bread* was discussed earlier in this chapter.)

The Feast of First Fruits (in Hebrew called *Reshit Katzir*) occurs the morning following the Sabbath that follows the first day of the Feast of Unleavened Bread. This feast is more accurately *the beginning of the harvest* and it actually begins a 49-day countdown to the next feast. The Feast of First Fruits was given to thank God for the fertility of the land. Early crops from the spring planting were brought as an offering. Symbolically, this feast looks at Jesus as the *first fruit of the grave* because of His death and resurrection.

Summer Feasts:

Pentecost (in Hebrew called *Shavu'ot*) is the culminating day of the countdown that began at the Feast of First Fruits. Also called the Feast of Weeks, Pentecost is fifty days after the Passover and, according to the book of Acts, coincides with the establishment of the Church. Pentecost celebrated the summer harvest and required an offering to God of two loaves of bread. In the history of Israel the countdown to Pentecost shows a connection between the first Passover and the giving of the Torah on Mt. Sinai seven weeks later. The countdown between the first day of the Feast of First Fruits and the Feast of Pentecost culminated with the giving of the covenant of Moses. For the church there is the significance of the giving of the new covenant made possible through the sacrifice of Jesus. Symbolically the two loaves that were required as part of the feast represents that new covenant, made with both Jews and Gentiles, when the church began.

# Pictures of Christ in Specific Objects
## Autumn Feasts:

The Feast of Trumpets (in Hebrew called *Yom Teru'ah*), is probably better known today as *Rosh Hashanah*. Also referred to as the Day of Remembrance, this feast generally falls in September and is marked by the blowing of the shofar, which serves as a call to examine your life. Rosh Hashanah begins the ten-day period referred to as the High Holy Days that culminate on the Day of Atonement. For the Christian, the sounding of the trumpet brings to mind Christ's promise that one day He will come again, with a shout and the sound of a trumpet, to take His Church to be with Him in glory.

The Day of Atonement (in Hebrew called *Yom Kippur*) is a day of confession—the day when the High Priest would offer sacrifice for the sins of the people and their sins would symbolically be placed on the scapegoat and carried away for another year. Through our acceptance of Christ's sacrifice, the Church has no equivalent to the Day of Atonement—our sin has been obliterated, exonerated, forgiven—but the feast serves as a reminder to us of what Jesus did for us when He sacrificed His life on the cross.

The Feast of Tabernacles (in Hebrew called *Sukkot*) is also referred to as the Feast of Booths, celebrating the fact that God provided shelter in the wilderness. This feast was celebrated by building temporary shelters as reminders of God's care and provision. The greatest image seen for the Christian in this feast is the promise of Christ—"I am with you always." We know that whatever our circumstances He is with us, He will provide for us.

All of the feasts, instituted by God, point to Jesus. In each we can find images that bring Him vividly to mind. Beyond that, many Bible scholars believe that the feasts—their purpose and their timing—creates a timeline foreshadowing the things to come. *Hebrew for Christians* described that timeline:

> Looking at the Feasts, we see that Jesus was
> crucified on Passover, buried on the first day of the
> Feast of Unleavened Bread, and raised on the first

morning of the Feast of First Fruits. Then the new covenant was given on Pentecost.

In the timeline of the future, the fulfillment of the feasts stops at Pentecost. The interim (symbolized in the calendar between late May or June to September) is seen as the Church Age that will end when the trumpet sounds and the Church is called out of the world. The fulfillment of the Day of Atonement and the Feast of Tabernacles is then expected to be seen in the second coming of the Messiah.

## Light
II Samuel 23:4; Job 24:13, 33:23-30; Psalms 27:1, 43:3, 118:27; Isaiah 9:2, 49:6, 60:1, 19-20; Daniel 2:20-22; Micah 7:7-9

From the first "Let there be light" to Jesus' claim, "I am the light of the world" we see that that the word light envelopes us with imagery of light shone on the path to truth, light that overtakes and dispels the darkness of sin and death, and light that welcomes us into the glories of heaven. Like so many other word-pictures provided in the Old Testament, many evoke images of the coming Savior and many merely offer a detail of its current place in the Old Testament story. Above are the ones that specifically whispered the name of Jesus as I passed over them.

Light of the morning
II Samuel 23:4

This verse is part of a passage that records the last words of David. He began verse 2 saying, "The Spirit of the LORD spoke by me" and then went on to reveal some words the LORD spoke to him, telling him what the one who rules Israel should be like. In verse 4 he says the ruler should be like "the light of the morning when the sun rises," and then, "like the tender grass springing out of the earth." I realize there is no direct reference to Jesus here, for David even goes on to say in verse 5, "Although my house is not so with God, yet He had made with me an everlasting covenant." David understood that he and his whole house fell far short of what God wanted from them, and yet he trusted in the Lord's promise of the everlasting covenant. We, of David's future, know that God could promise the everlasting covenant because He knew that one would come from the line of David that would indeed be like the "light of the morning when the sun rises." God knew that the Light would come in the person of Jesus Christ, a son of the house of David, a king forever of that line.

See the light of life
Job 33:23-30

In the 33rd chapter of Job, Job's friend Elihu is speaking. He suggests that if a mediator exists for Job, then the mediator would ask God to deliver Job from going down to the pit and to let his (Job's) life see the light of life. As a reason for the request he says, "I have found a ransom."

As I struggled through this passage (and am still unsure of how to interpret all of the uses of the word "he" correctly), I am surrounded by images of Christ—the mediator, the ransom, and the light. Elihu took a lot on himself to dare to speak for God, but in these words I feel that he is right—the mediator (Jesus) could ask God (the Father) to deliver Job from the pit because He (Jesus) is the Ransom and the Light.

My light and my salvation
Psalm 27:1, 43:3, 118:27; Isaiah 9:2, 60:1

In the psalms listed above we find that light is joined with salvation and truth. We are told, "The Lord is my light and my salvation." (27:1) God is asked to "send out His light and truth" (43:3). Then in Psalm 118:27, the psalmist reminds us that God has indeed given us light, bound as a sacrifice. In all of these psalms it is easy to hear the word *light* and think the word *Jesus* for He is our salvation; He is the Light that has come from God.

Isaiah continues the image, prophesying that the "people who walked in darkness have seen a great light." (9:2) He goes on in 49:6 to tell us that "to restore the preserved ones of Israel," God will send the Light, and in 60:1 he calls on Israel to "Arise, shine, for your light has come." In 60:19-20, Isaiah explains that the "Lord will be the everlasting light." In each of these verses we see *light* as a picture of *one* who would come to dispel the darkness of sin. We see the person of Jesus Christ. Matthew later quotes Isaiah, identifying Jesus as the "Light that has come to all who live in the darkness of sin." (Matthew 4:16)

## Light dwells in Him
Daniel 2:20-22

In this passage Daniel is interpreting Nebuchadnezzar's Dream. He describes God and ends in verse 22 by saying that He (God) knows what is in the darkness and light dwells in Him. Light dwells in God because He *is* light—by Him light *is*. It seems only reasonable, then, that we realize that Jesus is called the *Light of the world*. Jesus is light—the light that dispels the darkness of sin, the light that conquers the darkness of sin.

## Brought out to the light
Micah 7:7-9

In the seventh chapter of Micah, the prophet acknowledges the sin of Israel and looks forward to the time when God will send His salvation. Though the sins of Israel have led to destruction and exile, Micah is confident that the Lord is the light. In verse 9 he accepts the punishment given by God because he knows it is deserved, but he rejoices to say, "He will bring me out to the light, and I will see His righteousness." We can look back on Micah's prophecy and see that God did indeed show Israel the *light*. In sending Emmanuel to earth, God brought light to mankind. In Jesus we do indeed see God's righteousness, and more than that, we are allowed to experience God's righteousness.

## Ransom
Job 33:23-24; Psalm 31:5, 69:18; Jeremiah 31:11; Hosea 13:14; Micah 6:4

Ransom in the Psalms and in Jeremiah is linked with redemption. The psalmist asks that the Lord "ransom him from his enemies."

# Pictures of Christ in Specific Objects

Jeremiah records that "the LORD has ransomed Jacob and redeemed him from the hand of him who was stronger." These verses seem to carry with them the idea that in some way mankind has fallen into bondage—bondage of evil, of sin. When the idea of a ransom is mentioned, it is in the context that one who has the right and the power to pay for the redemption of man is being asked to do so. That payment—the ransom—must be paid before the redemption can be accomplished.

Undoubtedly, man has indeed fallen into bondage and a ransom is needed in order to buy him out of that bondage. As I contemplate what that actually means, I am reminded of all the kidnapping stories I've read and seen on television. There's always a ransom note—a note that tells how much must be paid and how it is to be delivered. In the backstory of the situation, we also always see the final component: to whom it must be paid. We always have to be careful that analogies are not taken too far, but I think Scripture does indeed provide us with a ransom note, many in fact. One is found in John 3:3, "Except a man be born again, he cannot see the kingdom of God." What is the price?—ultimately the price to be paid is the *rebirth of mankind* in order to return to a righteous relationship with God. How is the ransom to be delivered?—the sacrificial system has taught from its inception that payment for sin could only be made through a sinless sacrifice. What then is the real price of the ransom?—the ultimate price is, of course, the life of the Son of God.

> Here is a side thought for you to ponder. What of the final component of the ransom demand? To whom is it paid?—that's a harder question to answer. Many would automatically say that the soul is being *bought back* from Satan. I'm not so sure that is entirely accurate; the soul is bought back from the bondage to sin, but does Satan really *own* those who have succumbed to sin, or does he just try to make us think he does? I think perhaps that is a study for another day; for now, for the purpose of this study, I am content to recognize the presence of Christ in these verses because my heart assures me that only He could pay the ransom to restore the fallen soul.

## Rock/Foundation (also: Fortress, Refuge)

Exodus 17: 1-7; Numbers 20:8-12; II Samuel 22: 2, 3, 33, 47; Job 38:4-6; Psalms 18:2; 19:14; 28:1; 31:3; 62:1-2, 6-7; 71:3; 78:35; 95:1; Isaiah 17:10; 26:4; 28:16

Let's talk about rocks—in all their various forms. The image of a rock brings up visions of solidity, of stability, of firm resolution to never change or be altered, of permanence, of strength and unwavering certainty. All of these images can evoke a picture of Jesus, the foreshadowed Messiah, the unchangeable God. As I encounter some of the various verses that mention some synonym of rock, I see new images of my Lord unfold before me. To encounter the word *rock* (or its synonyms) in the Scripture does not necessarily remind me of Jesus, but often in my journey it did, for there is so much in the nature and characteristics of God that is symbolized through this word.

Moses struck the rock
Exodus 17: 1-7; Numbers 20:8-12

At our first stop, we pause before a rock in the wilderness, in a place that came to be called Meribah. In Exodus 17, the Israelites have been wandering a while in the wilderness and they have begun to complain, for there was no water to be found. As they grew more and more thirsty, they grew angry at Moses and at God, questioning God's care and provision. In verse 6, God pointed out a large rock and told Moses to strike it with his staff. When Moses obeyed, water came from the rock—water that was life to the thirsty Israelites.

Looking at the *water of life* flowing from the rock brings an automatic picture of Jesus, as the *Living Water*. But as I look closer, I see that before God told Moses to strike the rock, He said, "I will stand before you there on the rock." God stood right there on the rock and Moses struck the rock! Suddenly the image has changed a little. Instead of seeing only that living water is flowing from the rock, I realize *that God allowed Himself to be struck by the staff*, just as Jesus, so many years later, would allow Himself to be beaten and crucified so that eternal, living, water could come to us.

## Pictures of Christ in Specific Objects

In the 20th chapter of Numbers, the scenario is repeated. Again the Israelites are grumbling, again God says that He will provide water from the rock. But this time He told Moses to speak to the rock, rather than strike it. But Moses was angry with the people and he let that anger translate into disrespect and disobedience when he struck the rock again. It seems like a small infraction, but it cost Moses his chance at entering the Promised Land. God told him, "Because you have not believed Me...therefore you shall not bring this assembly into the land which I have given them." "Because you have not believed Me"—I can only assume God is referring to the fact that He had said that only speaking to the rock would be needed and Moses, in his own anger, chose not to believe that God could deliver water for the asking. He struck the rock again.

As I contemplate that apparently simple mistake, a vision comes to mind. I look again upon the horrid scene of whips, knotted together with sharp jagged pieces of bone, rock, or metal, flying through the air, and coming to rest on the torn flesh of Jesus. In a flash of understanding I experience a sense of déjà vu. This foreshadowing has happened before. The first time (back in Exodus) God gave Moses a picture of the Messiah, scourged, crushed, and afflicted to bring about our healing. That sacrifice would only be required once. Then I begin to comprehend the significance of Moses' mistake, for when he struck the rock a second time, he was in essence saying that God's sacrifice the first time was *not enough*. A chill runs through me as I consider what it would mean for me if that were true.

<u>My rock and my salvation</u>
II Samuel 22: 2, 3, 33, 47; Isaiah 17:10, 26:4; Psalm 18:2, 19:14, 31:3, 62:1-2, 62:6-7, 71:3, 78:35, 95:1

The Lord is my rock, my fortress, my refuge, my stronghold, my deliverer, my redeemer, my salvation. He is all that and more. These verses and so many more bring comfort because of their absolute, matter-of-fact certainty. *My Lord is.* There is no doubt. Psalm 62:1-2 perhaps sums up the image of all these references: "My soul waits in silence for God only; from Him is my salvation. He only is my rock and my salvation, my stronghold; I shall not be greatly shaken." I realize that I cannot encounter any verse in the Old Testament that speaks of salvation from the Lord without knowing in my soul how that salvation will be provided. In each verse I know that the words speak of Jehovah God—creator and sustainer of the universe; but in that knowledge is a whisper, "I AM; I, Emmanuel, will bring My salvation down to you." Then truly, I can say with the psalmist, "My soul waits in silence for my God, my Savior."

**Sacrificial System**
Leviticus (multiple chapters), Exodus 29:38-42; Numbers 28:1-8

Lest we fall into an allegorical quagmire attempting to equate every detail of the sacrificial system to Jesus, I would like to offer a word of caution. Accept my opinion or undertake an exhaustive study for yourself, but at least understand that accepting that the *sacrificial system* serves as a picture of God's redemptive plan does not require that we be able to equate each detail of every sacrifice to later actions of Jesus. In fact, sacrifices had multiple purposes and required multiple types of offerings. Animal sacrifices required bulls, goats, lambs, turtledoves, or pigeons, (sometimes male, sometimes female), depending on the type of sacrifice and the circumstances of the individuals who were bringing it.

As I understand it, a *very* simplified description of the overarching purpose for the sacrificial system was to provide a vehicle through which God's people could maintain some kind of relationship with the Lord until the Messiah came to restore the relationship that had been destroyed by *sin*. Through the sacrifices the people acknowledged their unworthiness, proclaimed their dedication, and obtained a temporary covering of their sins.

Jesus fulfilled the overarching purpose of the sacrificial system when He allowed Himself to be the Sacrifice that would completely cleanse all sin and restore mankind to a place where he could once again maintain a relationship with Jehovah God. Thus, the full system of sacrifices serves as a picture of the coming Messiah who would be sacrificed one time, bringing full forgiveness through His blood.

## Pictures of Christ in Specific Objects

That being said, there are also more specific images within the sacrificial system that also serve as pictures of the Messiah: the goat sacrificed for the atonement of sin on Yom Kippur, the scapegoat that is release during the celebration of Yom Kippur to carry the sins of the people away for another year, the sweet aromas of sacrifices that call to mind the sweetness and purity of the Christ who will come, and more.

One particular sacrifice that fills me with overwhelming images of Jesus is the burnt offering, also sometimes referred to as the perpetual sacrifice, that was executed twice daily—the third hour (9:00 am) and again at the ninth hour (3:00 pm). This was a daily sin offering that was established as part of God's covenant with Moses. These sacrifices were to be male lambs without blemish and Exodus 29:42 explains what is happening in this sacrifice: "It shall be a continual burnt offering throughout your generations at the doorway of the tent of meeting [later the temple] before the LORD, where I will meet with you, to speak to you there." *I will meet with you.* God promised to be present at this sacrifice—a promise that was not given lightly.

So besides the obvious image of the sin sacrifice, why do references to these daily sacrifices so poignantly recall the face of Jesus? That answer lies in information that I found as I studied about the sacrificial system. The first of the two sacrifices was set up at dawn and sacrificed at the third hour (dawn and 9:00 am) and the second was set up at the sixth hour and sacrificed at the ninth hour (noon and 3:00 pm). I find it interesting that God's instruction was so exact in this sacrifice—it almost seems to be unnecessary, merely detail for the sake of detail. But God's details are never superfluous, as we find in the account of the crucifixion: Matthew 26:66-75 relates that Jesus was condemned at dawn; Mark 5:25-26 relates that He was crucified at the third hour, 9:00 am; Matthew 27:45 describes how the sun turned dark at noon, and then in verses 46-50 declares that Jesus died at the ninth hour, 3:00 pm. When I realize that my Lord was sacrificed at the same time that the daily sin offering was made, is it any wonder that references to that offering flash an image of the cross into my mind? God had promised to *be there* for the daily sacrifice, and on that day more than two thousand years ago, His promise, and His presence, was literal.

## Sanctuary
Isaiah 8:14

Isaiah 8:14 explains that "He [the Promised One] shall become a sanctuary," giving us the promise that one would come who would provide a place of safety, a place of assurance, a place where we can forever abide in the presence of God. In that simple declaration, we are given a lifeline—a hope—a promise. We are told why safety and assurance are possible: because "He shall become a sanctuary."

## Scapegoat
Leviticus 16:10

The Day of Atonement, Yom Kippur, was (and is for the Jewish people) the most holy day of the year. On that day, during the time before the destruction of the second temple, the high priest would go into the Holy of Holies to offer sacrifices to atone for the sins of Israel. The sacrifices of the high priest did not bring forgiveness of sin; they only removed the sin for another year. Before offering the sacrifices inside the tabernacle (and later inside the temple), the high priest would stand at the entrance with two goats. He would cast lots to determine which goat would be the sacrifice and which would be the *scapegoat*. Following the sacrifice, the high priest would lay both his hands on the live goat and confess all the sins of Israel. Then the goat, carrying the sins of Israel, would be taken outside the camp and released into the desert. In this way, God symbolically removed the sins of Israel for that year.

Many centuries later, Jesus, the true scapegoat, was taken outside the city to the hill called Golgotha. There He carried the sins of all mankind away forever because His sacrifice provided full forgiveness of the sin.

> Though probably unnecessary, I'll still point out: BOTH goats served as symbols of the coming Messiah. The goat

that was sacrificed died for the sins of the people—unlike Jesus' death, the goat's sacrifice only symbolically served as a placeholder, a reminder that sin existed and Death would be required to pay its price. Nevertheless, that goat served as a yearly reminder of the price that would eventually have to be paid for sin.

## Tabernacle
Exodus 25-27

Spread throughout the pages of the Old Testament, more than a hundred references of the tabernacle can be found. Not always, but frequently, when I come across the word, my mind drifts to the purpose and the design of this structure, both of which bring to mind the Messiah.

For a moment, consider the purpose for which God directed the building of the tabernacle. This structure would be the seat of sacrifice; it was the focal point of the tribes of Israel as they related to Jehovah. The tabernacle, by its very design, illustrated that there was a distinct separation between God and man. In its function, the tabernacle taught the Israelites that *sin requires a sacrifice*. The whole sacrificial system, meticulously described by God, pointed to a time that *sin* would ultimately, once and for all, be conquered. There is no doubt in my mind that God designed this foundational component of Jewish life to point the way to the Messiah.

Beyond the overall function of the tabernacle, it provides almost a serendipitous illustration of Jesus for us. Like a set of nesting dolls, layer upon layer of the concept of the tabernacle projects images of Jesus, as God designed feature after feature to show us various facets of the true Tabernacle—the Holy One of Israel.

As we pause in our journey, try to comprehend all the threads that created the tapestry that He called the Tabernacle. Inside the layers of cloth that formed the walls was found simple, explicitly designed furnishings:

# The Scarlet Thread

• the ark of the covenant that represented the presence of God and promised that He would meet His people there, reminding us that Emmanuel, God with us, is still with us as the Spirit of God makes His home in our hearts
• the table of showbread that continually held the *bread of the Presence*—another continual reminder that Jesus, the *Bread of Life*, is always with us
• a golden lampstand, from which we recall that Jesus is the Light of the World
• the bronze altar that speaks of sacrifice, even as the corridors of time echo, "It is finished."
• the thick, heavy curtain that created the Holy of Holies reminded Israel that Jehovah God, while a loving God, is unreachable by human efforts. In our moment of reflection, we who know the Christ of the New Testament, recognize immediately that *only* Christ could make it possible to reach God, as is evidenced by the tearing of the veil in the temple when Christ died—only then was man provided a way to come into the presence of Almighty God.

## Vine
Jeremiah 2:21

In the second chapter of Jeremiah, God, through Jeremiah, is detailing Judah's apostasy. Then in the midst of all the sin and failure on the part of Judah that is being chronicled, God slips in, "Yet I planted you a choice vine, a completely faithful seed." Amid the condemnation, we see a flicker of hope, a promise to which we can cling. We see, not that God plans to plant a vine, not that He is considering preparing a solution, but we have the past tense promise that "He planted the *vine*"—even before sin came into the world, even before the foundation of the world was laid.

In this verse Jesus silently whispers, "I am the Vine," and indeed He has been that Vine, planted even before mankind was placed upon the earth, because God knew that only He, as the coming Messiah, could be that "completely faithful seed."

# Pictures of Christ in Specific Objects

**Water**
Jeremiah 2:13, 17:13; Zechariah 13:1, 14:8; Exodus 17:6;
Numbers 20:8, 10, 11; Nehemiah 9:15, 20; Psalm 78:20, 105:41;
Isaiah 48:21 (Refer to Rock above); Zechariah 14:8

Fountain of Living Waters
Jeremiah 2:13, 17:13; Zechariah 13:1, 14:8

In Jeremiah 2:13, Jeremiah 17:13 and Zechariah 13:1, we are
shown Jesus, as the *fountain of living waters*, and in Zechariah
14: 8 we are told that "living waters will flow out of Jerusalem."
Living water—water teeming with life—this is the water that is
offered through Jesus (John 4:10 and 7:38), water that would fill
the soul of man so that he would never thirst again. In this image
I see movement, purity, cleanliness, life with a purpose, never-
ending satisfaction and contentment.

For a moment, I stop to consider just what *living* water really is.
My mind jumps to rushing rivers and cresting waves, to
meandering streams that cut their way through mighty canyons,
and even tiny gurgling springs whose waters bubble up from deep
within the earth. I think perhaps that all those images taken
together may help us understand the living water Jesus offered—
water that vehemently shouts of power that fills the soul with
confidence and assurance in the one who commands the waves,
water that whispers of persistence because that one will never
leave us, and water that laughs in the face of adversity because
that one provides the strength it needs to push through the
ground to reach the surface of the earth. Such is the living water
that Jesus offered.

Sadly the people of His day, and so many today, would rather
drink from stagnant muddy pools that offer only a weary, wasted
life rather than claim the fountains of living water.

# The Scarlet Thread

<u>Water from the rock</u>
Exodus 17:6; Numbers 20:8, 10, 11; Nehemiah 9:15, 20; Psalm 78:20, 105:41; Isaiah 48:21 (Refer to Rock above)

Of the water brought forth at Meribah, I have little to add that was not already discussed when speaking of the rock that was struck to produce water in the wilderness, except that the references speak of water flowing out or gushing out. The image that is presented is one of abundance, of thirst being fully satisfied. I can't help but think of the Samaritan woman at the well. Jesus said that if she had asked, He would have given her *living water* so she would never thirst again. We know that the Israelites did thirst again, repeatedly, but I have to wonder: If they had asked (instead of grumbling), how much more of the *living water* would have been available to them. They would still have had the physical need for water; but, filled with His true *living water*, would they have done a better job of keeping their grumbling and disobedience under control?

<u>Deliverance through water</u>
Genesis 6-9; Joshua 3:8-16, 4:7-23, 5:1; II Kings 5:10-14; II Samuel 22:17; Isaiah 43:2; Exodus 14:13-30; Deuteronomy 11:4; Joshua 2:10; Isaiah 51:10, 63:12

Deliverance in the Old Testament is often seen through images of water. Knowing that fact, we can perhaps understand the New Testament command to be baptized a little better. Besides the concept of cleansing and changing, there is an element of trust associated with the situation. Going *through* the water takes us from the confident reliance on self to an understanding that the deliverance is only possible through the power of God.

Noah and his family found deliverance through the waters of the Flood (Genesis 6-9). To a certain extent, the Israelites found deliverance again through the crossing of the Jordan River (Joshua 3:8-16; 4:7-23; 5:1) when they were allowed to cross into the Promised Land. Naaman found deliverance from leprosy by going down into the Jordan River (II Kings 5: 10-14). In II Samuel 22:17, David attributed his deliverance to the Lord, saying, "He sent from on high, He took me; He drew me out of many waters." Isaiah 43:2 promises that we also have the certainty of deliverance through the waters: "When you pass through the waters, I will be with you; and through the rivers, they will not overflow you."

Probably the most prominent mention of deliverance through the waters is seen in the description of the Israelites crossing the Red Sea (Exodus 14: 13-30, Deuteronomy 11:4, Joshua 2:10, Isaiah 51:10, Isaiah 63:12).

Exodus 14:21-22 records, "Then Moses stretched out his hand over the sea; and the LORD swept the sea back by a strong east wind all night and turned the sea into dry land, so the waters were divided. The sons of Israel went through the midst of the sea on dry land, and the waters were like a wall to them on their right hand and on their left."

Having read the story many, many times, I thought I knew it well. I know that it is certainly a picture of deliverance—the kind of deliverance that only God can give. I contemplate for a moment the power of Almighty God that could cause this huge body of water to divide and leave a wide, dry pathway from one shore to the other. I think for a moment that Jesus spoke to the storm, "Peace be still" and the storm obeyed (Mark 4:3-39), because when the Master of creation speaks, creation must obey.

Still, on this particular journey with my Lord, as I pondered this miracle of deliverance, an image came to my mind that has forever changed the way I look at this story.

Coming from the generation that watched in amazement as Charlton Heston pointed his staff at the water and Hollywood's finest created huge walls of deep blue-green water, I have a vivid visual image of this scene. When I read the Biblical account of the crossing of the Red Sea, I automatically see those towering walls with millions of water droplets glistening in the sunlight. I see the pathway, so dry that a strong wind would blow up a dust storm in a matter of seconds. I see the Israelites approach with fear and trembling. Their eyes turn to the left and to the right. Inwardly, they measure the strength of those walls. They are terrified that they will reach the center of the path only to have the water come crashing down upon them.

Moses said, "Move," because God said to move. They trusted God, but there was still fear in their hearts.

Suddenly, in my contemplation of this passage, I realize that it is not the Israelites that are being asked to walk forward through the path. I am the one standing before the liquid walls. I'm standing there, hesitant, frozen with fear of the unknown. It's much easier to look at Scripture and think, *they should have trusted more; they should have known that God wouldn't let the water fall down upon them.*

I stand there, staring at the water. I watch as droplets break from the wall and dance upon the edges of the path. I wonder: *what power can possibly hold back those massive walls of water.*

Then, while I fearfully gaze at the glistening, shimmering spray, it seems to me that God's Spirit slowly, deliberately, draws back the invisible veil that separates His realm and mine. For just an instant He gives me a glimpse of the *only power* that can bring deliverance to mankind. Amid a backdrop of brilliant light, much brighter than the sun, I see a figure standing in the path. In that moment, I realize that two nail-pierced hands are stretch out— one toward the right wall of water and the other toward the left. Then, I understand what power can hold back the water. I understand what power can bring deliverance from the water *and from sin.*

Then, just before the veil falls back into place, I hear His voice. He speaks softly, but the words reverberate through the corridors of time, from eternity past through eternity to come. Gently, lovingly, He calls, "Come. I am the way."

# IV.   Pictures of Christ in His Titles

## *Revisiting the definition of the category*

Again looking at a modified version of typology, in this chapter of *The Scarlet Thread* I examine descriptive titles that are frequently applied to Christ, though they obviously have their roots in the Old Testament.

## *Specific Examples—Stops along my journey*

### Advocate/Mediator
Job 16:19-20; 33:23-24

The struggles of Job are legendary. Synonymous with suffering, his name dredges up images of agony and sorrow. Of all men, he is most pitied. His story is confusing. We have no answers for the trials that came upon him. We speak of the *patience of Job* as though it was his patience that saw him through the great troubles of his life. We wonder at his perseverance, how he could continue to hold to a hope that seemed lost amid the clamor of accusing voices and unrelenting pain and heartache. In truth, we struggle to understand the suffering of Job, so that in some small way, we can understand the trials and sorrows that are found in ever-increasing levels in our world today.

Reading through the book of Job, I was reminded again of the unfairness of his situation and the apparent futility of his own efforts to understand. Then in Job 16:19-20 (and again in 33:23-34) I found the source of the hope to which he held. As I came to this passage, I paused, struck by an almost visible light so bright that it threatened to hide the words. 'My witness is in heaven, and my advocate is on high." What a statement from a man who lived many centuries before Jesus came to earth! And yet in those words I can see Christ Jesus standing at the doorway to heaven, watching—measuring the strength of Job's resistance, smiling down on him as he continued day by day, hour by hour, firmly holding to his love and devotion to the maker of the universe. I don't think Job understood his situation any more than we do all these years later, but he knew with unfailing certainty that an *advocate* stood in heaven—and therein was the strength to which he held.

Looking back through the centuries, we can trust in the cross to guarantee that our Advocate stands in heaven. We know that the Messiah is there by the throne of the Father, advocating for us when our courage fails and our resolve to walk with the Lord weakens. I marvel at this man called Job, who, without benefit of our knowledge of Jesus, looked into the heavens, and trusted that one was there that was his Advocate.

### Anointed One
Psalms 2:2

I laughed as I came upon Psalms 2:2. The image created by this verse is astonishing. "The kings of the earth take their stand against the LORD and His Anointed. "How preposterous! It's like a vast paper doll army trying to face down a tornado. It's no wonder that only a couple verses later we read, "He who sits in the heavens laughs."

The Anointed One—how can we not see Jesus in such a title? Beyond the fact that we know that Jesus is called the Anointed One, the Messiah, the Christ, the very title suggests that a single *person* exists who will embody the power of God and will accomplish the plan of God. The psalmist, in this verse, reminds readers of the Holy Word that there is a *promised one*—He is God's Anointed and as God, He will face down the kings of this world.

### Faithful Priest
I Samuel 2:35

In I Samuel 2:35, in a context of rebuke for the behavior of the sons of Eli, we find a promise—a hint—at a different priest who will come. Through the Holy Spirit, the writer of Samuel records a message from Almighty God, "I will raise up for Myself a faithful priest." Here we are allowed to witness God's promise that one day a great priest, our High Priest, will enter into the lives of mankind. As I think about this verse I am struck by the "*I will*" that is used—it comes on the heels of failure in the priesthood of Aaron. In these words I see God, like a parent looking down at a child with a broken toy, shaking His head and whispering, "*It's alright, I can put it back together. I can fix it. It won't be easy, it will be costly, but I can restore what is broken.*" Then, as only He could, He makes a promise: "One day I will raise up the perfect priest—the faithful, forever High Priest that will not fail."

## First and Last
Isaiah 48:12, 44:6

Isaiah records the words of the Lord as He speaks to Israel and proclaims, "I am He, I am the first, I am also the last." In 44:6, Isaiah repeats this same refrain, attributing it to "the LORD, the King of Israel and his Redeemer, the LORD of hosts." As I pause at this verse, the whisper in my head is undeniable. I hear my Lord distinctly say (Revelation 22:13), "I am the Alpha and the Omega, the first and the last, the beginning and the end."

## Hope of Israel
Jeremiah 14:8, 17:13; Psalm 39:7, 62:5, 71:5; Lamentations 3:20-22; Ezekiel 37:11-14

*Hope of Israel* is a title that stretches deep into the souls of those who clung to Jehovah through the centuries when the promised Messiah was only a dim figure in a distant future! Only Jeremiah (14:8 and 17:3) actually calls the Lord the *hope of Israel* (which Luke picks up on in Acts 28:20), but writings from Job and the psalmists to the prophets echo the reality that they recognized that the *hope* of Israel lay in the hands of Almighty God and that it was personified in the promised Messiah.

Thus when I read "And now, Lord, for what do I wait? My hope is in You" in Psalm 39:7 or "My soul, wait in silence for God only, for my hope is from Him" in Psalm 62:5, I have a glimpse of Israel's hope, my Lord.

# The Scarlet Thread

In Lamentations 3:20-22, Jeremiah records that his "soul remembers" and therefore he has hope. He knows that the lovingkindness of the Lord will never cease and there is hope; he has hope because he knows the source of hope—the one who is the Hope of Israel.

Further considering the idea of the one who is the Hope of Israel, I paused at the description offered by Ezekiel in Chapter 37. Known to Bible students as *Ezekiel's Vision of the Valley of Dry Bones*, this passage offers a beautiful picture of the hope of Israel. As Ezekiel looks over a valley filled with bones that are bleached and dried by the sun, he is told that the bones are the house of Israel—seemingly dried, abandoned and without hope. But what seems to be and what is, in the hands of God, are not always the same.

As Ezekiel prophesies to the bones, they rose up from the ground and came together to become a vast army. In verses 11-14, Ezekiel explains what has happened. Though the house of Israel (the bones) thought they were without hope (dried up and scattered), the true Hope of Israel breathed life back into them, as described in verse 14, "*I will put My Spirit within you and you will come to life.*"

When Jesus Christ, the true hope of Israel, brings His life into us, we are alive, indeed!

## Horn of my Salvation
II Samuel 22:2-3; Psalms 18:2
Also: Psalm 132:17-18, 148:14, Lamentations 2:3 (KJV); Ezekiel 29:21

Had I not been acquainted with Luke 1:69, "And has raised up a horn of salvation for us in the house of David His servant," I might not have paused at II Samuel 22:2-3 or Psalms 18:2. But I was, and so I did. In fact, I paused for many moments as I quietly contemplated just what is being revealed in these verses.

What is a *horn of salvation* and why is it a name that is applied to Jesus? Most likely, we are looking at the horn of an animal, rather than a musical instrument. The image of the horn proclaiming victory or issuing a call to action would certainly apply to Jesus but, in the Old Testament context, it is apparent that the horn is a symbol of power, particularly in the context of the power of truth and in some cases, the power of evil. We see this referenced in Psalm 75:10, that says, "*And all the horns of the wicked He will cut off, but the horns of the righteous will be lifted up.*"

*Horn of David* or *horn of Israel* could be applied in like manner to *horn of salvation*. In Psalm 132: 17-18, God says He will cause the "horn of David" to spring forth; in 148:14, the psalmist says "God has lifted up a horn for His people." In Ezekiel 29:21, the prophet, speaking for God, says "God will make a horn sprout for the house of Israel." In each of these verses we see the promise of the one who will be the *horn of salvation*—the one who *because He IS truth*, will bring truth to the world, and with it He will offer the means of permanently cutting off the horns of the wicked.

All that being said, what did the Spirit show to me as I paused upon II Samuel 22:3 and Psalm 18:2? Oddly enough, in both verses I picture neither the musical instrument, nor the horn of an animal. While I agree with the interpretations mentioned above, what I actually visualized as I paused at these verses was the horn of a saddle. I remember sitting upon the back of a huge horse (at least he seemed so at the time) and gripping the reins, but also holding tightly to the horn of saddle. (Should I mention that I am far from being an accomplished horseperson?) In this particular memory, sitting upon a friend's horse, I was acutely aware that holding to that horn was, at least in my mind, a definite link to the likelihood of my survival. As I pause upon II Samuel 22:3 and Psalm 18:2, both of which refer to "my refuge, my shield, the horn of my salvation," I remember the mounting anxiety I felt on that horse. Only by holding onto Jesus, the horn of my salvation, can I ever hope to conquer the fears and anxieties that threaten to encroach upon my life.

# The Scarlet Thread

## Holy One of Israel

II Kings 19:22, Psalm 71:22, 78:41, 89:18; Isaiah 1:4, 5:19, 5:24, 10:20, 12:6, 17:7, 29:19, 30:11-12, 30:15, 31:1, 37:23, 41:14, 41:16, 41:20, 43:3, 43:14, 45:11, 47:4, 48:17, 49:7, 54:5, 55:5, 60:9, 60:14; Jeremiah 50:29, 51:5; Ezekiel 39:7

Many times the Scriptures refer to the *Holy One of Israel*, and a few others to the *Holy One in Israel*. As I look at these verses, I almost see a coin spinning in the air, for in approaching the verses as they appear in the Scripture I find that I must flip back and forth between some that seem to raise up the name like a gavel condemning the actions of the people and others that seem to stretch it out like an open hand, biding welcome and comfort to those who will accept Him.

Some of the verses in the list above condemn those who sin against the Holy One of Israel or record that they hated His law and His word. II Kings 19:22 reminded the people that their sins were against God. Isaiah 1:4 declared that they have provoked Him to anger. Psalms 78:41 suggests that the act of turning away from God limits—or set boundaries shutting God out of their lives. In these verses the title Holy One of Israel brings an image of the Messiah as accuser and judge. In the verses on this side of the coin there is something very haunting or disturbing, evoking a sadness that seeps deep into my heart. Holy One of Israel is such a personal description, conveying God's desire for a personal connection between the Almighty and the people of Israel, but the people just turned their backs on Him. As I ponder that idea, I am reminded that people today do the same. He is *still* the Holy One of Israel—the Holy One of all creation—and *still* so many just turn their backs on Him.

Then I consider the other side of the spinning coin, the verses that seem to hold the title like an open hand, offering comfort, peace, and hope. In these verses the title is *often linked with* Savior, Ransom, and Redeemer. Isaiah 12:6 reminds us that the *Holy One of Israel* will be in our midst and in Isaiah 48:17 the prophet tells us that God promises to lead us in the way we should go. In the verses on this side of the coin I see not the Judge but the Advocate, the One who both argues for my defense

74

and serves as witness to my forgiveness. Isaiah 47:4 leaves no doubt who the *Holy One of Israel* is: "As for our Redeemer, the LORD of hosts is His name, the Holy One of Israel."

There is something fundamental about that title, in whatever manner it is used, that automatically brings Jesus to my mind. I envision that point at which all mankind looks at the Holy One of Israel (or the Holy One of Heaven) and recognizes Him as the King of Kings. And as one, we fall to our knees before Him. Though the title is not used in his verse, Paul's words to the Romans come to my mind. When Paul says in Romans 14:11 that "every knee shall bow, and every tongue shall confess" he is talking about Jesus, but he is quoting Isaiah 45:23 that clearly is prophesying about Jesus. God, the Father, has accorded this honor to the Son: (Philippians 2:9-11) "For this reason also, God highly exalted Him, and bestowed on Him the name which is above every name, so that at the name of Jesus every knee should bow, of those in heaven, and on earth, and under the earth, and that every tongue will confess that Jesus Christ is Lord, to the glory of God the Father."

**King and Other Royal Titles**
Psalm 10:16, 29:10; Jeremiah 10:10; Psalm 47:2, 7; Zechariah 14:9; Psalm 2:6, 16:10, 24:7-10; Isaiah 42:1; Jeremiah 23:6; Daniel 7:13-14, 9:25-26; Zephaniah 3:15

King forever
Psalm 10:16, 29:10; Jeremiah 10:10; Psalm 47:2, 7; Zechariah 14:9

All of us are certainly aware that Jesus is referred to as the King of Kings (Revelation 17:14 and 19:16). If we think about that title we will realize that it is not likely to be found in the Old Testament. It connotes a superlative expression that would have no equal before Jesus comes a second time, a time when He will permanently conquer the forces of evil and reign forever. Still, as I read through the Old Testament during my journey to find images of the coming Messiah, I did notice some verses that evoked just that image.

# The Scarlet Thread

When the psalmist wrote, "The LORD is King forever and ever" in Psalm 10:16 and "the Lord sits as King forever" in Psalm 29:10, my heart immediately turned to Christ and I can see the King of Kings sitting at the right hand of the Father. When Jeremiah wrote (10:10) that "the LORD is the true God, He is living, and He is the everlasting king," that same image came to mind.

Reading the phrase "king over all the earth," as found in Psalm 47: 2 and 7, brings that image too. God is the king over all the earth; no man can fill that position. In those words is a promise that though rulers rise and fall, and mankind attempts to dominate the earth, there will come a time when Jehovah God will stand and be seen in all His glory. There will come a time when all eyes will see God—in the person of Jesus Christ, the King of Kings, stand as king over all the earth. Zechariah 14:9 says it most clearly: "And the LORD shall be King over all the earth. In that day it shall be—'The LORD is one, 'And His name one.'"

Other royal titles
Psalm 2:6, 16:10, 24:7-10; Isaiah 42:1; Jeremiah 23:6; Daniel 7:13-14, 9:25-26; Zephaniah 3:15

Studiously examining the rise and the fall of the kingdoms of the earth throughout the years of history, we can witness the posturing of earthly rulers, as they attempt to elevate their own rank, prestige, or authority. Meanwhile, through all the ages of man, Almighty God watched as the frail creatures of earth sought to claim the honor and glory due only to Him.

As I think on this, I can almost see Jehovah looking down upon the world—sometimes amused by our huffing and puffing, sometimes angered and offended by our presumptuous actions, and always patiently calling us to wake up and see how foolish we are.

Through the Scriptures, God let us know, beyond any doubt, that He alone is King, Ruler, and the one having all Authority. As I read the "holy resume" described in these verses, I can almost see the crowd of mighty monarchs shrinking in size and fading, as their stature and glory is revealed for the sham that it is.

• Psalm 2:6 records, "I have installed My King upon Zion, My holy mountain."
• Psalm 16:10 reports, "Nor will you allow Your Holy One to undergo decay."
• Psalm 24:7-10 speaks of the coming of the King of glory.
• Isaiah 42:1 explains that "My Servant" will bring justice to the nations. (Though "My Servant" would not be considered a royal title, I believe in this context it is, for it is identifying the only one who would have the authority to act for God to bring justice to the world.)
• Jeremiah 23:6 tells readers that Judah will be saved by one that is called "the LORD of righteousness."
• Daniel 7:13-14 describes the coming of the "Son of Man," and "the Ancient of Days," describing Him as having everlasting dominion.
• Daniel 9:25-26 refers to the coming of "Messiah the Prince."
• Zephaniah 3:15 calls the coming one the "King of Israel, the LORD" and explains that He is [will be] in our midst.

## Lamb of God/Passover Lamb

Genesis 22:7-8 (discussed in a prior chapter of *The Scarlet Thread*); Exodus 12:3, 12:5, 12:21; II Chronicles 30:15, 35:6; Ezra 6:20; Isaiah 1:11, 16:1, 40:11, 53:7; Jeremiah 11:19; Ezekiel 46:6

Probably one of the most recognized descriptive titles of Jesus comes to us only in the book of John (1:29, 1:36): "Behold! The Lamb of God! " The crucifixion of Jesus generates vivid images of the Passover lamb and of lambs being sacrificed in the context of the sacrificial system that was set in place through Moses. Thus it is potentially possible that every Old Testament verse relating to lambs, sheep, and other sacrificial animals could at times bring to mind our suffering Christ, who died so we could be restored. A search for *lamb* at *biblegateway.com* brings nearly 150 Old Testament references.

Above I have listed those that caught my attention in this journey, but in the text of this book I have only commented on a few of them.

# The Scarlet Thread

<u>The Passover Lamb</u>
Exodus 12:5, 12:21

Earlier in this chapter we looked at the image that was brought to mind through the unleavened bread on the night of the Passover. The context of the passage also describes the lamb—one of the most obvious of pre-Christ images. Because of the sacrifice of those lambs, because of their blood that was sprinkled on the doorposts, because of the fact that the entire scenario was designed by God—we cannot help but see in that night the foreshadowing of God's ultimate sacrifice, the true Passover Lamb. Exodus 12:5 reminds us that the lamb was to be without blemish—symbolically sinless, just as Jesus was sinless and perfect.

Exodus 12:21 is also a subtle foreshadowing of mankind's part in the horrid drama of the crucifixion. Moses told the elders of Israel, "Pick out and take lambs for yourselves according to your families, and kill the Passover lamb." Every family had a part in the Passover; each family had to choose the lamb and kill it. In a manner of speaking, though God designed the plan and ultimately saw it through, *man* had a very large part. Mankind, every family, chose to accept God's deliverance; they chose to accept that deliverance through the manner in which God prescribed; and through the killing of the lamb, they marked themselves as being instrumental in the deed.

Through the eyes of the Spirit I am again transported to that fateful weekend in Jerusalem. I hear crowds of angry people cry out for blood, "Crucify him, Crucify Him." As the shouts of the crowd ring in my ears, my gaze drops to my hands. I see the blood of the sinless Christ, and I remember that the Israelites marked us all; for though our hands did not bring down the hammer to the nails, our sin bound Him to that cross. However hard it is for us to comprehend, we were instrumental in that deed. But then, as I mourn my part in the horrible event, I watch the blood fade from my hands. I look up to glimpse a smile on the face of the one hanging between heaven and earth. Then I remember that the Israelites on that Passover night were given a choice: they could follow God's direction and claim the deliverance, or they could stubbornly refuse to mark their doorposts and fall to the fate of Egypt. In that moment, I recall my choice was the same: accept this Savior and claim my deliverance, or one day fall to the fate of the world. That smile on the face of my King assures me that my choice was made and my deliverance is sealed by the very one who smiles down upon me—the Passover Lamb—the Lamb of God.

## He will gather the lambs
Isaiah 40:11

In Isaiah 40:11, the lamb in question is not the Lamb of God, is not even representative of Christ at all. Instead, *I* am the lamb, and He is my shepherd. Nonetheless, I have encountered a beautiful picture here. Isaiah says "He will gather the lambs with His arm." As I read that line, I can picture the plains of Judea where crowds gather to hear the words of the Rabbi. I watch as He softly speaks to the people, explaining the words of life, urging them to understand. I watch as He tenderly gathers the little children around Him and lovingly explains that we must all become like little children, little lambs, in order receive the kingdom of heaven.

## Led as a lamb to the slaughter
Isaiah 53: 7; Jeremiah 11:19

Finally, I pause at Isaiah's prophetic image of Jesus—well known to nearly all who have ever heard the Easter message. The whole chapter describes the Messiah who would one day come, but in Isaiah 53:7 Isaiah says, "He was led as a lamb to the slaughter, and as a sheep before its shearers is silent, so He opened not his mouth." Jeremiah phrases it, "But I [the coming Messiah] was like a docile lamb brought to the slaughter."

Both these verses bring visions of the trial of Jesus described in the gospels. We see Jesus standing before the Sanhedrin and before Pilate. We know that He said little: He did not beg for mercy. He did not rant and rave and call down punishment upon those who unjustly accused Him. He did not try to explain away the actions that led to that moment. He stood silent before the caustic accusations and the shouts of the crowd that called for His death. Then, when He finally spoke, the few words He uttered sealed His fate—and the fate of all mankind, as well—for His words served only as fuel to fire the rage that carried Him to the cross. In those final words before the authority of Israel, Jesus restated what He had said all along—"I am the Son of God. I am God. I AM."

## Lily of the Valley/Rose of Sharon
Song of Solomon 2:1; Isaiah 35:1-2; Hosea 14:5

I must admit that I paused at Song of Solomon 2:1 in my journey through that book because I have often heard Jesus referred to as the *Rose of Sharon* and the *Lily of the Valley*. There is even an old song refrain from my childhood that says, "He's the Lily of the Valley, the bright and Morning Star, he's the fairest of ten thousand to my soul." (*The Lily of the Valley*, Charles W. Fry, 1881).

I also have to admit that I find no direct reference in the Scriptures to explain how or why these titles should be associated with Jesus. Such application could originate from an allegorical interpretation of the Song of Solomon that was held even before the church began. First interpreted as an allegory for God's love for the Jewish people, it was later seen by early Christians as a prophetic allegory of Christ's love for the church. This type of interpretation has become less prevalent in the century.

To satisfy my own curiosity I did a little research and found that very little has been written on these titles. Their use seems to come down to traditional views of the flowers—the regal image of the rose, as chief among blossoms, and the purity and humility seen in the white bell-shaped lily that bows downward. Later prophetic verses relating to the coming reign of the Messiah may lend some support to the tradition.

As I ponder these flowers, I consider a few of the facts I discovered.

• Sharon was a large, fertile plain on the Mediterranean coast, between Joppa and Caesarea. Many varieties of flowers grew there. (It should be noted that some translations suggest that the flower in question was more likely a type of crocus, rather than a true rose.)
• The rose is a fragrant, sweet smelling flower that is often considered to be among the most-favored of all flowers.
• The lily is also a sweet, fragrant flower. It typically is a brilliant white bell-shaped flower that hangs downward.
• The lily spreads easily and commonly grows in many areas.

In the Song of Solomon, the king is describing his relationship with his new bride. The first verse of the second chapter of the Song of Solomon is actually relating the words of the bride. None-the-less, Christian tradition has considered these two flowers as images of Jesus; so I lingered a little longer at this stop.

Regarding the Rose of Sharon: Isaiah's reference to the Plain of Sharon (Isaiah 35:1-2) could perhaps explain how Rose of Sharon can be seen as an illustration of the coming Christ. Isaiah says, "The wilderness and the wasteland shall be glad for them, and the desert shall rejoice and blossom as the rose; it shall blossom abundantly and rejoice even with joy and singing. The glory of Lebanon shall be given to it, the excellence of Carmel and Sharon. They shall see the glory of the LORD, the excellency of our God." In this passage Isaiah is describing the glory of the coming reign of the Messiah.

As for the Lily of the Valley: Hosea (14:5) picks up the reference to the lily, describing the time when God would heal the apostasy of Israel. He says, "I will be like the dew to Israel; He will blossom like the lily, and he will take root like the cedars of Lebanon." (The *He* apparently refers to the Anointed One who will one day settle the accounts and make it possible for Israel to be forgiven.)

As I contemplate these two flowers, I begin to see that each in their own way suggests an elevation or honor. The rose, singled out among the vast array of blossoms in the plains of Sharon, perhaps calls us to remember that His purpose is higher than ours and that honor surpassing that attributed to anyone else is due to the Lord of Lords, the Holy One of Israel. Then, in the lily, whose blossoms bow downward, I am reminded that though He is the pure, sinless, Son of God, He chose to be the humble servant of mankind.

## Lion of Judah
Hosea 5:14

When I hear the title Lion of Judah, the image of a huge lion comes immediately to mind, large mane and gentle eyes—Narnian style. But, as I encountered the one and only semi-direct Old Testament reference, I found that to immediately jump to that quick picture is really too simple and would be an injustice to the powerful title that Revelation applied to Jesus.

Considering how prominently the title of Lion of Judah is used and how often the Lion appears in Christian art, it is odd to realize that the name only appears in two direct references (*almost* direct references)—Hosea 5:14 and Revelation 5:5. Never having had reason to study that particular title, I had expected to encounter several references in the books of prophesy.

So, as I consider this stop in my journey, I feel compelled to detour, to look past the mere image of a friendly Lion, to see what else the Spirit will show me about the *Lion of the tribe of Judah*. Please join me for a few moments of investigation.

Genesis 49:8-10 records Jacob's prophetic blessing to his son Judah. He essentially says to Judah (my paraphrasing, not directly quoted):

> (verse 8) Y*our brothers shall praise you. Your hand shall be on the neck of your enemies. Your father's sons shall bow down to you.* At this point, Jacob, through the guidance of God's Spirit, has essentially

given notice to all the other brothers that Judah—the fourth son—will rise up and rule over them. The brothers (and their descendants) would bow to the tribe of Judah.

(verse 9) *Judah is a lion's whelp. After killing his prey, the lion goes up and lies down, and none will dare to rouse him.* Verse 9 suggests that the lion, relentless in his search for the prey will continue until the prey is caught and devoured and then will go back to the lair to rest in the knowledge that none would dare oppose him. Oddly, Judah is not called a lion, but the *offspring of the lion*. Perhaps the reference merely means to call him a young lion as is mentioned in Hosea. Or perhaps there is a subtle suggestion that in some way the tribe of Judah (and eventually the whole nation that would come to be called by that name) is being given the symbol of the lion, but that even as the head of the tribe, Judah is vastly inferior to the ultimate member of the tribe of Judah that would bear the name *Lion of Judah*.

(verse 10) *The scepter or the ruler's staff will never depart from the line of Judah until Shiloh comes. The obedience of all people will be given to Shiloh.* This prophecy that was given through Jacob was later confirmed in a promise to David: the scepter would not depart from the house of David until the coming of Shiloh, the promised Messiah.

Years later, Balaam looked out over the wilderness and saw the camps of the Israelites. Instead of cursing them, as Balak wanted, he delivered a blessing from God in Numbers 24:3-9. In that blessing (verses 8-9), Balaam essentially repeats verse 9 of Jacob's blessing, referring to Israel as a lion who "shall eat up the nations who are enemies."

Even later, Moses issued a blessing over the tribes of Israel as well, in Deuteronomy 33. He said nothing about Judah being a lion, but asked the Lord to "help against his adversaries."

# The Scarlet Thread

Many, many more years passed before Hosea wrote the words of Hosea 5:14: "*For I will be like a lion to Ephraim and like a young lion to the house of Judah. I, even I, will tear to pieces and go away, I will carry away, and there will be none to deliver.*" Hosea is delivering God's rebuke for the apostasy of the people. Using the same symbol that He blessed them with, through Jacob's blessing, God was assuring them that He would judge Judah for its sin.

As I think of the verses above, it occurs to me that even in Jacob's blessing I see a double image—I see the power and majesty of the royal Lion of Judah, even as I realize that the savage instincts of a warrior must hover in the background. Then I begin to understand the meaning of "going up from his prey" in Jacob's blessing or what Balaam meant by "eating up the nations." I remember that David was a warrior before he was a king. I even remember that the image of the Narnian-style lion that comes to mind so quickly is altered slightly when I consider that C. S. Lewis included the line, "He's not a tame lion" several times.

So I come back to Hosea 5:14 and ponder this *Lion of the house of Judah*. I contemplate the righteous anger that burned in Jehovah as He witnessed the sin of His people over and over and I see Him, so very reluctantly, transition from the tender shepherd of Israel to become the Lion of the house of Judah. I see the great mouth open to reveal the razor-sharp teeth and I remember that judgment and destruction was necessary before repentance could come.

As I prepare to leave this stop of my journey, I look one last time on that great lion with the large mane and the gentle eyes; but this time I can see the sorrow that lingers in the eyes. There is something so powerful and so comforting in the picture of a savage beast that is gentle by choice—like the meekness of a Savior who, with the power of the universe in His hands, humbles Himself to walk among His creation.

# Pictures of Christ in His Titles

## Redeemer/Deliverer

Job 19:25; Psalm 19:14, 78:35; Proverbs 23:11; Isaiah 41:14, 43:14-15, 44:6, 24, 47:4, 48:17, 49:7, 26, 54:5, 8, 59:20, 60:16, 63:16; Jeremiah 50:34, II Kings 13:5

From Job's declaration in Job 19:25, "I know that my redeemer lives," to the psalmist and the prophets who unequivocally link Redeemer with the LORD, I see in each of these verses the absolute assurance that only the Most High God, the Holy One of Israel has the authority to be named Redeemer. Therefore, in each of the verses, I linger over the words and rejoice in the certainty that I, too, KNOW that my redeemer lives!

All the *Redeemer* verses call me to pause in gratitude and appreciation, but Isaiah 54:5 *stopped me in my tracks,* so to speak. We, in the Church Age, are fully aware that Jesus is the bridegroom and the Church is His bride, but until I began this focus on places in the Old Testament where I recognize my Savior among the passages, I had not remembered that the same analogy was used even there. Isaiah says, "For your husband is your Maker, whose name is the LORD of hosts; and your Redeemer is the Holy One of Israel, who is called the God of all the earth." Isaiah leaves no doubt. Our Maker, the Creator of the universe, wants that loving, husband/wife relationship with His creation. And He wants to help us to understand the all-inclusive reality of *who* He is—He (the Lord) is the Maker, He is the Lord of hosts, and He (the Redeemer) is also the Holy One of Israel—the God of all the earth. Even though we cannot fully understand how Jesus can really *be* God incarnate, we have to admit that He is!

## Shepherd

Genesis 48:15; Psalms 23:1, 28:9, 80:1; Isaiah 40:11; Ezekiel 34:23, 37:24; Micah 5:4

Some titles or descriptions of Jesus so clearly span the bridge between Old and New Testaments that to make mention of the situation, the casual observer may not even be able to tell from which side of the bridge the reference comes. This is true of the term *shepherd*—Shepherd, Good Shepherd, Shepherd of Israel. Time and again the loving God of Israel is referred to in terms of *shepherding His people*. Time and again, Jesus lovingly spoke of people as sheep in need of a shepherd, told parables about sheep and shepherds, and called Himself the Good Shepherd. Therefore, as we approach *shepherd* verses in the Old Testament, we do so in the unquestionable knowledge that many of them will indeed bring to mind striking images of the Good Shepherd, who before His incarnation guarded the flock of Israel and afterward sought to bring the resistant, rebellious people back to the fold.

In his blessing to the sons of Joseph (Genesis 48:15), Jacob began, "The God before who my fathers Abraham and Isaac walked, the God who has been my shepherd all my life to this day." There is a certain solemn assurance that is seen here, as an aging grandfather passes on the secrets of his success. He places his hands upon the children and confidently assures them that the God who has stood by him and watched over him throughout his life is standing in the wings to be their shepherd too. Such a scene was common in the Old Testament; the passing of the blessing was a significant ritual, and having it here coupled with the description of a shepherd caring for his flock gives us a vivid picture of the Good Shepherd.

Probably the most well-known Old Testament shepherd verse is Psalm 23:1, "The Lord is my Shepherd, I shall not want." What a glorious promise. Under the care of the Good Shepherd—God Himself—I need not worry, for I know that He cares for me. Whenever I read that Psalm, I am transported to a gently rolling meadow where the soft grasses edge up against a quiet stream with water as clear as the morning dew. I see a single, lone figure standing guard. His hand stays any storms that threaten, and his smile warms my heart. Though the psalm was written many centuries before Jesus came, it is His image that I see on that shepherd. None other could know my wants and my needs, and none other can give the assurance that they will be met.

Later, when Israel has divided and its people continue to turn away, Ezekiel calls forth the image of the shepherd, too. "Behold, I Myself will search for My sheep and seek them out." "I will care for My sheep and will deliver them from all the places to which they were scattered." Ezekiel (34:11-16) describes what the Lord God will do as He restores Israel. Then he continues to relate a description that can only be speaking of Jesus: "Then, I will set over them one shepherd, My servant David" (Ezekiel 34:23). King David was dead long before Ezekiel prophesied, so the one shepherd can only be the one true Shepherd of Israel—the coming Messiah, King of Kings. It is somehow very appropriate that Jehovah, God of Israel, so clearly reminds us that *He is the Shepherd of Israel* and practically in the same breath lets us know that *one—He Himself in the person of Emmanuel*—is coming to be that physical Shepherd that His people so desperately need.

As a final stop amid the Shepherd verses, I pause at the fifth chapter of Micah. The prophet is describing the birth of a king who will one day be born in Bethlehem. Do we even have to ask who that king will be? It was such a joy to stop here for a few moments, for so often we remember that Micah foretold of Jesus' birth in Bethlehem, but never go farther to hear him promise that "He (Jesus) will arise and shepherd His flock in the strength of the LORD."

As I look at this passage and reflect on the full impact of this title, the Spirit reminds me that to recognize that Jesus is truly the Shepherd of Israel, the Shepherd of all mankind, I must also recognize myself as a sheep, foolish, prone to wander, and so-often selfish and self-centered. I must also recognize that, but for the worth ascribed to me as His sheep, I am only one insignificant creature among the flock. As I stand amid millions of other sheep, my heart rejoices to see that single, lone figure standing guard over my life.

## Son (of God)
Psalms 2:7-12

Prophetic in nature, the second Psalm describes the reign of the Anointed One. In verse 7, I pause at the simple statement of fact: "You are My Son." We don't fully understand how Father and Son can be one or how the Son can be said to be born even though He is eternal, but in passages like this one we are, in fact, confronted with that father/son connection. Through the psalmist, God describes the world that leads up to the reign of the Anointed One. Then, just as He did centuries later at the Jordan River, the

## The Scarlet Thread

Father declared His pride and pleasure in the Son, saying in verse 7, "You are My Son" and in verse 12 calling for homage to be paid to the Son.

"Do homage to the Son." What does that look like? Perhaps, like me, you can visualize a multitude of people that in synchronous motion all bow to the King of Kings. Perhaps, like me, you can hear God's word through His servant Paul thundering down through the corridors of time, "Every knee shall bow to me and every tongue shall give praise to God."

# V. Prophecies of Jesus' Birth and Ministry

## *Defining the category*

Probably the most well-known places that we encounter Jesus in the Old Testament are through the voices of the prophets. Our childhood lessons about the birth, life, death, and resurrection of Jesus are filled with references to passages where the prophets foretold that the Messiah would come.

The New Testament writers consistently record that specific incidents or circumstances during the life of Jesus were a fulfillment of a specific prophecy. Thus, it comes as no surprise as we journey through the pages of the Old Testament that we frequently encounter Jesus in verses that describe an event or situation that immediately brings to mind similar details described in the New Testament.

Even for one who has never seen the pages of the New Testament, these verses, if approached with a seeking heart, dramatically reveal the promise that a Messiah—the Messiah—the Anointed One of God—IS coming.

So in this journey through the Old Testament, I found that I made frequent stops to encounter Jesus through the prophecies that were recorded centuries before the incarnate Lord stepped into the stream of humanity. Of course, in addition to the actual prophetic passages that were set among the writings, there are often single verses that, because of the words or phrases that are used, seem to foreshadow an incident to come later, even if the passage itself is not specifically intended to do so.

When we think about prophecies about Jesus, references that come most quickly to mind are those prophecies that have been repeatedly cited over the years as proof-texts that validate Jesus' claim as the one and only true Messiah, the anointed one of God, prophesied through the ages of Israel's history and destined to become the Savior of the world. Besides giving us many word pictures of what the Anointed One would do and how He could be recognized, the Old Testament prophets foretold many circumstances or details that would help reveal the Messiah. These details, scattered among the words of the prophets, became the criteria or conditions by which one could verify the truth of His claim.

Frequently among these passages or verses is the typical prophetic tone of *this will be so*, but this is not always the case. Rather, sometimes the words that call to me from the prophets do so only because they carry a phrase or image the New Testament writers later used. Such references may more accurately be termed as prophetic words rather than true prophecy of a circumstance to come. Whether such verses or passages are indeed prophecy or merely prophetic by virtue of their repetition in the New Testament, they undoubtedly remind me of Jesus.

As I pondered the verses of these next three chapters, I found that the Spirit frequently called me to linger among verses I thought I knew well, and there opened to my heart new insights to awaken an ever-increasing desire to know my Savior better. I pray that you will discover the same truth as you continue to journey with me.

To systematically look at the prophetic verses, I have grouped them based on similarities in either words or concepts that are conveyed. To better manage the collections of verses, I have chosen to separate my selections into prophecies relating to the birth and life of Jesus (Chapter V), prophecies relating to the death, resurrection, and ascension of Jesus (Chapter VI), and additional prophetic passages, which refer to general details or to prophecies regarding the second coming or the millennial reign of Jesus (Chapter VII).

## *Specific Examples—Stops along my journey*

### Born in Bethlehem
Micah 5:2-4 (Matthew 2:1-6; Luke 2: 4-15)

"O Little Town of Bethlehem" has always been one of my favorite Christmas songs. The words and the music create a sense of peace—a sense that *all is well* rather than *all will be well*. The words and the music wrap around me to create a sense of silence, of patiently waiting for the God of the universe to fulfill His plan, but filled with an understanding that in the context of eternity His plan is already considered complete. In that song I recognize one simple fact: In those moments before the sacred realm touched the physical world, there is a discernable whisper of the incredible impact that the coming birth will have on that world.

The birthplace of the Christ strikes me as an oddity among the prophecies. The Old Testament sprinkles a number of references to Bethlehem and its inhabitants among its pages, but none describe a place of prominence.

- Rachel died and was buried, according to Genesis 35:19 and 48:7, "on the way to Ephrath (that is, Bethlehem)."
- Naomi left and then returned to Bethlehem; her daughter-in-law, Ruth, married Boaz there.
- David was anointed in Bethlehem, which was the home of his father Jesse.

Looking at the matter from a 21st century perspective, I would have guessed that the birthplace of Israel's greatest king would have grown to hold great significance to the people of Israel, but Micah says of Bethlehem, "too little to be among the clans of Judah," as though this little village had no value, no significance at all. Perhaps the fact that Jerusalem came to be called the *city of David* (II Samuel 5:7, 9; I Chronicles 11:7) completely overshadowed the historical reality that Bethlehem was also the *city of David*, as Luke cites twice in his gospel (Luke 2:4 and 11).

Still, after Micah specifically told the people of Israel that Bethlehem would be the birthplace of the Promised One, the little village never grew to become a leader in the political arena of the day. Indeed, so obscure was its importance that Herod had to ask the chief priests and scribes where the Messiah was to be born.

Micah's prophecy, however, goes deeper than just telling us where the Savior would be born; he lets us see that the one who is coming forth to be ruler in Israel is the Lord—everlasting, from the days of eternity. In verse 3, Micah almost whispers the chilling prediction that He (the Lord) will give them (the house of Israel) up until that *One* comes. The promise of Israel returning to the Lord hangs suspended in the future—linked irrevocably to the coming of that child, for only through Him will that restoration be possible.

What an amazing prophecy! In two simple verses, Micah sweeps the totality of time, from eternity past to eternity future. The Savior, the Messiah, who has *always* been, will be born in Bethlehem and He will then, one day, arise to become the shepherd to the restored nation of Israel *to the ends of the earth*.

**Born of a Virgin**
Isaiah 7:14, 9:6-7 (Luke 1:26, 27, 30-35)

Isaiah provides many familiar prophecies about the coming Messiah. In Isaiah 7:14, we read, "Behold a virgin will be with child and bear a son, and she will call His name Immanuel." It is interesting that the verse introduces that common prophecy by saying that "the Lord Himself will give you a sign." In Chapter 9 (verses 6-7) of Isaiah, the prophet continues to tell us about the child that would come. "For a child will be born to us, a son will be given." In the remainder of that passage Isaiah reveals some of the significant names that will be applied to this Child—the Incarnate Christ.

Often, when I read Isaiah's prophecies about the coming of the Messiah (or the New Testament record of the fulfillment of those prophecies), I get the image of an orchestra conductor. In my mind I watch the scenes unfold with precision, as God stands at the edge of eternity, carefully directing the movement of the realities that will accomplish His long-awaited plan.

**Called Out of Egypt**
Hosea 11:1 (Matthew 2:13-15)

"When Israel was a youth I loved him, and out of Egypt I called My son." I am reminded that Israel, besides being a person (the patriarch Jacob), was the chosen people of God (the people of the promise). It is interesting to notice that God, through the prophet Hosea, was giving us a comparison between the young Israel—the early years of the people of the Lord—and His own Son. I am reminded that Israel was in Egypt because of the hand of God. On the surface, the primary force that drove the people of Israel into the land of Egypt was the famine that was devastating their homeland; but in reality, it was the guiding hand of the Lord that sent them into the foreign land, to ultimately accomplish the greater purpose of God. In Egypt they waited for the right time to come forth as the nation that would forever make its mark on the area we now call the Holy Land. As they waited, their desire for Jehovah grew; even in the bonds of slavery, they trusted that the God of Abraham, Isaac, and Jacob would save them. Then, at the right time, God, through the voice of Moses, called His people out of Egypt.

Similarly, God sent His Son into Egypt. Mary and Joseph, at the warning of the angel in Joseph's dream, fled Bethlehem with their young child. We don't know how long they remained or what they did while they lived there among the descendants of those who had enslaved their people. We know only that at the right time, God called His Son out of Egypt.

## Great Weeping in Ramah
Jeremiah 31:15 (Matthew 2:16-18)

When Jeremiah weaves the image of Rachel weeping over the death of children, two Biblical references come instantly to mind—the massacre of children by Pharaoh during the time of Moses and Herod's similar massacre when Jesus was a baby. These images, of course, explain why I am moved to stop at this verse in my journey through the Old Testament. Matthew's use of Jeremiah's words supports the labeling of this verse as a prophetic image.

I've often struggled to understand what Matthew expected me to grasp when he used Jeremiah's words in his gospel. In the first place, Rachel lived and died long before Jeremiah prophesied. Beyond that, what does Rachel have to do with the Christmas story? What is this land called Ramah? I trust you will forgive a little meandering off the trail while I try to satisfy my own curiosity at this place.

From a little web hopping, I have come to a few conclusions:

• The Rachel that is mentioned is most likely the favorite wife of Jacob, the mother of Joseph and Benjamin. Rachel died in childbirth on the way to Bethlehem (perhaps near the city of Ephraim, just outside of Bethlehem, or perhaps near Ramah which lies between Jerusalem and Bethlehem) and was apparently buried at Ramah.
• The descendants of Rachel were the tribes of Benjamin, Ephraim, and Manasseh—Benjamin being a part of the Southern Kingdom with Judah, and Ephraim and Manasseh being a part of the Northern Kingdom, sometimes referred to as the *lost* tribes of Israel.
• The Northern Kingdom fell to Assyria around 722 BC. The Southern Kingdom was taken captive by Babylon around 586 BC.
• The Southern Kingdom (Judah) returned from captivity about 70 years later; the Northern Kingdom (Israel) remained dispersed.
• Perhaps most important to its reference as a prophecy, Ramah was apparently a kind of staging area as Babylon orchestrated the trail of captives from their homeland to their exile.

Quoting Jeremiah, Matthew referred to "Rachel weeping for her children and refusing to be comforted, because they [the children] were no more." He seems to be suggesting that Herod's killing of the children in some way had a profound connection to Rachel. Perhaps as Jacob's favorite wife, Rachel held some kind of *mother of all the tribes of Israel* status. Or perhaps it is the fact that Rachel was deprived of any future children by her untimely death during the birth of Benjamin that sets her up as one who would mourn so exceedingly in the face of such a massacre of children.

Looking beyond the *why Rachel* concept, I am drawn to Jeremiah 31:16. Immediately after telling the reader that Rachel refuses to be comforted "because her children are no more" Jeremiah lets us know that the LORD confronts her, telling her to stop weeping, promising that "her work will be rewarded" and that "her children will return to their land." I can't help but wonder: What work? Which children will return?

In all my meandering, I think what I have discovered is this: as Jeremiah prophesied, he spoke of the agony of a people who were being torn from their home. The image of a young mother who would never see her own sons grow to manhood became the representation of all those who mourned the senseless tragedies encompassed by the exile. Rachel mourned and would not be consoled because there seemed no hope left to her. Then the words of Jeremiah 31:16 came along and she (Rachel) was given a promise—a promise that was fulfilled amidst the senseless injustice of another time. Matthew reminded readers that at his time in history Rachel "still wept for all the children"—because the child from the manger in Bethlehem had not yet grown to fulfill the promise she had been given.

## Proclaim the Acceptable Year of the Lord
Isaiah 61:1-4 (Matthew 4:17; Mark 1:14-15; Luke 4:17-21)

Isaiah gave a resume, so to speak, that would help future generations recognize the Anointed One. The coming Messiah would "bind up the brokenhearted, proclaim freedom to the prisoners, and declare the favorable year of the LORD." "Favorable year" in Isaiah 61:2 and "favorable time" in Isaiah 49:8 are both linked to salvation, the freedom from sin that had plagued the earth since the time of Adam and Eve.

Jesus told the crowds that He had come to declare that the kingdom of God was at hand, that the time to repent was now. Luke even quotes Isaiah and explains that Jesus openly told the people that He was the fulfillment of Isaiah's words. He told all who would listen to His words that the salvation that Jehovah had promised so many centuries before was *now* being accomplished.

# The Scarlet Thread

## People in Darkness See the Light
Isaiah 9:1-2, 10:17 (Matthew 4:12-17)


Isaiah 9:2 reveals that "The people who walk in darkness will see a great light." As I read this verse, I can picture a grey, washed-out, desolate valley with thousands of people hopelessly, mindlessly, wandering about, unable to find their way out of the gloom. Then in an instant, a bright light cuts through the gloom to light every corner of the land. In a very real sense, that is exactly what occurred. The world was locked in the darkness of sin, blackness so thick and mind-numbing that most people could not even comprehend that they were in a place of such utter desolation. Then Jesus, the Light of the world, stepped down from the glories of heaven to split the darkness and light the way to repentance.

Sometimes, the phrase, "the people who walk in darkness will see a great light," rolls off our tongues easily, for we have heard the prophecy many times and know it to be associated with the birth of the Messiah. But as I look at this prophecy, I see something else; I see a second wonder being given to me from the mouth of Isaiah. He recorded, "in earlier times He (the LORD) treated the land of Zebulun and the land of Naphtali with contempt, but later on He shall make it glorious, by the way of the sea, on the other side of Jordan, Galilee of the Gentiles." Matthew, verses 15 and 16 of the fourth chapter, recalls those words, but only after telling us that Jesus withdrew into Galilee, leaving Nazareth, to settle in Capernaum, which lies in the region of Zebulun and Naphtali. Then Matthew closes this passage by letting us know that it was at this point that Jesus began to preach that the kingdom of heaven was *at hand.* The prophecy of Isaiah was fulfilled; the land of Zebulun and Naphtali was indeed made glorious, for from that land the Messiah began His campaign to usher in the salvation of the Lord.

Isaiah 10:17 carries the image further: "the light of Israel will become a fire and his Holy One a flame." As I look back at the image that came to mind as I read Isaiah 9:2, I am reminded that those of us who wander around in the darkness must make a choice: we must embrace the light that reveals our sin and accept its cleansing, or we will instead be caught up in the holy fire that will "burn and devour his thorns and briars." Isaiah 10:17 records an indisputable certainty of the outcome that will follow the wrong response to the *light that pierces that darkness*; for mankind has received generations of warnings of the choice to come.

## Messenger Sent to Prepare the Way

Isaiah 40:3-5; Malachi 3:1 (Matthew 3:3, 11:10; Mark 1:2-3; Luke 1:76, 3:2-6, 7:27; John 1:23)

Undoubtedly, reference to the one who came *to prepare the way* for the Messiah brings to mind the out-spoken preacher who came out of the Judean deserts to challenge hearers to "Repent." John the Baptist is seen in only a few pages of the New Testament, but the impact of his presence shakes the fabric of history, for his story essentially drew a line in the sand marking that point where God's promise of salvation intersected man's timeline.

We are introduced to the miraculous circumstance of John's birth in the opening chapter of Luke's gospel. About 400 years after Malachi completed the pages of the Hebrew Scriptures God spoke, through an angel, to a priest named Zacharias. In that moment, the silence of God's formal communication with man came to an end and God let the world know that the time had come for Emmanuel to come into the world.

Little is known about John the Baptist. We are told that he was clothed in camel's hair and he ate locusts and wild honey. We know he was somewhat reclusive, attending little to the social graces, single-mindedly proclaiming the message of repentance. And, on the word of all four gospel writers, we know that he was, without a doubt, the forerunner of the Messiah. It was John's job—his privilege—to break the silence and carry forth God's message: the Lord is coming, the Lord is here.

> As a side point: The 400 years between the Old and New Testaments is often referred to as a *period of silence*, during which there is no written records to suggest that God communicated with His chosen people. Lest we fall prey to the notion that this implies that God turned His

back on His people or otherwise remained removed from them, consider:

• After Malachi, the canon of the Old Testament closed. Though several Apocryphal books were written, no more books would be considered to be inspired (until the writing of the New Testament books). Though the writings ceased, the hand of God is still evident as Israel changed politically and culturally, setting the stage for the coming of the Messiah.
• At the close of Malachi, about 435 BC, the nation of Israel is back in Palestine (after the Babylonian Captivity), and is under the rule of the Medio-Persian empire. With the rise of Alexander the Great, about 330 BC, Greece became the prominent power of the world. After Alexander's death in 323 BC, the empire was divided among his four generals. By 63 BC the Greek empire had fallen to Rome.
• So by the close of the 400-year period of silence, the political and cultural circumstances of the nation of Israel had changed dramatically. Israel was merely a puppet-state of Rome. The king (Herod the Great) was a descendant of Esau, rather than Jacob. The God-ordained line for the priesthood had been replaced.
• Three major political/religious groups—Pharisees, Sadducees, and Essenes—had emerged.
• The stage was set for the greatest event in history to take place!

As I look at the verses that declare that the Lord will provide a predecessor, a messenger, who comes before the Messiah, I am struck with the thought that in a very real sense God still sends messengers before the Messiah. Rarely is anyone convicted of their need to accept and follow Jesus after their first encounter with Him—it happens, but not often. Instead, analysts tell us that a person may need to encounter the message of Christ many times before their hearts are softened and their brains are prepared to really consider the reality of their need for salvation.

Who then are the messengers that go before Jesus now? Who prepares the way in the wilderness of our fast-paced modern culture? Who lifts up the valleys of despair and confusion that hinder a person from listening to the Lord? Who brings down the barriers of doubt and uncertainty that will allow a person to be ready to hear the call of Christ? Though we so often fail to see ourselves there, as I pause to ponder these verses, my heart tells me that *we are the messengers,* you and I and all those who have heard and have chosen to follow Jesus. As Isaiah and Malachi prophesied of John the Baptist, I think perhaps they prophesied about us, the Church, as well, for it is the Church now that is sent to prepare the way for Jesus to be introduced to the next generation of souls that need to hear and respond to Him.

### Speak in Parables
Psalms 78:2-4; Ezekiel 17:2; Ezekiel 20:49 (Matthew 13:34-35)

The definition for *parable* given to me as a child was *an earthly story with a heavenly meaning.* Filled with stories of parables from the New Testament, I can't help but stop for a moment whenever I encounter that word in the Old Testament. After all, that was His trademark—Jesus, the master storyteller, could weave an image from the common elements of nature that would either cut to the heart and soul of the hearers or leave them scratching their heads in wonder.

When the psalmist utters, "I will open my mouth in a parable," the words echo through time until I can see the Master walking along the dusty road, speaking in parables to His followers. Whether the verse is a prophecy or merely a prophetic statement does not really matter, but the verse does make us ponder the question as to whether the writers of the Old Testament were truly telling us that the Anointed One to come would indeed speak to the people through parables.

Ezekiel prompts the same question in 17:2 when he says "Son of man [a name Jesus applied to Himself], propound a riddle and speak a parable to the house of Israel." Perhaps Ezekiel 20:49 would serve as a stronger prophetic statement: "Then I [perhaps meaning Jesus in the future] said, 'Ah Lord GOD! They are saying of me, "Is he not just speaking parables?"'"

## Enter Jerusalem on a Donkey
Zechariah 9:9 (Luke 19:35-37; Matthew 21:8-11)

The image presented in Zechariah 9:9 clearly parallels that of New Testament events known as the Triumphal Entry. Zechariah is, through the utterance of the Spirit of God, obviously laying the foundation for that moment in history when God, in physical form, would choose to ride into His city not on a mighty steed, declaring the imminent conquest of sin, but rather on a simple, lowly donkey, quietly reminding His followers that the conquest to come was in the spiritual realm rather than the physical one.

This prophetic fulfillment was perhaps one of the most striking of any found in the pages of Scripture. For generations, Jews had looked for that moment—the moment when their *king* would ride into the holy city of Jerusalem. As the hosannas rang through the air and the fevered pitch of excitement climbed, the crowd would likely have recalled Zechariah's words, though perhaps not as he intended them—

> • "Shout in triumph, O daughter of Jerusalem!" he said—and they did. They shouted and rejoiced, believing they stood on the brink of a military conquest.
> • "Behold, your king is coming to you;" Zechariah said—and the crowd tossed down their palm branches and pledged in their hearts to follow this Messiah to the very throne of Herod.
> • "He is just and endowed with salvation," the prophet said—and the frenzied crowd saw freedom from tyranny and oppression now within their reach.
> • "Humble, and mounted on a donkey," Zechariah said—and the crowd saw only that prophecy was being fulfilled. The crowd did not stop to wonder why Jesus did not choose to ride into Jerusalem as a conquering hero on the back of more regal beast. They did not recognize the subtle message that only days before their Passover, the Lamb of God was in their presence.

Even as the people acknowledged that Zechariah had said the Messiah would ride into Jerusalem on a donkey, they failed to understand what that choice meant. They saw only what they wanted to see.

## Lord's House Called a Den of Robbers
Jeremiah 7:11 (Matthew 21:13; Mark 11:17; Luke 19:46)

Jeremiah's reference to the *den of robbers* obviously brings to mind Jesus' angry words to the Jews when He cleansed the temple, overturning the tables, for Matthew, Mark, and Luke all reference the fact that Jesus quoted (almost) Jeremiah's words as He drove the money changers out of the temple.

I ponder, though, why Jesus did not quote the words more closely. Perhaps He was calling to mind writings of the Rabbis of the past who may have altered the words, or perhaps He was merely looking back to the *question* of Jeremiah and acknowledging that it had indeed come to pass. The temple—His house of prayer—had become a den of robbers.

Much of my childhood recollection of this story created the impression that Jesus' anger was predominantly directed at the unjust sales practices that were forcing visitors to the temple to pay exorbitant prices for sacrificial animals. Were this true, it would certainly be justified anger, for the purpose of the temple was to focus attention on Jehovah, not to become a seat of commerce for the people of Jerusalem.

However, as I thought through these verses, it came to me that Jeremiah (and Jesus) referred to the temple becoming a *den of robbers*, not necessarily a place where robbery was occurring. This caused me to take a new look at my understanding of these verses. There may indeed be thievery going on in the den—the home base—of the robbers, but is that really the definition of a *den* of robbers? Rather, the den, or home base, of the robbers is the place where the *society* of the band lives—they gather as a unit of like-minded individuals with a common purpose; they trust in the security they have set up for themselves; they plan the ongoing evil that they will perpetrate for their own gain of riches and glory.

Then I read Jeremiah 7:11 with this new understanding, "Has this house, which is called by My name, become a den of robbers in your sight? Behold, I even I, have seen it, declares the LORD." Jehovah, through the mouth of Jeremiah, seemed to be asking the people of Judah, "Has this house become a den of robbers in your sight? [Have you allowed My temple to become a den of robbers?]" And then He immediately answers the question Himself, "Behold, I even I, have seen it."

Jesus is really combining Old Testament references. He said "It is written, 'And My house shall be a House of Prayer'" (Possibly from Isaiah 56:7). Then He refers to Jeremiah when He essentially restates His words from centuries before, "You [house of Israel] *have* made My house to be a den of robbers. I [God incarnate] have seen it."

When Jesus' anger burned against the Jews, it was not just because unjust commerce was being done. Jesus saw that His house was no longer a house of prayer, a house truly dedicated to God; instead, temple worship and operation was permeated with the influence of those who trusted in their own power rather than in God's, those who sought their own glory rather than the glory of God. Indeed, the house of God had become a *den of robbers*.

**Rejected by His Own**
Isaiah 53:3; Psalm 118:22 (John 1:11)

As I pause to consider Isaiah 53:3, "*He was despised and forsaken of men,*" my mind drifts onward to the conclusion that is found in John 1:11, "He came to His own, and those who were His own did not receive Him." Isaiah sets up the image that the One who would come will be despised, He will be forsaken. For a moment I look upon the scene and I realize that those who met Jesus and listened to His words were faced with a dilemma— either they embraced His message and act accordingly, or they would have to reject that message. There seems to be a point at which a conscious choice has to be made—or perhaps a series of choices that blend together to obscure the true choice, causing some to reject not just the truth but what they fear the truth would mean to their lives.

It is at that point in my thought that the words of Isaiah 53:3 are boosted by those found in Psalm 118:22, "The stone which the builders rejected has become the chief corner stone." What's the result of being "*despised and forsaken*"? Ultimately, the result is rejection—rejection of the very one upon whom eternity's choices rest. I follow the chain of emotions and find that because they despised the implications of His words, because they didn't want to accept what accepting Him would mean to their lives, the people of Israel made the choice to reject that message, and to reject Him. They despised Him because His presence forced them to confront the realities of God's expectations. They refused to accept His path because they had to in order to protect the life they had created for themselves.

Pondering the whole of Isaiah 53 more closely, I still struggle to see how it could be true. How can mankind's sense of right and wrong, good and bad, be so distorted that Jesus is not immediately seen for who He is—the very Son of the living God, God in the flesh, Emmanuel? How could those who knew Him reject Him and the precious gift He was offering? How can so many today do the same?

As I think further on the matter of rejection, I realize that it basically comes down to personal desire to cling to the temporal power and position they had or to deception. Either the people recognized that Jesus must be the prophesied Messiah and chose to ignore it rather than turn over the power and position they had or they were so wrapped up in the circumstances of life that their minds were deceived to the point they truly did not recognize who He was.

Perhaps the saddest truth is the reality that God instructed Isaiah to write, "He was despised and forsaken of men," because He knew it to be true. He knew that His own people would despise and reject Him. And He knew that ultimately that rejection would open the doors for all the rest of His people—those not of the chosen nation of Israel.

As hard as it is to visualize the condition of the man described in these verses, my heart reminds my head that it is necessary. I need to be reminded, on occasion, that He was, as Isaiah predicted, "a man of sorrows." He took my sorrows from me; He was smitten, crushed, scourged, and pierced, for He took the punishment for my sin.

Perhaps the hardest of the verses in this chapter for me to read was the 10th, "But the LORD was pleased to crush Him, putting Him to grief; if He would render Himself as a guilt offering, He will see His offspring, He will prolong His days, and the good pleasure of the LORD will prosper in His hand." My first reaction to the words is shock, perhaps even tinged with anger. I can accept that all this must be so, but to say that the Lord was *pleased* is more that my sense of right and wrong can handle—until I remember that *pleased* does not necessarily mean that pleasure was gained. It also means that the *will or desired goal of the recipient has been met*. The Lord (the full Godhead—Father, Son, and Holy Spirit) was indeed pleased that Jesus endured all that Isaiah described, for in so doing, He executed the plan of salvation that had been set in place before creation began.

### From the Line of David
Isaiah 11:1, 11:10; Jeremiah 23:5, 33:15; Amos 9:11 (Matthew 1:6; Luke 3:31) (Isaiah 4:2, 53:2 and Zechariah 3:8, 6:12 also refer to Branch, but not specifically to branch of Jesse or David.)

As I pause at this cluster of prophetic verses, I acknowledge that they could as easily have been listed in Chapter II. They speak of the physical image of a branch or a root, the parts of a plant or tree that prompt us to think about the continuation of a family line.

Both Matthew and Mark make a point to record the genealogy of Jesus because it was imperative that prophecies connecting the Messiah with the line of David be fulfilled.

# Prophecies of Jesus' Birth and Ministry

God promised that a *branch*—a family connection, a blood relative—of David would one day come to save the world. Prophecies about *the branch* or *the root* of Jesse (or of David) serve as reminders of that promise.

Thus, as we pause to read "In that day the Branch of the LORD will be beautiful and glorious" in Isaiah 4:2; "I will raise up for David a righteous Branch" in Jeremiah 23:5; "In those days and at that time I will cause a righteous Branch of David to spring forth" in Jeremiah 33:15; and "I am going to bring in My servant the Branch" in Zechariah 3:8, we can know without doubt that the *Branch* is the Messiah who would come from the line of David to be the king forever.

## Called a Nazarene
Isaiah 11:1, 11:10; Amos 9:11 (Matthew 2:23)

> As a side note:
> Matthew 2:23 records that He (Jesus) lived in a town called Nazareth *so the prophecies would be fulfilled* that the Anointed One would be called a *Nazarene*.
>
> Complications are introduced when we realize that this is one of many verses that make scholars scratch their heads and debate about the depth of its content. The verse clearly says that "prophets foretold He [Jesus] would be a Nazarene," but nowhere in the Scripture [our English Scriptures] can such a prophecy be found. The debate then is whether, as some believe, Matthew was making reference to oral prophecies that were traditionally accepted, or if the lack of direct reference to that prophecy results from ancient uses of certain words.
>
> Many Bible scholars tend to think that Matthew was referring to Isaiah 11:1 (and perhaps Isaiah 11:10 and Amos 9:11, as well), which speaks of a shoot springing up from the stem of Jesse and a branch from his roots. The Hebrew word *netzer* (meaning branch) is used. *Netzer*, containing the NZR combination of letters, would then in this theoretical use become NaZaReth, leading to the term

105

Nazarene. In essence, these scholars assume Matthew was using a play on words to describe the prophetic reference that Jesus would be the branch of the line of David.

## Visited by Wise Men from the East
Psalm 72:10-11; Isaiah 60:3-6 (Matthew 2:1-2, 7-11)

Matthew describes a scene in the opening years in the life of Jesus that suggests that the magi (*wealthy, educated, possibly very religious, high-ranking men from the lands to the east of Palestine*) were not only aware of prophecies about a coming King of Israel, but were possibly, at least on a periodic basis, actively engaged in looking for the time when those prophecies would be fulfilled. We find that when these *prominent men of the east* saw evidence in the sky of the coming of the promised one, they immediately set about preparing for the lengthy journey that would bring them to their knees before the *child from the manger*. (For those of us who take great delight in including wise men and camels in our nativity scenes, note that child *from* the manger was deliberately referenced here in preference to child *in* the manger, for Matthew 2:11 clearly tells us that they came to the *house* where Mary, Joseph, and Jesus were staying.)

It is interesting to note that we sometimes have the idea that a small group of wise men (maybe three, which of course has no scriptural foundation) came quietly into Jerusalem to find the new king. Matthew 2:3, sometimes lost amid the other verses, assures us that was probably not the case. We are told that Herod was troubled, *and all Jerusalem with him*. In the past I have raced past that verse to move on to Herod's calling of the scribes and chief priests to get answers, but in this reading, I am called upon to stop. As I read the verse I realize that these travelers have essentially come hundreds of miles to pay homage to a foreign dignitary; the trip could have required a massive caravan of supplies, not even considering the great treasure that would have been brought as a gift for the royal child. This would have been a major happening! It is no wonder that *all* of Jerusalem was concerned about

the unexpected presence of representatives from the lands
to their east.

Unlike the other prophetic descriptions found in this chapter of
*The Scarlet Thread*, this section was a post-sighting. Reference to
a *star* in Numbers 24:17 may have brought a momentary glimpse
of the star of Bethlehem in our Christmas narratives ("a star shall
come forth from Jacob"), but that verse more accurately turned
my attention to the person of Jesus, rather than to the sign of His
coming. Thus, in my initial journey through the verses of the Old
Testament, I would not say that I actually encountered a verse
that propelled me to Matthew's narrative of the wise men.

However, since these characters were so prominently a part of the
Christmas story, I was certain that I must have missed some such
reference and I felt the gentle nudging (though at times it did not
seem so gentle) to pursue the matter further. If you will follow me
along a little detour to return to some passages I at first
overlooked, I would like to share what the Spirit showed me when
I followed His urging to take a second look.

In this second look, I first noted that in Isaiah 60:3 I caught a
glimpse of the star of Bethlehem: "Nations will come to your light,
and kings to the brightness of your rising." This reference would
almost satisfy my need to account for the foreign visitors that
Matthew describes, but somehow I was sure that there should be
a more definitive picture of the wise men in the Old Testament.

> In an old book of Bible promises (*Promises of the Messiah*,
> Barbour and Company, Inc., 1987), I found that the
> author/compiler, Abram Kenneth Abraham, suggested that
> Psalm 72:10-11 prophesied the coming of the magi: "Let
> the kings of Tarshish and the islands bring presents; the
> kings of Sheba and Seba offer gifts. And let all kings bow
> down before him, all nations serve him." On the surface I
> almost agreed that this could speak to me of the wise
> men, but then I tried to identify where Tarshish, Sheba,
> and Seba would be. Tarshish appears to be a place far
> across the sea from Israel, perhaps in what is now Spain;
> Sheba and Seba appear to refer to kingdoms in regions

from Ethiopia to Yemen—south and east of Israel, but not as far east as I had always thought the land of the wise men would be. So the reference in Psalm 72 really did not seem to be speaking of visitors *from the East* who brought gifts. After all, from most of what I have studied the *eastern regions*, when spoken of in Scripture, most frequently referred to lands lying far to the distant east— Persia, or what is now the area around Iran. I dismissed this reference as a prophecy of the wise men, even though the "bowing of the kings" did bring a momentary picture of kings bowing before the King of Kings.

As I wandered about through various Internet sites describing where the wise men may have actually come from, I eventually discovered two primary possibilities.

First, I was drawn into a drama my limited knowledge of ancient history had never conveyed. At the time of Jesus' birth, the Roman Empire ruled the Mediterranean region of the globe, but regions to the east, from the Euphrates River and beyond, were ruled by the Parthian Empire. It has been suggested that the origins of the Parthians may have included descendants of part of the ten *lost tribes* of Israel that moved through Assyria into Parthia around 721 BC, so knowledge of Jehovah's promise to send a king for the throne of David could have been known to the Parthians.

In the closing centuries before Christ's coming, the two empires had fought many battles. For a short period of time the Parthians had even laid claim to the area of Palestine. After Mark Antony defeated them, that claim was crushed and Palestine remained under Roman rule. Thereafter it appears that the two empires seemed to settle into a sort of quasi-peace, each holding claim to lands on their own side of the Euphrates and neither venturing to cross the boundary. It was into this climate of uncertainty that God set the greatest event of all history— the birth of the Messiah. If Parthia (ancient Persia) was the homeland of the magi, then the drama of their visit to

## Prophecies of Jesus' Birth and Ministry

Bethlehem is increased by the possibility that they may also have been very distantly connected to the holy child through the ancient bloodlines of Israel.

As I returned to the Scriptures, looking deeper into Isaiah 60 where I found the reference to the "kings coming to the rising light," I found that the prophet whispered that perhaps I had been too hasty in dismissing the psalmist's words in Psalm 72. In that chapter Isaiah describes the glorious kingdom to come, when Zion will be reborn and the Messiah will be King; but in building the image, he includes the first coming of the Messiah as well. In verses 3-6 he seems to be speaking directly to the baby that will lie in a manger:

"Nations will come to your light" –
> the wise men of the east (the magi)

"The wealth of nations will come to you" –
> the gifts from the magi

"A multitude of camels will cover you" –
> the eastern visitors would use camels to come

"They will bring gold and frankincense" –
> the gifts of the magi

*How could I possibly have failed to see this when I first journeyed through the verses?!*

Isaiah also provides insight into the homeland of the wise men: "*The young camels of Midian and Ephah; all those from Sheba will come.*" The question then is: Where are Midian, Ephah, and Sheba? According to Father Dwight Longenecker in "*We Three Kings" Who were the Magi?*, Midian was the Old Testament name for what would now be Jordan, Ephah was a city in the Arabian Peninsula, and Sheba, as noted earlier, was centered in what would presently be Yemen (south and east of Israel). Following this line of reasoning, the magi would have come from Arabia, rather than from Persia. The use of camels and the choice of gifts lend credibility to this opinion. Midian was famous for its use of camels and the Arabian Peninsula is one of the few places (if not the only one) in the world where the plants needed to make both incense and myrrh were grown.

# The Scarlet Thread

So what has my Lord shown me in this detour? I have no definitive answer for where the homeland of the wise men was located—noted scholars seem to line up on both the Persia and the Arabia sides of the issue. It may be that this is another one of the great Bible debates that modern students of the Scripture like to bat around. Still, my humble observation whispers that hints, however small, deliberately sprinkled into the prophecies by the Holy Spirit, should perhaps carry more weight than the mere understanding that *eastern regions* generally refer to lands in the distant east.

More than receiving a little better understanding of the magi's homeland, I think my detour—or my need for the detour—has reminded me yet again that the Bible is "living and active." It continues to call me deep into its words and continues to reveal new messages from my Lord.

I wish I could convey the depth of the impact this particular encounter has had on me—not because of the subject, but because of the personal calling: the text of *The Scarlet Thread* was otherwise complete, I was content to leave the wise men out because those verses had not initially spoken to me during my gathering of materials, and one more pause in the journey would not change the overall outcome of the purpose of the study. But the Holy Spirit reached into my heart and mind and commanded me to seek more. I can't explain why He compelled me to include this, or even whether it was merely a test of my desire to obey His voice, but I can tell you that the hours shared in this encounter with Jesus have been some of the most blessed of this journey. Dear readers, I urge you all: whenever you feel the Lord calling you to look deeper into His Word or merely to come and sit at His feet—do so: nothing can compare to the joy you will find with Him in that obedient act.

# VI.   Prophecies of Jesus' Death and Resurrection

## *Re-Defining the category*

As we continue to wander through the prophecies, Chapter VI lingers over passages and verses that prophesy about the death, burial, and resurrection of Jesus. At many of these stops I find it hard to look at the raw truth that God, the all-seeing, all-knowing deity, so graphically laid open to man the reality of what sin would cost many, many years before it came to pass. As my journey slowly led me through these verses, I am acutely aware of Christ's sacrifice, and I am humbled at the inadequacy of my gratitude for His gift. Even so, the tender compassion of Jesus reaches through the hurt and shame that sometimes threaten to overtake me to remind me once more that all He asks of me is to accept His offer.

But prophecies of death and burial, as vivid and painful as they are, are followed by the promise of the resurrection—the promise that the grave is not the final stop. Thus, in this chapter, I found that the Holy Spirit continued to remind me, even amid the images of despair, that God's story was not through yet—the victory of the cross broke the darkness, and the ultimate victorious return will scatter it into oblivion.

## *Specific Examples—Stops along my journey*

### Betrayed by a Friend for 30 Pieces of Silver
Zechariah 11:12-13; Psalm 41:9 (Matthew 26:14-16; Luke 22:47-48) (Psalm 41:9, referenced by John 13:18 also refers to the betrayal by a friend.)

While Psalm 41:9 speaks of the betrayal of a friend, prompting a potential connection to Jesus, Zechariah fleshes out the full image. Zechariah, under the command of God, lived out the image of what was to come. In Zechariah 11:4, God told Zechariah "Pasture the flock doomed to slaughter." The flock, of course, in this case was the people of Judah, since Zechariah was born in Babylon and lived and taught during the period that the restoration of Jerusalem and the temple was taking place.

When Zechariah says "so I pastured the flock doomed to slaughter" in verse 7 (of Zechariah 11), he was looking ahead to a future scenario when Judah (the chosen people of God) would again choose sin and self over the shepherd appointed by God. In Zechariah 11:7-14 the prophet is *acting out* the part of the Good Shepherd, but the *sheep* will not follow. As this image closes, Zechariah asks of the people, to "give him his wages" as he severs his relationship as their shepherd. The response of the people was to give him 30 shekels of silver. Then God, factitiously tells Zechariah, in verse 13: "Throw it to the potter, that magnificent price at which I was valued by them."

Thirty shekels of silver—the value of the life of the shepherd! (It should perhaps be noted that 30 shekels of silver in the time of Zechariah was a high price, indeed. By the time of Christ it was not so great a price at all.)

Luke 22:47-48 describes the scene in the Garden of Gethsemane when Jesus was betrayed by a friend, and Matthew completes the picture in Matthew 26:14-16. Judas Iscariot asked the chief priests what they would pay for Jesus. There was no negotiation; there was no hesitation. Thirty pieces of silver was weighed out to him. I can almost hear the echo of the clinking of the coins that were dropped into his hands. I can see the resolution in his eyes as his hand closes over the coins.

The price paid for the betrayal of Jesus is considered to have been the going rate for a slave at that time and place in history. The price of one slave was paid for the one who would purchase all mankind from the slavery of sin and death!

**Led Like a Lamb to the Slaughter**
Isaiah 53:7; Jeremiah 11:19 (Acts 8:32)

Both Isaiah 53:7 and Jeremiah 11:19 use the phrase "like a lamb that is led to slaughter," which so clearly describes the coming Savior. Luke quotes this same phrase in Acts 8:32.

# Prophecies of Jesus' Death and Resurrection

"Like a lamb that is led to slaughter": the phrase evokes the haunting image of an innocent lamb quietly walking a well-worn path that leads to the slaughterhouse, perhaps even being led by one it trusted. The lamb is meek and obedient. It does not struggle, for it does not comprehend what lies ahead. Such an image does not entirely parallel Jesus' walk to Calvary, for He knew where He was going—and why. Even so, like the lamb, He walked meekly, without struggle, quietly placing one foot in front of the other, each step taking Him nearer to His own kind of slaughterhouse. The image is a dark one, fashioned in greys and blacks, and my heart is troubled as it forms in my mind. As I envision this scene, I hear the echo of John the Baptist's words, "Behold, the Lamb of God, who takes away the sin of the world." (John 1:29). When I visualize those words, I generally see sunlight and promise; the path to the cross is somehow hidden in the words. But in Isaiah's words I am forced to confront the reality of what it cost for the Lamb of God to "take away the sin of the world."

## Not Open His Mouth to Defend Himself
Psalm 38:13-14; Isaiah 53:7 (Matthew 26:63, 27:12-14; Mark 14:61; Acts 8:32)

Psalm 38, another psalm of David, in the NASB, is titled *Prayer of a Suffering Penitent*. "I am like a mute man who does not open his mouth," he says in verse 13; and in verse 14, "and in whose mouth are no arguments." In the prior verses David has explained that his friends have left him and his enemies lay snares for him. But the reason for his response in verses 13 and 14 is perhaps seen in verse 15: "For I hope in You, O LORD; You will answer, O Lord my God." Simple as it is, this may explain, at least a little, why Jesus could stand before His accusers and say nothing—for He knew that God would have the last word. Indeed, even the very mockery of justice that He was forced to endure played a part in the intricate plan Almighty God had set in motion before He laid the foundation of the world.

Of course the more common passage about this concept is found in Isaiah 53:7: "He was oppressed and He was afflicted, yet He did not open His mouth; like a lamb that is led to slaughter, and like a sheep that is silent before its shearers, so He did not open His mouth." As I pause to consider these verses, I find myself wondering about whether sheep are really silent when they are being sheared.

Out of curiosity, I hopped around various sites on the Internet to see if I could find and answer. As it turns out, many of the sites agreed that most sheep really are *silent before their shearers*. The process is complex and exacting, but typically, the sheep apparently does not struggle or resist the shearing.

## Convicted on the Word of False Witnesses
Psalm 35:11 (Mark 14:57-62; Luke 23:8-10)

Psalm 35 is another cry of David. Perhaps it is the closeness of David to his Lord that causes so many of his words to whisper of things to come. In this psalm, David prays for rescue from enemies that have risen up against him. "Malicious witnesses rise up against me," he says in verse 11.

David has already, in verses 1-3, prayed that God Himself would take up the fight against his enemies. He pled for God to take it all in His hand and searched his own soul to feel God's assurance. But then he sank once more into the fear and despair, enumerating the circumstances around him that seems to block his prayer and threatened to rob him of the very assurance to which he tries to cling.

It was at that point that David wrote the words that seem to echo in the ears of those who know what is to come: "Malicious witnesses rise up against me." The words seem to linger in the air. They seem to thrust me forward in time to think of other witnesses—false witnesses who maliciously seek to convict an innocent man in a sham of a trial.

God had set the standards of trials when He gave the law to His people. It was He who proclaimed, "On the evidence of two witnesses or three witnesses, he who is to die shall be put to death" (Deuteronomy 17:6). Then, centuries later, in a twisted mockery of a trial, false witnesses came forth to condemn the Son of God to death.

## Struck by the Authorities
Zechariah 13:6-7 (Mark 14:27; Matthew 26:31)

In the 13th chapter of Zechariah, the prophet is detailing a time when God Himself promises that a remnant of His people will be brought through the fires of refinement and will be restored to Him. Leading up to that declaration, God speaks to Zechariah (and to all who would hear), "'Awake, O sword, against My Shepherd, and against the man, My Associate,' declares the LORD of hosts. 'Strike the Shepherd that the sheep may be scattered.'"

"My Shepherd, My Associate" appears to refer to the Good Shepherd, the Messiah who would be the shepherd of the house of David. The shepherd would be struck down, and the sheep would be scattered.

As I ponder the words of Zechariah, I think on the words of the Lord. "*Awake,*" He says, as though someone or something was sleeping, waiting. Almighty God described a time in the future that would signal the beginning of the execution of the plan He had set in place before creation. Knowing, as no one else could, that the incarnate Lord, the Savior of the world, would have to be "struck down," God said, through Zechariah, that He would call "the sword" (those who would serve as His instruments) to awake and He would allow, even command, them to strike down the Shepherd—for that was the only way for salvation to be provided.

Both Matthew and Mark wrote that Jesus quoted this reference, as He prepared His disciples for what lay ahead. It is interesting, however, to note that Jesus did not quote Zechariah exactly. Zechariah said, "Strike the Shepherd that the sheep may be scattered." Jesus carried it farther, emphasizing the reality of the prophecy—"I [the God of the universe, Jehovah, the three-in-one] will strike down the Shepherd, and the sheep of the flock will be scattered." Jesus left no doubt that this was God's plan, and God was ultimately in command of its execution.

# The Scarlet Thread

In John 10, Jesus had given His disciples a glimpse of this same concept when He identified Himself as the Good Shepherd: (verses 17-18a) "For this reason the Father loves Me, because I lay down My life so that I may take it again. No one has taken it away from Me, but I lay it down on My own initiative."

## Lifted Up
Psalm 102:10 (John 3:14, 12:32)

Psalm 102 is a prayer given by one who has been afflicted, who is pouring out his sorrow and complaints before the Lord. The unidentified psalmist writes, "because of Your indignation and Your wrath, for you have lifted me up and cast me away."

In a prior chapter of *The Scarlet Thread*, we looked at the incident in the life of the Israelites in the wilderness (found in Numbers 21), where Moses lifted up a bronze snake on a pole. Those who had been bitten by snakes could be saved if they would *look up* to the form that had been lifted up. In this verse, the psalmist is perhaps remembering that time in his nation's history. Perhaps in his need for God to hear his cries, he grasped at an image that poignantly illustrated his need to be saved from the burdens he carried.

There amid the agony and despair that is being voiced, the Spirit slips in a foreshadowing of the ultimate solution, not only to the cries of this psalmist but to ours as well. In my mind, as the psalmist prays, an image of God Himself, in the person of Jesus Christ, is momentarily superimposed on the scene and I hear him cry out to God the Father, *Because of Your righteous indignation with all of mankind and Your wrath at all the evil they have done, You have lifted Me up to be the salvation of all.*

## Pierced
Zechariah 12:10; Psalm 22:16; Isaiah 53:5, 49:16 (John 19:34, 37, 20:27)

Pierced His hands and feet
Psalm 22:16; Isaiah 53:5

As I pause on Psalm 22:16 and Isaiah 53:5, I immediately note that images come to mind of the day when the soldiers would pierce the side of Jesus with a spear. The psalmist brings me to the foot of the cross, saying, "A band of evildoers has encompassed me; they pierced my hands and my feet." Likewise Isaiah, describing the coming Messiah, said "He was pierced for our transgressions."

See the One who was pierced
Zechariah 12:10

It is Zechariah 12:10 that John, the beloved disciple, quotes in John 19:37, "they will look on Me whom they have pierced." Oddly, it seems that Zechariah is not necessarily speaking of that moment at the cross; he's not referring to those at the foot of the cross who look up to see the pierced Lord. Rather, Zechariah is looking farther into the future, as he describes the scene at the time of the King's return. "In that day," in the day that Jehovah will finally settle the score, so to speak—in that day, when the nations of the world come against Jerusalem, "I [God] will pour out on the house of David and on the inhabitants of Jerusalem, the Spirit of grace and supplication, so that they will look on Me whom they have pierced." So what is happening in Zechariah 12:10? In the final pages of man's history, God will flood the house of David with great grace and understanding so they can recognize the one they pierced as being the promised Messiah— the Savior of the world.

As a side note, have you ever wondered why Jesus had to be pierced? The obvious answer of course was that the soldiers needed to hurry up the dying process because Passover was close. But Jesus appeared to be dead so the

117

soldier pierced His side, just to make sure. (That fulfilled another prophecy about *no broken bones.*)

Though there is no definitive explanation, my thoughts turn back to the Garden of Eden. I think of the sin that entered the world—the same sin for which the Lord's beaten body hung upon the cross. Genesis 3:21 tells us that the Lord made garments of skin for Adam and his wife. Skins—the skin of an animal! To clothe man, to cover his sin, God was forced to introduce the first step of His ultimate redemptive plan: He sacrificed an animal—He *pierced* an animal—not to provide food, but to provide a covering for the sin until the time that full redemption could be purchased. Perhaps the piercing of the body of Jesus was a visual seal to the promise, a visual sign that the sacrifice that began in Eden was complete.

Inscribed in His hands
Isaiah 49:16

Isaiah 49:16 also refers to the wounds to Christ's hands. This verse is found in a passage in which we are being told about Zion, but it brings forth a visual image of the crucifixion, recording, "Behold, I have inscribed you on the palms of My hands." As I read this verse, I consider what those words actually imply. The first point that jumps out at me is the "I" as in "I have inscribed." We know that the angry crowd called for His death, the Jewish and Roman authorities brought it about, and the soldiers actually pounded the nails into His hands and feet. Still, Isaiah says I, meaning the Lord Himself, inscribed the scar into His hands.

The second point that strikes home to me is that He says that "I inscribed you on the palms of My hands." The powers of the world may have torn into His flesh and applied the scars, but it seems that Christ figuratively wrote the names of all mankind into those scars. Jesus has inscribed the names of all the redeemed into the scars on His hands! Wonder of all wonders: my name was written into His palms!

Prophecies of Jesus' Death and Resurrection

**Lots Cast for His Garments**
Psalm 22:18 (Matthew 27:35; Mark 15:24; Luke 23:34; John 19:24)

Psalm 22, attributed to David, is one that is considered Messianic because it so clearly describes one of the critical episodes in the life of the coming Messiah. Interspersed between cries of anguish or pleas for help and declarations of praise and confidence, David, directed by the Spirit of God, shows us a picture of the fateful day when the incarnate Lord would die for His people.

This Psalm is filled with words that echo the voice of Jesus. Beginning with the familiar "My God, my God, why have You forsaken me?" in verse 1, the Psalmist begins to build a picture of the coming Savior and of the day of His sacrifice. Phrases like "a reproach of men and despised by the people" in verse 6 and "All who see me sneer at me" in verse 7 remind us of the mockery and humiliation Jesus endured on His way to the cross. Verses 16 and 18 clearly describe the scene that the gospel writers wrote of centuries later: "They pierced my hands and my feet. I can count all my bones. They divide my garments among them, and for my clothing they cast lots." (See Matthew 27:35; Mark 15:24; John 19:24.)

The casting of lots for Jesus clothing seems to be a simple act of expediency. The clothing would no longer be needed, so the soldiers claimed the garments for themselves. We aren't told specifically how many or what kind of garments were involved, but the gospel writers make it clear that while the Maker of all mankind hung upon the cross, the soldiers divided His few worldly possessions.

As I consider this stop in the journey I marvel at the detail that is provided in the prophecies. Sometimes we miss the simple statements, losing some of the precious details in the process. The psalmist wrote "They divide my garments among them, and for my clothing they cast lots," giving the impression that two acts are taking place—a dividing of garments and a casting of lots for clothing. Matthew, Mark, and Luke don't really shed much light on this apparent sequence of actions; they only record that the garments were divided by casting lots. If no other record of the incident was written, we could be left wondering about whether the prophecy really was completely fulfilled. But that is not the case. The Spirit of God gave us the substantiation that our legalistic minds would need when He inspired the writing of John's gospel. John very clearly tells us how the prophecy was fulfilled, when he included in John 19:23-24, "The soldiers, when they had crucified Jesus, took His outer garments and made four parts, a part to every soldier and also the tunic; now the tunic was seamless, woven in one piece. So they said to one another, 'Let us not tear it, but cast lots for it, to decide whose it shall be.'" Then, John specifically says that this action was to fulfill Scripture. Isn't it odd that the very ones who sought to destroy Jesus (the soldiers, the Jewish leaders, the Roman government) all performed acts that served as evidence to verify just *who* He really is?

## No Bones Broken
Psalm 34:20; Exodus 12:46; Numbers 9:12 (John 19:32-36)

In Psalm 34, David is praising the deeds of the Lord. He begins the chapter with "I will bless the LORD at all times; His praise shall continually be in my mouth." Then he goes on to describe the LORD as the deliverer—not just in saving him from those who sought to harm him, but ultimately rescuing his very soul.

By the end of the chapter, David is building an image that, to later generations, was understood to represent the promised Messiah. David speaks of the afflictions of the righteous and writes that the Lord delivers him out of them all. I think perhaps he is proclaiming his confidence that at some point in time the Lord will bring all those who are righteous (not by their own doing) out of their afflictions (sin and its consequences). Then David adds to the picture by explaining that He (God—the one who is doing the delivering) will keep all His bones, unbroken.

Partially I see this in these verses because I know the Easter story; I know that the gospel writers made a point of telling us that no bones were broken. But why would that make a difference, other than to fulfill Scripture? The answer to that question, and the rest of the reason I see Christ so clearly in this passage, lies in Exodus 12:46, where God meticulously commands that the Passover lamb was to be eaten in a single house, was not to be taken outside of the house, and that no bones were to be broken. So, I guess the question could be asked: aside from the *because God said so* answer, why was it important that the sacrificial lamb have no broken bones? Was God, even then, setting up a picture that would help verify the identity of the Anointed One? Certainly that became the case, for Numbers 9:12 tells us that same instruction was given when God told them to commemorate the Passover every year. By the time of the crucifixion, all Jews who were beginning to wonder if Jesus was indeed the Messiah that was promised would know the significance of the fact that *no bones were broken*.

### Offered Vinegar to Drink
Psalm 69:21 (Matthew 27:34, 48; Mark 15:23, 36; John 19:29)

Psalm 69 is another one written by David. So often David's psalms meander around from the pits of despair to the heights of joy; he wallows in grief and self-pity, only to once again confidently boast of the glories of his Lord. As we see so many facets of David revealed in his psalms, we also see the seemingly random verses or phrases that could as easily be God Himself speaking. It is perhaps those moments that most clearly show us a glimpse into the future.

Such is the case in verse 21 of Psalm 69: "They also gave me gall for my food and for my thirst they gave me vinegar to drink."

Matthew and Mark each points out in his gospel that Jesus was offered vinegar to drink, but that Jesus refused to drink it. Later, Matthew, Mark, and John all explain that just before He died, Jesus said "I thirst." Someone below His cross dipped a sponge into some vinegar, added some hyssop, and gave it to Him. It was at that point that Jesus drank, uttered His last words, and died.

Sometimes in breezing through the Easter story we fail to notice that Jesus was offered vinegar (wine) twice. Apparently it was the custom that the soldiers would give the prisoners vinegar mixed with a drug of some kind. The drink would lessen the torturous effects of the crucifixion—but, Jesus refused the mixture, facing the full agony of the cross.

It is perhaps the second time that vinegar was offered that is the most significant. As some writers describe the physical effects of the crucifixion, one thing that occurs is the drying out of the mouth. Thus, as Jesus neared His last moments, He was ready to make the final declaration that God's redemptive plan was at lasted completed, but His mouth was dry and cracked. So, He almost whispered, "I thirst," to which someone responded by dipping a sponge in a vessel of vinegar (wine) and adding some hyssop. With His mouth moistened, Jesus was then able to utter His last words, "It is finished."

Hyssop is an herb in the mint family that was used medicinally, for cleansing, and for flavoring. The significance of its use in these passages lies in the picture that is being portrayed. Hyssop was used in the sacrificial process, as well as in the process of marking the lintels of the doors at the time of the first Passover (Exodus 12:22). Thus, in those last moments, Jesus verbally proclaimed the completion of God's redemptive plan and at the same time symbolically demonstrated the end to the sacrifice of the Passover.

### Scorned and Laughed at by the Crowd
Psalm 22:6-7, 109:25 (Matthew 27:39-40; Mark 15:29-32)

I pause briefly at Psalm 22:6-7 and at Psalm 109:25. "I am… a reproach of men and despised by the people." "All who see me sneer at me; they separate with the lip, they wag the head."

The words bring images of Jesus' slow walk up the stony hill called Golgotha. All around Him, crowds mocked and sneered and laughed. The people shook their heads and pointed at the humiliating picture of the Rabbi, beaten, scourged, and crushed beneath the load of the cross He bore.

## My God, Why Have You Forsaken Me?
Psalm 22:1 (Matthew 27:46; Mark 15:34)

The question that is raised with this reference, as with many others, is this: Is an Old Testament verse a *prophecy* merely because the Spirit prompted someone in the New Testament to recognize the similarity of the historical utterances to the life or ministry of Jesus? The leading phrase of Chapter 22 of Psalms is certainly not written as a "*this will happen*" kind of statement, but it does make me stop to ponder. *Why did the Holy Spirit point out certain phrases to the New Testament writers, causing then to make the connections they made?*

As to this passage, Matthew and Mark both wrote what Jesus said. Jesus, of course, knew the words of the psalmist: He knew them from His study of the Scriptures as He grew up in a religious home. Even more, He knew them because He had been there. His Spirit had lingered near to David, had heard David pour out his heart to his God. So perhaps the verse has prophetic overtones because He listened to the agonizing cry of David. Perhaps, looking ahead to the fate that awaited Him, He even identified with that moment when David felt abandoned by God. Then, in His own moment of separation from the Father, He chose to repeat them, so all who knew the words of David would understand the depth of His pain.

Undoubtedly, the verse brings images of Jesus. In David's haunting cry, I remember that Jesus is the *son of David*, the *offspring of the house of David*, the *promise of an eternal king who would sit on the throne of David*. It was perhaps fitting that He chose those words, for just as David's groaning always gave way to praise, Jesus knew that true, everlasting victory was only a breath away.

## Sun Will Go Down at Noon
Amos 8:9 (Matthew 27:45)

*In that day* is always like a finger pointing to the future that signals followers of the Lord to take note, be alert, and watch for what Almighty God will someday do. Generally it refers either to

123

significant things that will occur at a time when the Messiah, in His first or second time upon the *first earth*, has stepped into the history of man.

Amos tells us that *in that day* God will make the sun go down at noon and will make the earth dark when it should be light. Matthew records the fulfillment of this verse when he writes that from the 6th hour to the 9th hour, the earth was held in darkness. From noon to three o'clock, the brightest part of the day, the sky became black. Perhaps there is a symbolism that we can find here, for the ninth hour was the moment when the agonizing cry of Jesus was heard: "My God, my God, why have You forsaken Me." It was at the ninth hour that He received a final drink of vinegar with hyssop. It was at the ninth hour that He calmly, perhaps even in a whisper, declared, "It is finished." In those hours of darkness—black as the sin that was gathering upon His shoulders—the forces of evil waited to carry His life away, and when that blackness reached its climax, Jesus Christ, the incarnate God, gave up His physical life in exchange for the spiritual lives of all mankind.

It is always fascinating when the Master of the universe demonstrates that even though He sealed creation, He is still its master. He created an orderly pattern to all of creation. Even though we don't necessarily understand it, nature behaves in a prescribed, logical, reliable manner—because God designed it that way. That order, however, in no way stands independent of its creator; God is still in charge of His creation, and when He chooses to exercise that right, the forces of nature bow to His supremacy.

So Amos, led by the Spirit, could prophesy of a time when God would *shut down the light*, because of the devastating pain in witnessing the death of His Son.

### Death, Where Is Your Sting?
Hosea 13:14 (I Corinthians 15:54-56)

Like the line quoted from Psalm 22:1, I again question if a mere statement that is quoted in the New Testament can automatically be called *prophecy*. Perhaps in this case it is not the statement that is prophetic, but rather the fact that there seems to be some underlying hint that the question will be answered in some distant time.

Hosea 13 is expounding the idolatry of Ephraim and the consequences that will follow. In verse 4, God clearly tells the people that He has been their God and now they have chosen to turn their backs on Him. The destruction is promised—but God holds out a glimmer of hope. He asks, "Shall I ransom them? Shall I redeem them?" and then turns from speaking to the people to speak to Death itself, "O Death where are your thorns? O Sheol, where is your sting?" Therein lies the prophecy of the Messiah—God asks, "Shall I redeem them?" and then in the next breath hints at the answer—of course He will redeem them, and His questions to Death suggests that Death itself will figure into the act of redemption.

On that forsaken hillside, when the Son of God hung upon the cross, Death stood ready to claim victory over the creator, over man, over life itself. But then the *sting* of Death—sin—was defeated! Through His own death and resurrection, Jesus destroyed the power of sin and conquered Death.

Paul, quite graciously, finishes the explanation for us. "The sting of death is sin, and the power of sin is the law; but thanks be to God, who gives us the victory through our Lord Jesus Christ."

**Grave with the Wicked, with the Rich in Death**
Isaiah 53:9 (Matthew 27:57-60)

I pause so many times in the 53$^{rd}$ chapter of Isaiah! So many of his word pictures fill my mind with pictures of Christ—pictures that all too often cause me pain as I recognize myself among the crowds. Still, those images bring joy as well, because I am given a front-row seat at the greatest illustration of love that was ever displayed.

In verse 9, Isaiah almost speaks out of both sides of his mouth, so to speak. After telling us in prior verses that the Promised One

# The Scarlet Thread

will be oppressed and afflicted unjustly, in our stead, he then tells us that His (the Promised One's) "grave will be assigned with the wicked," but that He "will be with a rich man in His death—because He had done no violence, nor was there any deceit in His mouth." The phrases don't seem to be fit together as nicely as I would like. Isaiah seems to imply, even while looking at the text in a pre-Christ context, that this person will receive a rich man's burial because He had done no wrong. So, where does the "grave with the wicked" fit in?

Matthew doesn't really shed much light to answer my question either. Aside from at some point showing us that Jesus *died* in the presence of thieves, Matthew's description of His grave consists of letting us know that a rich man named Joseph of Arimathea gave his own tomb to be used by the Master.

So again, I wonder, what did Isaiah mean by saying the Promised One would have his "*grave assigned with wicked men?*" One web source I consulted suggested that perhaps it was the *intention* of those who would crucify the Christ that was being predicted. Thus a different way of writing the verse (using my own amplification) would be: *His executioners will plan that His death will be with the wicked—the thieves and robbers with which He will share the hillside execution. But instead, a rich man will intervene and allow Him use of his very own tomb.*"

Far be it for me to argue with learned scholars who have contributed to trusted commentaries (and I agree that the interpretation is probably true.) However, a tiny whisper in my head reminds me that wherever Jesus would have been lain—in a shallow pauper's grave or a luxurious marble sepulcher—He would have been lain with the wicked, for we are all *wicked sinners* in desperate need of the saving grace of that very "man" who was buried in a tomb that could not hope to hold Him.

**Raised on the Third Day**
Hosea 6:2 (Matthew 28: 5-7; Luke 24:36-48; John 20:19, 24-29)

*Three days* almost takes on a mystical tone in the Bible sometimes, appearing over and over in events of importance. We are never really surprised when something connected with God takes three days to be accomplished.

Yet, as I pause at Hosea 6:2, I see the "He will raise us up on the third day," as a kind of indirect reference to the promised Messiah. The us appears to be the same us that had to return to the Lord, but at the same time, I recognize that it is only because He was raised on the third day that I (or anyone else) can be raised from out of my sins to live before Him (forever).

I go back to the last verse of Chapter 5, where Hosea said that essentially God said to Himself, "I will go away and return to My place until they [the Jewish people] acknowledge their guilt and seek my face; in their affliction they will earnestly seek Me." God pulled away from His chosen people! Like a father that realizes that his child must sometimes learn hard lessons the *hard* way, God pulled back to give the people time to realize their need for Him.

Then beginning in Chapter 6, we see a glimpse into the future when the people eventually respond. Verse 1 states the decision they are realizing they must make—"Let us return to the LORD." They acknowledge that God has allowed them to be torn and wounded—torn from their land and afflicted both physically and spiritually—but they remember that He promised to heal them and bandage their wounds. Then Hosea writes (verse 2), "He will revive us after two days." (Various commentaries appear to agree that *two* or even *two or three days* was probably a Hebrew idiom that basically means *in a short time*, meaning that the time of God's disfavor with them will not last forever, that in a short time He will make it possible for them to be revived.)

As I contemplate the remainder of the verse, I catch a glimpse of the salvation that is possible only because the Holy One of God shouldered the burden of sin and carried it to the grave and because He then conquered Death and sin when He rose on the third day. Thus, in my own amplified version, I see Hosea's closing words for this verse as: "He [Almighty God] will raise us [all those who seek His forgiveness] up on the third day [because we are raised with Christ], so we can live [forever] before Him."

# The Scarlet Thread

## Ascend to Sit at the Right Hand of the Father
Psalm 110:1 (Hebrews 1:3; Acts 2:34-35)

Again, a psalm of David points our attention to the heavens. *The LORD* is Almighty God and Father, Jehovah, Yahweh, the One whom David served. Who then is *my Lord*? *My Lord* suggests supremacy—one whom David considers to be of higher rank and importance than himself—a feat not easily accomplished at that time in Israel's history. David, through the prompting of the Spirit, gives us a glimpse of a King that would be greater and higher than King David, who was thought by all to be the greatest king ever to rule Israel.

And, of course, *right hand of God* brings to mind Hebrews 1:3: "When He had made purification of sins; He sat down at the right hand of the Majesty on high." In his first sermon on the Day of Pentecost, Peter emphatically explained that David was most certainly not speaking of himself when he penned that psalm, for it was not he (David) who ascended into heaven.

> As a side note—another small detour—there is yet another idea that Psalm 110:1 brings to my mind. As I look at the verse, I ponder for a moment on the *footstool of God*: The LORD tells the Son to sit at His right hand until He makes His (the Son's) enemies a footstool for His feet. I wonder just what would the *footstool of the Lord* actually be?
>
> The first mention of a *footstool* of God is in I Chronicles 28:2, where King David is telling the people that he wants to build a permanent home for the Ark of the Covenant and for *the footstool of our God*. Apparently then the *footstool* is either the Ark of the Covenant, or perhaps the temple itself that will be the home for the Ark. Psalm 132:7 says, "Let us go into His dwelling place; Let us worship at His footstool." *His dwelling* would be the temple, but again the *footstool* could represent either the temple or the Holy of Holies, which was to hold the Ark. Isaiah 66:1 expands the interpretation, "Heaven is My throne and the earth is My footstool." (Matthew 5:35 and Acts 7:49 make reference to the earth being God's

# Prophecies of Jesus' Death and Resurrection

footstool, as well.) Lamentations 2:1 describes the anger of the Lord and says that "he has not remembered his footstool in the day of his anger." A note in my NIV Study Bible says that the footstool could be the Ark of the Covenant, but more likely is Mount Zion. Nearly all other references to the footstool of God (Luke 20:43, Acts 2:35, Hebrews 10:13) are essentially quotes of Psalm 110:1, referring to a time when His (Christ's) enemies would be His footstool.

So, again I wonder: *What is the footstool of God?* As I flipped pages back and forth to try to understand, a hazy idea began to take shape in my mind. I first begin to see the Ark of the Covenant. This was the object that God chose to represent His presence with the Israelites. Later, when the temple was built, that became the place where His presence would be. Since the temple was in Jerusalem, which is sometimes referred to as Zion or Mount Zion, I can understand how any of those terms can be seen as the *footstool of God*—especially after the last temple was destroyed. Then, as I consider the references to the earth being the *footstool of God*, I begin to get a clearer picture. Isaiah 66:1 sharpens the image for me: *Heaven is God's throne and earth is His footstool.* Earth is the jewel in His creation. It was there that He put man and it was there that He placed a figurative connection to Himself. As the image becomes less hazy, I seem to see God sitting on His throne, but resting His feet on the earth—suggesting the promise that He would indeed one day set His feet upon the earth. Thus, the Ark, the temple, and even the city of Jerusalem (Zion) become pictures of the relationship that exists between God and His created beings. The earth is *His footstool*—emphasizing not that it is held in servitude under His feet but that it serves as the connecting point between the physical and the spiritual realms.

Why then does Scripture say that the Father says to Christ, "Sit at My right hand until I make your enemies a footstool for Your feet."? I wonder if perhaps this verse is more prophecy than I have ever before considered—speaking

129

not only of the ascension of Christ, but of His return. Perhaps the key is *until*. How long will Christ sit at His right hand? *Until*—until I (Almighty God) make your (Christ's) enemies a footstool for your (Christ's) feet—until that moment comes when the enemies of the Lamb gather in Israel for that final battle—until that time when Jesus, the King of Kings, rises from His seat at the right hand of the Father and comes back to the earth—*the footstool of God*—to once and for all deal with the enemies that have gathered there.

# VII. Additional Prophetic Passages

## *Re-Defining the category*

In Chapter VII we pause at passages and verses that refer to general prophecies that bring Jesus to mind.

In a very real sense, this chapter of *The Scarlet Thread* represents a hodge-podge of stops, with little connecting them but the fact they were included in the books of prophecy. Most, but not all of them, refer to the second coming of Christ or to His millennial reign.

## *Specific Examples—Stops along my journey*

### Woman's Offspring
Genesis 3:15

Before the new world had barely had a chance to experience the life that had been given it, God began to reveal a glimpse of His ultimate plan to rescue mankind from the devastating choices that would soon separate him from his Creator. Genesis 3:15, the first Messianic prophecy, provides a glimpse into God's plan of salvation. "And I will put enmity between you and the woman, and between your seed and her seed; He shall bruise you on the head, and you shall bruise him on the heel." The *He* of course, is the Anointed One—the coming Savior, the one who will execute the plan that Almighty God set in place before creating mankind.

The *you* and *your seed* in this verse is of course the serpent— Satan, the deceiver. As I pause to think of Christ, I find myself thinking of Satan, too. I can't help but wonder if he had any idea that his fate was already sealed. Did he understand the ultimate end to story? Did he know that in the end his apparent triumph over God, seen when God incarnate hung on the cross, was just one more step in God's ultimate plan?

I wonder too if those who repeated the history of man until it could be written down, or those who first recorded it on papyrus

131

scrolls, actually understood just how important this simple declaration was to their survival. I wonder when the followers of Jehovah began to realize that this was indeed a prophetic statement and that it had vital significance to the promises made later to Abraham and David. Having already seen Jesus as Creator it is somewhat chilling, only a few pages into the Scripture, to suddenly catch a glimpse of Him bruised, beaten, and hanging on a cross. I can almost see the ecstatic joy of that serpent, in his single moment of triumph. Even knowing that his triumph was indeed for just a moment, it is heartbreaking to think about what that moment cost.

**A Certain Man (and subsequent references to the "man")**
Ezekiel 9:2-4, 11, 10:2, 40:3; Daniel 10:5, 16-19, 12:7

References to *a certain man* appear in both Ezekiel and Daniel. Both prophets record visions in which they mention *a certain man* and in subsequent verses refer back to him.

Those verses initially prompted an image of Jesus in my mind, but a closer study of the surrounding text suggests the *certain man* was most likely an unnamed angel, rather than a vision of the physical person of Christ. Nevertheless, I pause here for a while to contemplate what it was about the references that initially made me think of Jesus.

In Ezekiel 9:2-4, Ezekiel records that the man was given an assignment to *mark the people*—to distinguish between the ones who still serve the Lord and the ones who don't. The task brought memories of Matthew 25:31-46, when he records that "He (the Son of Man) will separate them from one another, as a shepherd separates the sheep from the goats." Perhaps it was the memory of this New Testament passage that prompted me to see Jesus in Ezekiel's *certain man*.

The ninth chapter closes with the *man clothed in linen* reporting back to the Lord that all had been accomplished as He directed. What I heard as I read verse 11 was, "It is done. It is finished." The echo of Christ's words filled my mind.

## Additional Prophetic Passages

Daniel (10:16-19) also refers to *a certain man*, or *one who resembled a human being*, that was seen in a vision. This *man*, when Daniel was weakened by the vision, touched him and gave him strength, saying, "Peace be with you. Take courage." As I read the words, I hear: "Peace I leave with you." (John 14:27) and "Take courage; I have overcome the world." (John 15:33).

So, as I study the surrounding text and realize that the *certain man*, spoken of by Ezekiel and Daniel was not likely Jesus at all, I wonder if I have stopped at these verses in vain. But then I recall that the visions were given by the Lord, and the Lord directed the actions of the *certain man*. I also remember that the job of the servants of the Lord (the angels) were to speak for the Lord and do "as He would do." It is no great wonder, then, that I recognized the presence and the voice of my Lord through the actions of His angels.

As I prepare to leave this stop, I am reminded that throughout the Scripture His messengers communicated His words and deeds for me to hear and see. It is for me to "rightly divide the word of truth" to discern the subtle distinctions (II Timothy 2:15, KJV). It is also for me to learn that I, like His angelic messengers and His prophets of old, am expected to carefully communicate His words and deeds to future generations.

### David's Crown or Kingdom

Genesis 49:10, 24; Numbers 24:17, 19; II Kings 8:19; II Kings 19:30; Psalm 14:7, 53:6, 80:15, 108:8; Isaiah 9:6-7, 11:1, 10, 22:22; Jeremiah 23:5, 30:9; Ezekiel 37:25-26, Ezekiel 17:22-23; Amos 9:11; Nahum 2:2, I Chronicles 28:7, II Chronicles 21:7

Beyond the prophecies that the Anointed One would be a direct descendant of David, as discussed in a prior chapter, many prophecies in the Old Testament connect the image of the Messiah to the person of David—to his kingdom, his reign, his crown, etc.

David was the most beloved king of Israel—by the Jews and by God. God singled David out to be the king, anointing him and naming him as the king while Saul still held the throne. Through all the high and low points of his reign and in his personal life, through his struggles to obey his God, and even through his many failures as a man and as a king, one constant remained in David: he loved the Lord.

The relationship that existed between God and David has been held as a model for those of us who came later. Indeed, in that relationship we can clearly see that when we honestly, humbly seek to follow God, all our failures, mistakes, and disobedient choices are forgiven. God wants to love us; His desire is not dependent on anything that we do.

Thus, as I stop to ponder the verses that I have placed in this category, my mind quickly recognizes the link between David and Jesus and my heart immediately responds, creating images of the great King who came, as promised, from the line of David.

The scepter shall not depart from Judah
Genesis 49:10, 24; Numbers 24: 17, 19

As early as the blessing of Jacob that is recorded in Genesis 49:10, we begin to see the prophecy of the *forever* king who would come from the tribe of Judah, "The scepter shall not depart from Judah, nor the ruler's staff from between his feet." Verse 24 continues the image, "from the hands of the Mighty One of Jacob (From there is the Shepherd, the Stone of Israel.)" A similar description is given in Balaam's blessing in Numbers 24:17, 19: "a star shall come forth from Jacob, a scepter shall rise from Israel. One from Jacob shall have dominion."

The promise of a lamp
II Kings 8:19, 19:30

As the history, not always a prosperous history, of the tribe of Judah continued, God never forgot His promise, nor did He cease reminding the descendants of Judah of that promise. Even after the house of David had divided and neither branch was consistently following the ways of the Lord, we find verses in II Kings that call us to remember.

# Additional Prophetic Passages

II Kings 8:19 recalls, "He had promised him [David] to give a lamp to him through his sons always," and II Kings 19:30 promises, "The surviving remnant of the house of Judah will again take root downward and bear fruit upward." In the first of these verses I recognize the *lamp* that is promised to David is none other than Jesus, the Light of the world. In the second, an image is formed in my mind of the man, Christ Jesus, standing like the cross on which He died. His feet are rooted into the earth for He chose to leave the glories of heaven to become a part of the race of man. His arms, outstretched, reach upward, for in His death and resurrection He bears the souls of all who will receive Him upward.

A King would come from David's line
Psalm 14:7, Psalm 53:6, Psalm 80:15, Psalm 108:8

Beyond its historical records of the house of David, Scripture records through the psalmists and the prophets that the time will come when God will fulfill His promise to David—a King will come (did come) whose reign will be from everlasting to everlasting, forever and ever.

From the depths of despair, Psalms 14:7 and 53:6 both exclaim, "Oh, that the salvation of Israel would come out of Zion!" as the psalmist remembers that the LORD has promised to restore His people. Other psalms that record similar reminders of the promised connection between David and the coming Messiah include Psalm 80:15 which speaks of the "shoot which Your right hand has planted," and Psalm 108:8 which recalls the promise that "Judah is My scepter."

Connecting the King of Kings to the house of David
Ezekiel 37:25-26; Isaiah 9:7, 22:22; Jeremiah 30:9

Jeremiah emphatically connects the King of Kings to the house of David when he writes in 30:9, "But they shall serve the LORD their God and David their king, whom I will raise up for them." In Jeremiah's time David had already been dead for a long time, so when he writes of *David their king* he can only be referring to the promised one, who will one day reign over all Israel, and the entire world. Isaiah carries the message as well, writing in Isaiah 22:22, "Then I will set the key of the house of David on his [the Messiah's] shoulder." In Isaiah 9:7, we find further promise of the reign of peace that has no end, "There will be no end to the increase of His government or of peace, on the throne of David and over his kingdom, to establish it and to uphold it with justice and righteousness from then on and forevermore."

Ezekiel 37:25-26 speaks of the land, the physical land of Israel on which the people of God had lived for generations only to lose it because of their repeated disobedience. Ezekiel describes a time when that land will again come into their hands: "They will live on the land that I gave to Jacob My servant, in which your fathers lived; and they will live on it, they, and their sons and their sons' sons, forever; and David My servant will be their prince forever. I will make a covenant of peace with them; it will be an everlasting covenant with them. And I will place them and multiply them, and will set My sanctuary in their midst forever."

God says that He will make a covenant of peace with them forever. There is no doubt, amid the tempestuous history of Israel, that the promised *forever peace* has not yet come to them; there is no doubt that it can only come when it is ushered in by the Prince of Peace.

The parable of the branch
Ezekiel 17:22-23

One of the most interesting stops in my journey through the prophets was found in Ezekiel 17:22-23: "Thus says the Lord GOD, 'I will also take a sprig from the lofty top of the cedar and set it out; I will pluck from the topmost of its young twigs a tender one and I will plant it on a high and lofty mountain. On the high mountain of Israel I will plant it, that it may bring forth boughs and bear fruit and become a stately cedar."

On the surface, taken completely on its own, this little passage would possible not have drawn my attention at all, but there is something about Ezekiel quoting God, saying "I will also take," that pulls me into the picture. When I read of God *taking, giving, raising up*, etc. a *shoot, a branch, a root*, etc., I automatically think of Jesus, the root of the house of Jesse, the branch of the house of David; so, I simply must pause at the *sprig* as well.

As I read and re-read these verses, I begin to watch a tender story unfold, almost in slow motion. I see a tall, straight cedar standing proudly among a cluster of lesser trees and shrubs in the foothills of a towering mountain range. The cedar is a powerful, majestic tree—I think that it must symbolize a ruler or perhaps a long line of rulers. As I watch the cedar pass through the seasons, it sways and bends; sometimes it bends almost to the point of breaking, but then stands again. As I watch, I notice God standing to the side of the picture, also watching the cedar, and I see tears in His eyes. Finally, Jehovah reaches out and takes a sprig, a tender shoot, from the very top of that cedar. I watch as He slowly, carefully, lovingly, carries the shoot to the top of a high mountain and plants it. I watch and wait as more seasons, more years, seem to pass. The little sprig grows, reaching its branches toward heaven. It sways in the mountain breezes but never bends, always standing straight and strong. The young cedar grows and produces branches and bears fruit, and off to the side, the Lord God watches and smiles. I smile too, for in my soul I recognize the tender sprig as the humble Christ, coming from the line of kings of Israel, becoming the King of kings who reigns forever.

> (As I look back to the beginning of Chapter 17, I find that the image my heart created as I read those two little verses was not too far removed from the one that is described in Ezekiel's prophesy. The first 21 verses were written as an allegory or parable in which Ezekiel told of King Zedekiah's faulty foreign policy, which eventually led to the Babylonian captivity. At the end of the allegory, Ezekiel continued the same style of writing to provide the beautiful Messianic prophecy that appeared in verses 22 and 23.)

# The Scarlet Thread

<u>Promise of restoration, even amid the devastation</u>
Nahum 2:2

Nahum is such a small book, filled with the ultimate promise of destruction of Nineveh. Yet, in Nahum 2:2, I find the promise that in the end God will restore His people. "For the LORD will restore the splendor of Jacob like the splendor of Israel." Even as Nahum prophesies of the absolute, irrevocable promise that Nineveh will be destroyed, he takes a moment to remind the people that God will restore the splendor of Jacob and Israel—and ultimately He will restore all mankind to Himself.

Today, I sit here in a twenty-first century world that is collectively turning farther away from God. As warning bells seem to be sounding in my head at an alarming pace, I find it very comforting that God's Spirit whispered to Nahum that even as he declared the righteous judgment of the Lord, he needed to extend a thread of hope for anyone who finally hears and wants to turn back to Him.

<u>The lamp and the throne</u>
I Chronicles 28:7; II Chronicles 21:7

In I Chronicles 28:7, the writer says that God would "establish his [David's] kingdom forever." When I pause at II Chronicles 21:7, I am again given the image of light that was mentioned II Kings 8:19, for the writer reminds his readers that He [God] had promised to give a lamp to David and his sons forever. *A lamp*, the Light of the world, was promised to David because one day that light will carry on the kingship of the line of David, reigning from the physical throne that, even then, will be referred to as the *throne of David* because it demonstrates the fulfillment of the promises of the Lord.

## Eternal Throne
II Samuel 7:16; I Kings 8:25; I Chronicles 17:12, 14, 22:10; Psalms 89:27-29

Repeatedly Jehovah, Almighty God, promised that the throne of David will endure forever. The verses listed above emphatically declare that David's "throne would be established forever" and that David was told he would "not lack a man to sit on the throne of Israel." Of course wherever I read of such a promise, my mind immediately jumps to the Anointed One of God, the Savior and Lord, who will one day fulfill that promise. I see the throne of David, bathed in the brilliance of the light of heaven, for the Son of God sits upon it.

One of the most interesting passages about the eternal throne of David is found in Psalms 89:20-29. The psalmist describes the covenant that God made with David. At the end of the passage God's promise is recorded, the promise to establish his [David's] descendants forever and his throne as the days of heaven [forever].

But it is at a verse 27 that I am drawn to pause a while longer in my journey. "I also shall make him My firstborn, the highest of the kings of the earth" is written there. God is still speaking in that verse; He is at once bestowing a great honor upon David and giving future generations of readers a glimpse into the *forever* kingdom that will come. As I think on the verse, I remember that not only was David not the *firstborn* of the house of Jesse, but his household—the line of Jesse—was not in line to be king at all. When David was anointed by Samuel, there was only one king of Israel, Saul, and he was from the tribe of Benjamin. By appointing David as king, God dramatically reminded the Israelites that He had, through the prophetic blessings of Jacob (Genesis 49), told the people that Judah would be the line of kings.

In verse 27 of Psalm 89, the writer gives us a glimpse into the relationship between David and Jehovah. God gave David the position of *firstborn*, naming him as the royal son that would begin the royal line of kings that would ultimately be fulfilled in the Messiah, the King of Kings.

## Day of the Lord/Reckoning
Isaiah 2:12; Amos 5:18; Amos 5:20; Obadiah 1:15; Zephaniah
1:7; Malachi 4:5

The prophets speak many times of *the day of the Lord* or *the day of reckoning,* identifying a time that will come in the future—a time of judgment, of fulfilled prophecies, of a final conclusion to the earth, as we now know it. When those phrases are used, they convey a sense of urgency and a promise of justice. These verses don't generally speak directly of Christ. Indirectly, they do, not because He is present in the situation, but because the devastation they describe eventually ushers in the millennial reign. Even so, there were some of *the day of the Lord* passages that did vividly bring His image to my mind—and some of the prophetic warnings spoke directly into my heart.

Settling accounts
Isaiah 2:12; Obadiah 1:15

*The day of reckoning.* The phrase suggests a settling of accounts, like the full remaining balance being required immediately on debt that has lingered on and on because the debtor paid only a minimum amount each month. There is a sense of suddenness. There is an impression that, even though man knows the day is coming, he is caught off guard. I think of Jesus' parable of the prosperous man who was so wrapped up in himself that his only solution to more crops was to build a bigger barn (Luke 12), and of course he did not even consider the possibility that his own death was imminent.

Isaiah 2:12 carries haunting promises of doom, "The LORD of hosts will have a day of reckoning against everyone who is proud and lofty." But the record of man serves as evidence that few really take heed. As I ponder the words, I can't help think how easy it is for man to delude himself into thinking he has all the time in the world, even though the prophets have told us that God's day of reckoning will come. We are even told that Jesus will return suddenly—unexpectedly, even though we are indeed expecting it to occur. I Thessalonians 5:2 reminds us that He will come like a thief in the night.

# Additional Prophetic Passages

Obadiah continues Isaiah's thoughts. Isaiah suggested that the day of reckoning was leveling up the accounts, kind of like a *payback* for the selfishness that has been evidenced in the lives of mankind. In Obadiah 1:15, the prophet hints of a lesson that was later taught by the Messiah: "For the day of the LORD draws near on all the nations. As you have done, it will be done to you. Your dealings will return on your own head." Reading the words of Obadiah, I am immediately carried back to the shores of Galilee, hearing the words of Jesus as recorded in Matthew 7:2: "For in the same way you judge others, you will be judged, and with the measure you use, it will be measured to you."

## A prepared sacrifice
Malachi 4:5, Zephaniah 1:7

Malachi reminds the nations that God will send warnings before the day of His judgment comes. Malachi (4:5) prophesied of the first coming of the Messiah, noting that a forerunner in the spirit of Elijah would come—a forerunner that we recognize to be John the Baptist.

Amid all the dark warnings that are seen in verses that refer to the *day of the Lord*, Zephaniah 1:7, offers hope to those who have chosen to obey the Lord and to follow Him: "Be silent before the Lord GOD! For the day of the LORD is near, for the LORD has prepared a sacrifice, He has consecrated His guests." What a glorious promise—the Lord prepared a sacrifice (Jesus) and has consecrated His guests (me and you)!

## A warning for those who think they don't need it
Amos 5:18, 20

As I prepare to leave this cluster of verses about the *day of the LORD*, I look at Amos 5:18 and 20. I humbly take note of the prophet's warning, for Amos records, "Alas, you who are longing for the day of the LORD, for what purpose will the day of the LORD be to you? It will be darkness and not light." "Will not the day of the LORD be darkness instead of light, even gloom with no brightness in it?" Amos was prophesying to the nation of Israel—the chosen people of God.

The Scarlet Thread

As I read his words, I am reminded that the nation of Israel, at least in general terms, looked forward to the coming of the Lord, for the time that His day would come. But Amos asked *why?* He condemned those who, claiming to be the people of God, refused to obey Him. He prophesied destruction, a coming day of darkness and desolation, to the very people who thought they had it all together, who thought they were on the winning side. Amos essentially asked, *Why do you look forward to the day of the Lord, when that day will only bring darkness and devastation to you because you have sinned against the very Lord you claim to honor?*

As I read these passages about *the day of the Lord*, I must humbly admit that Amos' warning is for me as well. It is all too easy, as we rest in the blood of the Lamb, to begin to let a *you need to heed the warnings of the prophets* attitude grow in us. After all, *we* are the chosen priesthood; *we* are the heirs of salvation; *we* are children of the King! I think, in all honesty, we must guard against that nature in us that would cross the line from *confidence in Christ* to *confidence in self because we have accepted Christ.* I think that perhaps Amos' prophecy rings through time to remind me to be on guard that I never allow that to happen.

> [Other Day of the Lord/Day of Reckoning verses:
> Isaiah 13:6, 9; Ezekiel 30:3; Joel 1:15, 2:1-2, 11, 30-31,
> 3:14; Zephaniah 1:14-18]

**Days Are Coming-Warning**
Jeremiah 9:25

Another phrase, similar to *the day of the Lord*, that propels me into the future, is *the days are coming*. Sometimes the phrase is used in the context of judgment—used almost as a threat of what is to come. Those references carry the idea that *one of these days you will get what you deserve*. Of course, those of us who have claimed the salvation of the Lord know that when that day comes, we will not get what we truly deserve, for instead we have already been given the mercy of God and forgiveness for all our sin.

# Additional Prophetic Passages

Of the warnings described in the *days are coming* verses, only one spoke to me directly of Jesus, issuing a warning to carefully guard against pride. In Jeremiah 9:25 we find, "'Behold, the days are coming,' declares the LORD, 'that I will punish all who are circumcised and yet uncircumcised.'" I immediately wonder: *Who are the ones who are circumcised and yet uncircumcised? How can someone be both?* The NIV Bible renders this verse as "'The days are coming,' declares the LORD, 'when I will punish all who are circumcised only in the flesh.'"

My thought turns to the teachings of Paul in the 4th chapter of book of Romans for an explanation. Paul asked the question, in verse 9, "Is this blessing then on the circumcised or on the uncircumcised also?" Then he went on to remind his readers that righteousness was credited to Abraham before he was circumcised and that circumcision was given as an outward sign to the promise of the Lord. Going back to the original occurrences, we find in Genesis 15:6 that Abraham believed the LORD, and that belief was credited to him as righteousness. At that time the Lord made a covenant with Abraham—that he (Abram) would be the father of many. The command to be circumcised was not given until Chapter 17 (about 14 years later), when the covenant was re-confirmed. Circumcision was commanded to serve as a sign of the covenant God made with Abraham. Thus Paul, in Romans, reminded the people that the circumcision was a sign of the covenant that was based on the faith Abraham had expressed when he believed God would do as He said He would.

Why then does Jeremiah say that the days are coming when the Lord would punish all who were circumcised, but not circumcised? In the generations following the promise to Abraham, many of the Jewish people came to put more trust and confidence in the sign of the promise than in the promise. It was often seen as a *guarantee* of God's continued favor, regardless of whether they upheld their end of the covenant. Thus the physically circumcised often were not spiritual circumcised at all, and Jeremiah warned that such people would be caught up in the righteous judgment of God when *that day* comes.

So where is my image of Christ in Jeremiah's warning? I think, perhaps, that as the Spirit of God prompted Jeremiah to warn of the danger of relying on a physical circumcision without the accompanying heart relationship He was issuing a warning to those of the Christian age as well. I think Jesus warns that Christians, too, must be alert and guard that we do not allow ourselves to complacently rest on a promise that is given—that promise must be received, accepted, claimed as our very own before we can be considered among the spiritually circumcised. We must clearly understand that it is not enough to simply believe in God, for as James warned in James 2:19, *even the demons believe*. Jesus repeatedly warned that it is what is inside that marks us as His, not some outward sign, expression, or action.

[Other Days are coming verses that give a warning:
I Samuel 2:31; II Kings 20:17; Isaiah 39:6; Jeremiah 7:32, 19:6, 48:12, 49:2, 51:47, 52; Amos 4:2]

**Days Are Coming- Promise**
Jeremiah 33:14, 16:14-15, 23:7, 30:3, 31:31, 38, Amos 8:11

While many verses using the phrase *the days are coming* gave warnings, some instead spoke of promises and brought with them joyful images of my Lord.

<u>A light breaks the darkness</u>
Jeremiah 33:14, 16:14-15, 23:7, 30:3, 31:38

Jeremiah 33:14 records the promise from God that all the good that He has promised to Israel will be done. He says, "'Behold, days are coming,' declares the LORD, 'when I will fulfill the good word which I have spoken concerning the house of Israel and the house of Judah.'" In Jeremiah 16:14-15, Jeremiah 23:7 and Jeremiah 30:3 we find expansion of those words. Jeremiah records the Lord's promise that the people of Israel and the people of Judah (both kingdoms) will be brought back to the land of their forefathers to possess it again. Then, in Jeremiah 31:38, he refers to the rebuilding of the city of Jerusalem.

# Additional Prophetic Passages

In each of the verses above, I see the dark clouds that surround the warnings that appear in so many of the *days are coming* verses suddenly lose their darkness, as light shines through. I see that, even though the children of Israel failed to uphold their end of the covenant, God will still honor His promises. As I think on all the verses that called to me to think on the *days that are coming*, I hear a soft promise echoing from the cross, the grave, and the heavens: *the days are coming when I will return and I will make all things right again.*

## A new covenant
Jeremiah 31:31

Another bright spot in my journey through the *days are coming* verses is found in Jeremiah 31:31, where the Lord declares that the days are coming when He will make a new covenant with the house of Israel and Judah. He did just that, and Jesus, through the blood of the crucifixion, sealed that new covenant—the covenant that includes me!

It is such a joy to remember that the new covenant—the one that opened the doors of heaven for me—was not an afterthought. God's restoration plan, from the very beginning, included all the peoples of the earth who would claim the Son of God as Savior and King.

## A renewed hunger for the Word
Amos 8:11

Still another bright spot is found in the book of Amos, as he goes beyond the promise that there will be a new covenant to tell us that the Spirit will prompt a renewed hunger for the things of the Lord. Amos 8:11 reminds us that the days are coming when God will send a famine on the land, "Not a famine for bread or a thirst for water, but rather for hearing the words of the LORD." I can't help but ask myself: *Are those days here yet? Will they be here soon?* More to the point, I ask myself: *Are they here for me?* Lord, I pray that it is so! I pray that my thirst for His Word and my longing to be in His presence will never cease!

145

**Pour out His spirit**
Isaiah 44:3; Ezekiel 37:14; Joel 2:28

The promise that God will one day *pour out His Spirit* upon us is one that brought hope to the remnant that sought to cling to the God of their Fathers and brings confidence to all those of us who recognize that God's Spirit—the Holy Spirit—has indeed been poured out upon those who have accepted the Son and been baptized according to His Word.

Isaiah 44:3 records, "For I will pour out water on the thirsty land and streams on the dry ground; I will pour out My Spirit on your offspring and my blessing on your descendants." As I consider this verse I am reminded of Jesus' words to the woman at the well: living water was available for the asking; she did not have to live in the thirsty land, because the *true Living Water* was being poured out for man.

Ezekiel 37:14 and Joel 2:28 also remind us that with His Spirit within us we will truly come to life—eternal life. As we contemplate the promise of God's Spirit living inside us, we should perhaps remember that His presence is there for a purpose. The Spirit came to help us to continue in our spiritual growth and our service for His kingdom; He is our guide and our teacher.

**Messianic Kingdom**
Micah 4:7; Habakkuk 2:3; Haggai 2:6-7, 20-23; Jeremiah 3:15-18; Zechariah 8:3; Zechariah 14:4; Jeremiah 23:3, Isaiah 60:18-20, Daniel 2:;44; Daniel 7:9

As I journey through the books of prophecy, I often find that I stop to rest amid clusters of verses—sometimes whole chapters, for it is not just a single verse that calls on me to think of Jesus. This is especially true of those passages that describe the second coming, for the prophets weave their image of the days to come through many verses. Taken alone, a verse may give no hint of the depth of its message, but like a vibrant painting created by layer upon layer of colors, these clusters of verses form vivid pictures in my mind of the future kingdom of my Lord.

# Additional Prophetic Passages

Prophecies relating to the second coming tend to be more difficult to understand than those describing the birth, life, death, and resurrection of Jesus. Sometimes in these verses it is not the typical artist's rendering of the man who was called Jesus that fills my mind. Rather, it is a wispy, ethereal image, much like a fragmented picture that lingers in those moments when I awake from a vivid dream. It is the image, perhaps, that I would see if my human mind were actually able see the Spirit of God.

## A literal reign, lasting forever
Micah 4:7

"I will make the lame a remnant and the outcasts a strong nation and the LORD will reign over them in Mount Zion from now on and forever." Two things jump out at me as I read this verse—the reality of a literal Messianic reign in Zion and the fact that it will last forever. In our frail grasp of language and thought, humans tend to throw the word *forever* around quite haphazardly: we speak of a boring speech going on *forever*, of a man-made product lasting *forever*, of being placed on hold *forever* when we call customer service, or of a package we ordered at Christmas taking *forever* to arrive. I don't know that I can truly comprehend what *forever* means, but as I listen to the whispered voice of my Lord, here and throughout Scripture, when He tells me His love lasts *forever* and I can live with Him in the magnificent new world He will create *forever*, my heart and mind strain to grasp and hold on to that concept, for though I may lack the understanding to truly comprehend it, I know without a doubt that I want it.

## Another chance
Jeremiah 3:15-16

Jeremiah, in Chapter 3, records God's invitation to His people. He is speaking of a time in the distant future when Judah will be given another chance to follow after the God of their fathers. The words as he describes *that day* create such a marvelous picture—a promise that is given to Judah that those of us who came to Him in the Church Age will witness. Through the Spirit of God, Jeremiah writes in 3:15-18, "Then I will give you shepherds after My own heart, who will feed you on knowledge and understanding." Jeremiah suggests that Almighty God will supply a special measure of understanding that will turn His people back to Him.

Jeremiah continues, "It shall be in those days when you are multiplied and increased in the land," declares the LORD, "they will no longer say, 'The ark of the covenant of the LORD.'""

The Ark of the Covenant was one of the most important physical links to God that was given to the Israelites. The Ark represented the actual presence of God in their midst. Again Jeremiah continues, "And it will not come to mind, nor will they remember it, nor will they miss it, nor will it be made again." The Ark seems to have disappeared sometime just prior to the Babylonian conquest that led to the captivity of Israel. The last historical reference to the Ark of the Covenant in the pages of Scripture is found in II Chronicles 35:3, where King Josiah asked the Levites to return the Ark to the temple, but there is no indication whether this was ever done. The Ark's location has been the subject of quests and debates for centuries, but in the millennial kingdom, there will be no need to even remember it, for the Lord will be present with them, in resurrected bodily form.

Jeremiah goes on to say in verse 17 of Chapter 3, "At that time they will call Jerusalem 'The Throne of the LORD,' and all the nations will be gathered to it, to Jerusalem, for the name of the LORD; nor will they walk anymore after the stubbornness of their evil heart." Jerusalem—the New Jerusalem—will become the *Throne of the Lord*. From there, Jesus the Messiah will reign over all the kingdoms of the earth.

Verse 18 continues, "In those days the house of Judah will walk with the house of Israel, and they will come together from the land of the north to the land that I gave your fathers as an inheritance." The house of Judah will walk with the house of Israel—at last the tribes of Judah will be reunited—joined as one under the King of Kings.

# Additional Prophetic Passages

## Jerusalem
Zechariah 8:3

"Thus says the LORD, 'I will return to Zion and will dwell in the midst of Jerusalem. Then Jerusalem will be called the City of Truth, and the mountain of the LORD of hosts will be called the Holy Mountain.'" Zion, Jerusalem, the City of Truth, the Holy Mountain—the growing list of honored names given to this once war-torn land that we call the Holy Land reminds us of its value— this is God's chosen land and He will bring it back to the glorious state it was meant to be, and from it Messiah will reign.

## Certainty of that day
Habakkuk 2:3; Haggai 2:6-7

Both Habakkuk and Haggai assure us of the certainty that the day the other prophets have described will actually come to pass. "Though it tarries, wait for it; for it will certainly come, it will not delay," Habakkuk says in 2:3. *Though it tarries* reminds us that it seems in our finite comprehension to be taking a long, long, time, but *it will not delay* stresses that in the timeline of the Father there is no delay; everything is happening right on schedule. Haggai 2:6-7 reinforces Habakkuk's words. He quotes the Lord, "Once more, in a little while." To us *a little while* is so very different from what the Lord means. Perhaps it is a matter of perspective. A parent can say to a little child, "In a little while we will go for ice cream." The parent means in a few hours, but the child, after only a few minutes, can't understand why he can't go for ice cream. In like manner, Almighty God, who alone knows His timing, can say "In a little while I will return and make all things new." But we, those who not-so-patiently wait for His coming, struggle to understand how so many centuries can be *a little while*.

## Powers of this world will be overthrown
Haggai 2:20-23

Later in that same chapter Haggai describes the manner in which that day will come. God told Haggai to tell Zerubbabel, governor of Judah, "I am going to shake the heavens and the earth. I will overthrow the thrones of kingdoms and destroy the power of the kingdoms of the nations." "*I am going to*," God said. Though the manmade governments and their mighty leaders proudly claim power and dominion over their little corners of the globe, God emphatically reminds us that He is still creator and ruler of the earth—He will, in His time, in His way, bring all the political powers on the earth to their knees. When *that day* comes, there will be no doubt about *who* has brought it about!

Picture of Messiah's land
Isaiah 60:18-20

Violence will not be heard, there will be no devastation or destruction within the borders of the Lord's kingdom, there will be no sun, for the glory of the Lord will light the land, and the days of mourning will be over. What a wonderful picture of Messiah's land! We see the same general descriptions in the 21st chapter of Revelation, as it describes the new heaven and the new earth.

Looking at the description of Isaiah is like opening a window into the heart of God. As I sit by His side I can feel the cares of this world diminish in the light of His glory. I can breathe deep and catch the fragrance of eternity that waits just beyond. I can feel the rest and rejuvenation that His presence brings to my soul. I rest *in Him*, and in that moment I realize: this moment alone was worth the journey!

The Ancient of Days will take the throne
Daniel 2:44, 7:9

The prophet Daniel describes the eternal throne that was promised to David in terms that cannot be misunderstood. In Daniel 2:44 he explains how that kingdom will come to be: "In the days of those kings the God of heaven will set up a kingdom which will never be destroyed, and that kingdom will not be left for another people; it will crush and put an end to all these kingdoms, but it will itself endure forever." Then, in 7:9 Daniel describes the one who will occupy that throne: "I kept looking until thrones were set up, and the Ancient of Days took His seat; His vesture was like white snow and the hair of his head like pure wool." Of course there can be no doubt of whom Daniel is speaking, for John too uses this same description in Revelation 1:14: "His head and His hair were white like white wool, like snow; and His eyes were like a flame of fire."

## Millennial Reign
Micah 2:12-13, 4:1-7, 5:4-5; Joel 3:18; Amos 9:13; Habakkuk 2:14; Haggai 2:9

The following references, described by the prophets, sometimes share pictures of the Lord, but at other times only hint at the presence of the risen Messiah, as though He were standing just beyond the visual image of the description. Nevertheless, throughout the prophecies of the coming reign of Christ, the words continue to remind me that Jesus came once, just as the prophets had predicted, and they fill me with renewed certainty that He will return.

The Warrior King
Micah 2:12-13

Through the pages of the New Testament we are given a clear image of Jesus. We see Him as the Rabbi wandering the hills of Judea; we see Him as the Master of all nature; we see Him as a Friend to the outcast and as a Healer of the sick and afflicted; we even see Him as the beaten and bloodied sacrifice. With all the pictures that the New Testament writers provide, we only glimpse the majesty of the King in the closing chapters of the Bible; only John lets us peek into heaven to see the glory of the King. Thus, it is to the Old Testament that we turn to witness the King of Kings and Lord or Lords, as the prophets reveal *the end of story before it is written*.

The second chapter of Micah describes the calamity that is coming, ending with Micah 2:12-13 which creates a picture of the days that will come when the Messiah will assemble the remnant of Israel and gather them together like sheep in the fold. Then "The breaker [the Messiah] goes up before them [the remnant that has been gathered together]; they break out, pass through the gate and go out by it. So their king goes on before them and the LORD at their head." In these few verses we are allowed to glimpse that moment when the humble, suffering Savior becomes the fierce, warrior King who will lead the remnant into the new era of peace.

Judge and Lawgiver in Jerusalem
Micah 4:1-7

Micah begins by declaring "And it will come about in the last days that the mountain of the house of the LORD will be established as the chief of the mountains."

To me it seems obvious that the "*mountain of the house of the LORD*" refers to Mount Moriah, where the Temple in Jerusalem was built (twice). However, before getting too far into the image of this mountain when the LORD returns, it may be helpful to consider it in its earlier history.

Jerusalem was built at the crest of a low range of hills, or more particularly, it was built on two hills—Zion (which is also the name of the mountain range) and Moriah, creating a single city sometimes referred to as the upper and lower cities. There are other mountains that surround Jerusalem as well, as we see referenced in Psalm 125:2: "As the mountains surround Jerusalem, so the LORD surrounds His people from this time forth and forever." The temple, built on Mount Moriah, is located in the place where Abraham took Isaac to offer him as a sacrifice to the Lord (Genesis 22) and where David purchased the threshing floor so he could build an alter to God (II Samuel 24).

Getting back to Micah, we are told that this mountain, Mount Moriah, will essentially be the *seat of the Messianic government*. People will stream into the city to learn from the Master, and "from Zion will go forth the law, even the word of the LORD from Jerusalem." He (the reigning Messiah) will judge disputes, rendering decisions for all people.

Peace will reign: swords will be hammered into plowshares, spears will be made into pruning hooks, and never again will the people train for war. There is no one to make people afraid. The

Additional Prophetic Passages

Lord says, through Micah, that *in that day* the lame and the outcast will be a remnant and He will make them a strong nation.

Thus, in this chapter of Micah, we see Jesus as the Judge and the Lawgiver. In that time His people not only recognize His right to rule, they also realize that it is His justice and the rightness of His rule that actually brings about the peace that they experience.

Peace
Micah 5:4-5

Micah 5:2 prophesies that the final king of Israel—the Messiah—would be born in Bethlehem Ephrathah. The prophecy quickly shifts from the birth of the king to the reign of the king—thus beginning to give an image of the Messianic reign. In Micah 5:4-5, the prophet once again calls us to witness the Shepherd who will shepherd His flock. Micah explains that this One will be *our peace* and emphasizes that the people will remain there with Him, because "at that time He will be great to the ends of the earth."

Water flowing from the house of the Lord
Joel 3:18

Joel 3:18 paints a picture of peace and serenity. He says, "And in that day" –"all the brooks of Judah will flow with water; and a spring will go out from the house of the LORD to water the valley of Shittim." As I think on that verse, I visualize the spring, a stream of clear, sparkling water, flowing from the house of the Lord, spreading its living water to all those who dwell in the valleys below. I can picture the scene—an actual, physical scene, where all nature displays the grandeur and wonder, unseen since Adam and Eve were expelled from the Garden of Eden. I can picture the figurative scene, as well, a spring from the house of the Lord—living water flowing from the temple of God, and in so picturing it, I can hear Jesus challenging the Jewish leaders: "Destroy this temple (Himself), and in three days I will raise it up." (John 2:19) Jesus promised that He would provide water that would refresh the soul forever, and in Him we find that water.

# The Scarlet Thread

## Peace and prosperity
Amos 9:13


Amos 9:13 says, that "days are coming when the plowman will overtake the reaper and the treader of grapes him who sows seed; when the mountains will drip sweet wine and all the hills will be dissolved." In these words we see prosperity of such vastness that those who harvest are practically taking the mature crops from the garden before the plowman can finish plowing and the wine makers are treading grapes practically as soon as the seeds are sown. Amos uses the same imagery as Joel when he writes of a time when the "mountains will drip with sweet wine," again describing harvests of grapes so immense that the wine seems to flow from the mountains.

## The return of full knowledge
Habakkuk 2:14


Habakkuk goes beyond the physical provisions that are provided and speaks instead of that time when mankind will finally understand. "For the earth will be filled with the knowledge of the glory of the LORD, as the waters cover the sea." *The knowledge of the glory of the Lord,* what could that really be like! My mind is taken back to the Garden of Eden. I think that God wanted to share all the knowledge of heaven and earth with His new creation. I think that if sin had not ripped mankind from the presence of the Creator, Adam and Eve would have truly come to *know* and *understand* the full glory of the Lord. If the *knowledge of evil* had not become a part of them, permeating into their very souls, then the knowledge of good—the Good that is God—would have filled their hearts, their minds, and their beings. If the knowledge of evil had not come into the world, then perhaps evil itself (in the guise of the serpent deceiver) would have ended right there. But that was not to be, for sin did enter the picture, and man was left with a heart and mind that could not fully comprehend all that God is.

I think about what it must have been like to walk with God, to communicate with God, to understand all that He has placed before us, and my heart mourns for what we lost in that moment when mankind (yes, mankind—not just Adam and Eve) let sin sever our connection to the Maker. Here, in Habakkuk's words, I hear the whisper of words later spoken by Paul, "For now we see in a mirror dimly, but then face to face; now I know in part, but then I will know fully just as I also have been fully known" (I Corinthians 13:12). The Spirit, through Habakkuk reminds us that when our Lord returns, "the earth will be filled with the knowledge of the glory of the LORD"—we will truly *know* Him. What a joyous promise!

The coming of the true temple
Haggai 2:9

In Haggai 2:9, the prophet is speaking about the temple (Zerubbabel's temple), encouraging those who were rebuilding it. The original temple built by Solomon had been destroyed when the people were taken captive by Babylon. Then after seventy years of captivity, a remnant had returned to rebuild. The second temple was smaller, and it was not nearly as magnificent as Solomon's. In fact, Scripture tells us that those who had seen the former structure *mourned* at the sight of the new one. It was at that point that Haggai declared the words of the Lord of hosts, "The latter glory of this house will be greater than the former, and in this place I will give peace." The temple that was built when the remnant returned from Babylon was obviously not *greater than the former*. But then, God was not speaking about the temple built by Zerubbabel that was later modified by Herod. He was looking far into the future to a day that would come when the true Temple—the presence of the Lord in the flesh would come to Jerusalem to reign in peace and triumph. In that day, the temple will indeed be greater than the former!

**Names of the Messiah**
Jeremiah 23:3, 33:14-18; Daniel 2:44-45; Zechariah 10:3-4, 12:3; Isaiah 52 and 53

This collection of verses could easily have been included in Chapter VI, but because of the element of prophecy, they have been places here instead.

# The Scarlet Thread

## King and Priest
Jeremiah 33:14-18

Many of Jeremiah's words are bitter, declaring a bitter message for an unrepentant people. Still, rather than just promising judgment, Jeremiah 33:14-18 proclaims the promise of the Lord, "days are coming when I will fulfill the good word" and then goes on to reiterate that David will never lack a man to sit on the throne of the house of Israel and the Levitical priests will never lack a man to prepare sacrifices. In that one passage we see the unprecedented promise that, in one Man, both the King and the Priest shall be seen. Instead of a line of kings from Judah and a line of priests from Levi, God promised *one* who would be both King of Kings and High Priest.

## Stone
Daniel 2:44-45, Zechariah 12:3

Prior mentions have been made concerning the image of a stone or a cornerstone. Daniel makes reference to the *stone* as well. Prophesying of the divine kingdom to come, Daniel (2:44-45) reveals the meaning of one of Nebuchadnezzar's dreams, explaining that the "*stone that was cut out of the mountain without hands*" meant that God would set up a kingdom that would never be destroyed and that kingdom would crush all the powers of earthly kings. Zechariah (12:3) also includes cornerstone as part of his prophecy, indicating that Jerusalem will be a *heavy cornerstone* and all the people of the world who try to *lift* it will be severely injured, perhaps emphasizing that there will be no way to remove that stone and no way to prevent the prophecies from being fulfilled.

## Suffering Servant/Exalted Servant
Isaiah 52 and 53

Examined together, Isaiah 52 and 53 almost take on the appearance of mirror-image bookends. In Chapter 52 the prophet describes the *exalted servant* and in the very next chapter introduces the *suffering servant.* On quick glance, I wonder how the two can exist in the same person and then the Spirit seems to

## Additional Prophetic Passages

whisper—*Perhaps the better question is: How can they not?* Indeed, if Jesus had not been willing and able to be the suffering servant that Isaiah describes, would the exalted servant even exist? His place in heaven would surely be there, from everlasting to everlasting, but would there be a place in heaven for the sons and daughters of Adam who, when sin was chosen, threw away their right to be with their Maker.

Isaiah 52:13-15 identifies the exalted servant, who would be high and lifted up. As Isaiah reveals that the servant will be *greatly exalted* I am reminded of Philippians 2:9-11, where we are told that Jesus is given the name above every name. For a moment I try to visualize that moment when the entire world will exalt Jesus as King of Kings. I try to experience the joy of that triumph, but the image of celebration is dimmed by Isaiah's description of the physical appearance of this exalted servant. "Marred more than any man," Isaiah says, and my image of celebration becomes instead a picture of the scourged, beaten body of the Messiah. Even before Chapter 53 begins, I am already there.

Isaiah continues his description of the suffering servant in Chapter 53, noting that He has no stately form and no appearance that would attract us to Him. Then he writes the famous description of the coming Messiah (Isaiah 53:3-9) that includes "man of sorrow, acquainted with grief," and "pierced through for our transgressions," and the comparison that calls us "sheep who have gone astray." As vivid as this passage is in showing us a picture of the suffering Christ, my heart is drawn to verse 12: "Therefore, I will allot Him a portion with the great, and He will divide the booty with the strong; because He poured out Himself to death, and was numbered with the transgressors; yet he Himself bore the sin of many, and interceded for the transgressors." In that verse I find the undeniable promise that while He (Jesus) would choose to be counted among the transgressors (us), He would choose to carry our sins away, as the scapegoat carried the sins of the Israelites into the desert. And, because He would make those choices, He will stand forever as our intercessor.

# The Scarlet Thread

Zechariah, in 10:3-4, includes several names of the coming Lord—cornerstone, tent peg, bow of battle—indicating the one who is so described would come from the house of Judah. *Cornerstone* has already been discussed in *The Scarlet Thread*, but tent peg and bow of battle aren't found in other references.

Zechariah says that the Lord will visit His flock, the house of Judah, and will make them like His majestic horse in battle. The image that comes to mind is one of a mighty steed, racing at the front of the line, directly into an opposing army that spreads out across the land as far as the eye can see. But the implication is that the might and power of this commander is so great that defeat is inconceivable.

Then Zechariah goes on to say that from them (the house of Judah) will come the cornerstone, the tent peg, the bow of battle. He also says that from them (the house of Judah) will come every ruler, all of them together. I think Zechariah is building momentum in these verses, coming to the conclusion that Judah is eventually going to return to God, to again be His people.

Cornerstone brings to my mind the concept of the first stone, the central building block of God's plan, or perhaps of His will for Judah (and for us). Tent peg suggests support, describing the unyielding, unfailing power of the Anointed One to hold onto those who place their trust in Him. It also suggests the concept of home, of a dwelling place, a place where a person is content to reside, perhaps as a result of the assurance of the security provided through the relationship with the Holy One. Bow of battle seems to return to the earlier reference to the majestic horse in battle, perhaps again referencing the power of the one who leads us. In the same manner that the tent peg also has a component image of the one who is relying on the Messiah, the bow of battle seems to suggest a time of battle, a place of uncertainty, perhaps reminding us that whether in safe times or in trouble, our strength comes from the Lord.

As I ponder Zechariah's words, I see the strength and power of God incarnate, the person of Jesus, as He prepares to return. He is the support and strength that I need in times of peace and tranquility and in times of trials and fear.

## Zion, the place of the return
Zechariah 14:1-9

As I close this chapter of prophetic verses, I pause in Zechariah 14, for the richness of the image created in my mind in those opening verses seems to move me to the very edge of life as we know it.

Zechariah prophesies that all the nations will gather against Jerusalem and the city will be captured, but then in verse 3 he explains that the Lord will go forth and fight against those nations. It is at that point that Zechariah describes the moment when all history as we know it comes to a standstill. Verse 4 says: "In that day His feet will stand on the Mount of Olives, which is in front of Jerusalem on the east; and the Mount of Olives will be split in its middle from east to west by a very large valley, so that half of the mountain will move toward the north and the other half toward the south."

Zechariah goes on to describe the chaos that erupts. He says that the people of the land of Israel will flee as they fled before the earthquake in the days of Uzziah king of Judah. (Amos 1:1 also refers to the earthquake in the days of Uzziah.) He says that it will be a unique day where in the evening there will be light.

"In that day His feet will stand on the Mount of Olives." Jesus, the Christ, the incarnate Lord, will step out of heaven to once again stand upon the earth! What an amazing image—our finite minds cannot begin to grasp the power that emanates from the Holy One of Heaven. Then at the end of verse 5, Zechariah broadens the image to tell us, "Then the LORD, my God, will come, and all the holy ones with Him!" In that moment, the entire world will see Him, and know Him—there will be no doubt that He is the King of Kings and Lord of Lords. Then, stating the obvious, Zechariah writes in verse 9: "And the LORD will be king over all the earth; in that day the LORD will be the only one, and His name the only one."

As I ponder Zechariah's words and I think of that moment when the risen Christ will return to stand upon the Mount of Olives, I try to imagine looking up to suddenly see the brilliant light of heaven slice through the clouds. I try to imagine the clouds rolling back on themselves. I try to imagine Jesus, in bodily form, stepping down to earth again. And then I remember verse 5: "and the holy ones with Him!" and I realize my sight of that glorious moment won't be as one looking up, but as one looking down, already encompassed by the radiance of heaven, following my Lord and King, and I am filled with more wonder than I can possibly comprehend.

The mere thought of that moment takes my breath away. Awestruck by the glorious image of the gleaming light of heaven, I wait in breathless anticipation and, with John in Revelation 22:20, I whisper, "Come, Lord Jesus. Come.

# VIII. Concepts Relating to Jesus or His Mission

## *Defining the category*

In the pages of the Old Testament we find the definition and the history of the critical concepts surrounding the person of Jesus Christ. There we discover why He came, why He is the only one who could provide salvation, and why forgiveness is even needed in the first place. We find the foundation that anchors the path to salvation to the very heart of God, the Creator.

The teachings of Christ and His apostles rest on certain fundamental premises that were introduced in the Old Testament, truths and certainties that were woven into creation and the history of man as surely as threads are woven into an intricate tapestry. Mankind's sin-stained minds continue to question and challenge, limit and redefine, or even deny, the basic principles set forth *in the beginning*. Nevertheless, God is still God and the basic principles He set forth are still the same:

- Sin tore the relationship between God and man apart.
- Payment must be made if that relationship is to be restored.
- He is the only one who can provide a way to restore the relationship.
- The restoration must be accomplished in the manner He prescribed.

In this chapter of *The Scarlet Thread*, we pause to look at the foundation of some of the concepts that are critical to our understanding of why God incarnate came to earth and what His coming meant for us.

161

## *Specific Examples—Stops along my journey*

### Atonement for Sin
Leviticus 1:4-5, 16:10, and Chapter 8

Atonement is defined as *amends or reparation made for an injury or wrong*. A more archaic definition suggests that atonement is *reconciliation or agreement*. The word carries the connotation that 1) a definite *wrong* has been done, even hinting at the fact that it is a *serious wrong*, not a simple mistake and 2) that *someone* mends, repairs, or reconciles that *wrong* in a manner that brings the situation so fully back to its original state that it is *as if the wrong had never been done*. Atonement, by definition, is not a temporary fix, but a full, complete solution that *makes things right again*.

As I think on this concept, I find myself considering the entire, complex system of sacrifices that was set in place in the book of Leviticus. Why have sacrifices? Did God need the burnt offerings? Was there something physical about the aroma of the sacrifice that He needed in order to feel loved by His people? Was He trying to wrap the Israelites up in so many laws and practices that they would not have time to get into trouble (obviously that didn't work!) No—to all of the above! The sacrificial system was a dramatic picture to show mankind the concept of *one* (animal, person) giving the most important possession (life) in order to pay for the wrongdoing of another person (mankind).

Two key elements are seen in the sacrificial system—the concept of atonement (the broken relationship can be restored, the wrong can be made right) and the concept of substitution (someone having no part in the wrongdoing must willingly be the sacrifice that makes the atonement possible).

The first chapter of Leviticus lays the foundation of the burnt offerings. God told Moses to tell the people how to bring their burnt offering. In verses 4 and 5 we immediately begin to see God laid the groundwork that would help His people understand what was really happening. Those verses record, "He shall lay his hand on the head of the burnt offering, that it may be accepted for him to make atonement on his behalf. He shall slay the young bull before the LORD; and Aaron's sons the priests shall offer up the blood and sprinkle the blood around the altar that is at the doorway of the tent of meeting."

In these few words we see the concept of atonement laid out before us. "He shall lay his hand on the head of the burnt offering" in verse 4 and "He shall slay the young bull" in verse 5 forces mankind to recognize (and accept) the fact that he (or she) is the primary player in the drama of sin. He (*we*) must understand that it is because of some action or inaction on the part of mankind that there exists something that requires atonement or reconciliation. "That it may be accepted for him to make atonement on his behalf" suggests that man knows that this sacrifice is paying the price for his wrongdoing—he knows it and he is willing to allow that atonement to be made on his behalf. Verse 5 emphasizes man's part in the situation by requiring that he (the wrongdoer) slay the sacrifice, but then shifts the focus from the one causing the need for atonement to the priests, who "offer up the blood." As I look at that verse I am reminded that Jesus, our *forever* High Priest, was the one who offered up His own blood—the Jews cried out for crucifixion, the Romans carried out the deed, but it was God incarnate, Jesus the Messiah, that offered up His life as the ultimate, final sacrifice for the sin that began millennia before in the Garden of Eden.

Leviticus 16:10 tells of another picture in the sacrificial framework of the Israelites. It tells about the scapegoat (which we looked at in Chapter III). The goat that was chosen by the casting of lots to be the scapegoat was to be presented alive before the Lord. Each year a goat was sent out into the wilderness, symbolically carrying the sins of the people away and providing temporary atonement until the time the ultimate sacrifice would come to atone for those sins once and for all and then would stand, alive, before the Father.

# The Scarlet Thread

## Concept of Mercy
Ezra 9:13, 39:25; Jeremiah 33:26; Isaiah 63:9

At the close of Chapter 8 of Ezra, we learn that the new temple has been completed and the returning captives from Babylon have once again begun offering their sacrifices. Then Chapter 9 introduces a specific sin that has reemerged among the people. Ezra is confessing their sin of not separating themselves from the people of the lands around them, for they had again begun intermarrying with those tribes of people.

Ezra acknowledges their sin and describes in verse 13 a concept that we have come to understand as the *mercy of God*. Ezra wrote, "After all that has come upon us for our evil deeds and great guilt, since You our God have requited us less than our iniquities deserve, and have given us an escaped remnant as this." Recognizing the great sin of Israel that had led to captivity in the first place, Ezra is amazed by the fact that God *requited to the people less then they deserved*, and he is appalled that his people can again turn to sin.

Here we encounter the infancy of a concept that, when fully disclosed, shatters the power of evil in the world. Ezra knew his people deserved the consequences of their sins. He knew that the Babylonian Captivity (only 70 years in length) might well have been a total destruction of the nation of Judah. He knew that their continual disregard for the will of God and the laws He had given them had earned them that penalty. Even so, he understood that God had *charged to them less than was reasonable to be expected*. Instead of total annihilation, God had protected a remnant and restored them to the land of their fathers.

Mercy is defined as *compassion or forbearance shown especially to an offender or to one subject to one's power* or *a blessing that is an act of divine favor or compassion*. Another common understanding of mercy is *receiving something good that is not deserved* (grace). Thus, buried in Ezra's confession of the sins of his people, we realize that he understood the mercy of God, for he realized that God had indeed not given the nation of Israel what they deserved.

Some of the prophets, in recording the warnings and consequences of Israel's sin, also mention the concept Ezra describes, but they call it what it is—the mercy of God. Ezekiel 39:25 says that God will "restore the fortunes of Jacob and have mercy on the whole house of Israel." Jeremiah 33:26 repeats the promise, "I will restore their fortunes and will have mercy on them." Isaiah 63:9 provides a glimpse of the full force of the concept of mercy: "and the angel of His presence saved them; in His love and in His mercy He redeemed them."

The concept of mercy, sprinkled throughout the Old Testament, shows us that while sin leads to severe consequences (even death), the one who is sinned against can require less of the offender and that, in His compassion and love, provides this thing called *mercy* to alter the natural consequences of sin. *Saved them, redeemed them,* Isaiah wrote, and he hit the bull's eye, so to speak, for in his words we see the power of mercy: Death and destruction would rightfully be the consequences, but God, in His love for mankind, hands down mercy instead—mercy that brings with it life and redemption.

## Deliverance Comes at God's Time
Esther 4:13-14

The book of Esther, alone among the 66 books of the Bible, never mentions Jehovah directly. Yet, the hand of the Lord is seen throughout its story. Esther, living in Persia about a hundred years after the Babylonian captivity, rose to fame as the winner of a beauty pageant for which the prize was a crown of Persia. Esther hid her Jewish heritage and assumed her role as a favored wife of King Xerxes I.

Were it not for the evil ambition and vindictiveness of a man named Haman, the story of Esther would probably have faded into the pages of history and the book of Esther would never have found its way into the sacred scriptures of God. But God's plan included Esther. Haman, selfishly grasping for more honor and glory than he deserved, fell right into that plan.

# The Scarlet Thread

Through plot twists that included conspiracy and attempted assassination, lavish parties and secret meetings, and an edict that could mean the annihilation of God's chosen people, God's plan placed Esther at center stage in the Persian drama. In Esther 4:13b-14, Mordecai, Esther's uncle and former guardian, confronted Esther, saying, "Do not imagine that you in the king's palace can escape any more than all the Jews. For if you remain silent at this time, relief and deliverance will arise for the Jews from another place and you and your father's house will perish. And who knows whether you have not attained royalty for such a time as this?"

Two great realities jump out at me, as I pause at this verse. First, "relief and deliverance will arise for the Jews from another place," Mordecai said. I notice the decisive declaration—the absolute certainly of God's promise that His chosen people would be saved. Like Mordecai, I have no doubt that whenever the survival of the Jewish people stands in the balance, God's hand on the scale will determine the outcome. Historically this can be seen in the fact that, while all the great nations of the ancient world have come and gone, Israel is still here. The second reality is found in Mordecai's challenge to Esther, "And who knows whether you have not attained royalty for such a time as this?" As Mordecai stared into the fearful eyes of the young queen, a woman he raised, cared for, and educated in the ways of her people, he challenged her to remember that the God of Abraham, Isaac, and Jacob had always protected and guided His people—and He had always used willing people to bring about His will. The challenge—the reminder—did not fall on deaf ears. Esther stepped up to the climactic position God had given her and He brought salvation for His people through her obedience.

What then can we learn of God's timing for deliverance for His people? The answer: His timing is perfect, even when we don't understand it. Just as God, years before a threat existed, brought a young Jewish orphan into the Persian palace to save His people, He brought Jesus, the Messiah, into the world at the perfect time to save all mankind from eternal damnation.

## Concepts Relating to Jesus or His Mission

In our modern world, as we watch sin gaining greater footholds, Mordecai's challenge to Esther should continue to echo in our ears. *Relief and deliverance will arise ...from another place.* Whenever we are given an opportunity to act for the Lord, our failure will not change God's ultimate plan—it will only change the blessing that could have been ours.

God promised deliverance—and it came in the person of Jesus Christ. Jesus promised He would return—that, too, will come about in His time.

### Firstborn Is Owed to God
Exodus 13:1-2; Deuteronomy 15:19; Numbers 3:13, 41, 8:16-18

In Colossians 1:15 and 18 Jesus is called the *firstborn of all creation* and *the firstborn from the dead.* (In Revelation 1:5 He is also called the *firstborn of the dead.*) Luke even emphasizes that Jesus is the *firstborn* of Mary (2:7) and goes on in verse 23 to refer back to the Old Testament (Exodus 13) saying, "as it is written in the Law of the Lord, 'Every firstborn male that opens the womb shall be called holy to the LORD'."

So, I ask myself, *What is the significance of the firstborn? What is so special about this concept that it is carried over into the New Testament?*

As I look at references to the firstborn, I find little of note—other than genealogical references, until I read the details of the Passover. At that time, I am reminded of the slaying of the firstborn of all the Egyptians, which led to Pharaoh letting the Israelites leave. It is after that incident that I begin to find references to the firstborn that seems to have great significance to God. Exodus 13:1-2 records, "Then the LORD spoke to Moses, saying, 'Sanctify to Me every firstborn, the first offspring of every womb among the sons of Israel, both of man and beast; it belongs to Me.'" Later, in Numbers 3:13, the idea is repeated, "For all the first born are Mine."

Not long after the commands just mentioned, God changed His requirement. In Numbers 3:41, He told Moses, "You shall take the

# The Scarlet Thread

Levites for Me, I am the LORD, instead of all the firstborn among the sons of Israel, and the cattle of the Levites instead of all the firstborn among the cattle of the sons of Israel." Numbers 8:16 and 18 repeat this same message, "for they are wholly given to Me from among the sons of Israel. I have taken them for Myself instead of every first issue of the womb, the firstborn of all the sons of Israel." (Verse 16) and "But I have taken the Levites instead of every firstborn among the sons of Israel" (Verse 18).

As I look at the sequence of events laid out in these passages, I try to comprehend the significance of the firstborn being dedicated to God in the first place and then the Levites later being allowed to take the place of the firstborn.

The closest text I find to provide the explanation I sought is found in the rest of Numbers 3:13, where God told Moses, "on the day that I struck down all the firstborn in the land of Egypt, I sanctified to Myself all the firstborn in Israel, from man to beast. They shall be Mine: I am the LORD." *On the day I struck down the firstborn of Egypt*: why then? What was important about that particular plague over the other nine?

As I ponder these verses, the Spirit seems to light the words and I come to understand, if not THE reason, at least one possible reason, one that once again makes me marvel at the intricate images of my Lord that are woven into His Word.

Numbers 3:13 almost reads as *because I **had to** strike down the firstborn of Egypt, the firstborn of Israel will be Mine*. Immediately, I am reminded that our omnipotent God, before the foundation of the world, knew He would have to come as a Savior to restore the relationship that would be broken. Thus, at the moment in history that is recorded in Exodus, God knew that this act that He would bring about would set in motion the actions that would eventually lead to the sacrificial death of the incarnate Christ. I mentally walk through the verses and I see the promise of the Messiah emerge: To free Israel from the physical bondage of Egypt and to prepare the way for all mankind to be freed from the bondage of sin, the firstborn of Egypt was struck down (just as, many centuries later, the *firstborn* of heaven would have to be struck down). The firstborn of Israel being given to God became a symbolic picture of a retribution that would be required. That concept would help future generations of Israelites to understand how the death of the firstborn of Egypt made the way for their freedom, thus preparing the Jews (and us) to understand the need for the *firstborn of all creation* to be sacrificed. Later, the picture of substitution was introduced, as God chose to accept the Levites as a substitute for the firstborn of each family, thus showing future generations the picture of the High Priest becoming the substitutionary sacrifice.

## God Alone Provides Sin's Solution

Genesis 7:16; 22:8; Deuteronomy 12:5, 14; Psalms 3:8, 37:39, 62:1; Isaiah 43:1; Jeremiah 3:23b; Jonah 2:9 (Judges—all the judges are shown specific directions from God to solve the dilemmas that they faced.)

It is a condition among man that we tend to think that we can, through the application of intellect, reason, money, or merely hard work, find a solution for any problem that we face. In matters of the physical realm this may be true, but in matters of the spiritual realm it is not even close. Sin, and the consequences it brings, is a real problem—it is not necessarily something that we can touch or see, but it is a circumstance that severed the relationship between Jehovah and His created beings and literally shattered the spiritual walkway that connected them.

In the New Testament we see the solution—God incarnate dying on the cross as a substitution for man. In the Old Testament we find the roots of that concept and the certainty that God's solution is the only one.

Perhaps the most dramatic episode that illustrates this concept is found in Genesis 7:16. When the ark was loaded and the rain gathered in the heavens, ready to pour down upon the earth, Scripture tells us that, "the LORD closed it [the door] behind him [Noah]." This was not a case of Noah rigging some kind of pulley system to close the door behind him; nor did he pay one of the scoffers to close him and his family up inside the huge wooden structure. Instead, God, who conceived the project and designed the vessel, completed the act by *closing the door.* In this drama, unequaled to that point in man's history, God took center stage, demonstrating that He alone was the one who was providing the means of salvation (physical salvation) for the human race.

Another dramatic episode, which we have already looked at, was the event that so clearly illustrated the future sacrifice of the Son of God. As Abraham and Isaac walked the trail to Mount Moriah to offer sacrifice to Jehovah, but taking no sacrificial animal with them, Abraham spoke God's promise to his son, saying in Genesis 22:8, "God will provide for Himself the lamb for the burnt offering."

Psalms 3:8, Psalm 37:39, Psalms 62:1, Jeremiah 3:23, Jonah 2:9, and many more verses point to the fact that salvation comes from the Lord, that it was conceived by Him and that it was executed by Him. In Isaiah 43:1 we read of God's perspective, "But now, thus says the LORD, your Creator, O Jacob, and He who formed you, O Israel, 'Do not fear, for I have redeemed you; I have called you by name; you are Mine!'"

Deuteronomy 12:5 and 14 even required that the Israelites seek the LORD "at the place which the LORD your God will choose." In the very beginning of His relationship with the Hebrews, God clearly claimed the right to determine how, when, where, and in what manner the people were to come to Him—He established times and places to come before Him, and specific laws regarding how He was to be contacted. Since the coming of Christ, those temporal, physical conditions that pointed to the coming Messiah are now seen in the reality of a personal relationship with God, through the work done by Christ at Calvary. Even so, Jehovah still holds claim to His right to determine the manner in which His gift of salvation is received, as seen in John 14:6, when Jesus clearly says, "no one comes to the Father but through Me." Or when He says in John 3:3, "unless one is born again he cannot see the kingdom of God." Or when Peter stated God's command, saying, "Repent, and each of you be baptized in the name of Jesus Christ for the forgiveness of your sins" (Acts 2:38).

Concepts Relating to Jesus or His Mission

## **Life after Bondage**
Ezra 9:9

Is there life after death? Of course, we know that to be true
because the Bible clearly teaches it. But throughout the New
Testament promises we also realize that there is *life after
bondage*—not just spiritual life we are given in Jesus, not just the
promise of eternal life that continues beyond our earthly grave,
but rather life—the realization of a purposeful, meaningful,
worthwhile physical existence in the here and now, even after we
have been crushed beneath the power of guilt and sin.

This concept is perhaps one of the most precious of God's
miracles, for it builds an armor around us that can protect us from
the lies of Satan. Even though he has lost the battle for our soul,
Satan uses his sharpest weapons—guilt, feelings of inadequacy,
crippling fear that we will never be good enough—to try to make
us live less than victorious lives. When he is successful in his
battle plan, the result is seen in our ineffectiveness in the ongoing
spiritual battle on planet Earth.

Under the unending reminders of our failure and our
worthlessness, children of God so often find it much easier to
believe God can save us than that He can (and is willing to)
thoroughly cleanse us—turning us into righteous, worthy saints,
living in this fallen world. We find the idea of *life after death*
easier to understand and believe than *life after bondage*.

As I pause at Ezra 9:9, I realize that he spoke of this same
concept, saying, "For we are slaves; yet in our bondage our God
has not forsaken us, but has extended lovingkindness to us in the
sight of the kings of Persia, to give us reviving to raise up the
house of our God, to restore its ruins and give us a wall in Judah
and Jerusalem." The people of Judah were in a physical
bondage—they were slaves to Babylon, and later to Persia. But
God brought them out of that situation. He did not merely remove
them from the physical bondage, giving them their freedom; He
gave them a worthwhile purpose—rebuilding the temple and the
wall around Jerusalem. In His lovingkindness, He restored their

pride in their nation. He lifted them back to their place as the chosen people. He gave them life after their bondage.

He offers us life after bondage as well. The spiritual life is ours now, the eternal life that He promised has already begun, and then, like icing on the cake, He also gives us a meaningful, worthwhile purpose, as we anxiously await His return.

## No One is Good Enough
Psalms 14:3; Micah 7:2a; II Chronicles 6:36; Ecclesiastes 7:20

Paul reminds us that there is no one who is good enough to reach God by his own efforts. In Romans 3:10 he says, "There is none righteous, not even one" and further emphasizes the fact in 3:23, "for all have sinned and fall short of the glory of God." John speaks to the same idea in Revelation 5:2 when he records that the angel, in a loud voice, asked, "Who is worthy to open the book and to break its seals?" John apparently was filled with despair at that moment, for a few verses later (verse 5) he recorded, "and one of the elders said to me, 'Stop weeping; behold, the Lion that is from the tribe of Judah, the Root of David, has overcome so as to open the book and its seven seals.'"

Thus, we see in the New Testament the concept that there is no one among the race of man who is good enough to satisfy the righteous conditions set upon the debt of sin—no one except the Son of God, Himself.

In the Old Testament, the foundation of this concept was laid, that those in the ages to come would understand why God's own sacrifice was needed. Psalm 14:3 can be heard resonating in Paul's words in Romans 3:10: "They have all turned aside, together they have become corrupt; there is no one who does good, not even one." Ecclesiastes 7:20 and Micah 7:2a basically repeat the same text. In II Chronicles 6:36a, we find the idea expressed in Romans 3:23: "When they sin against You (for there is no man who does not sin) and You are angry with them and deliver them to an enemy."

172

## Concepts Relating to Jesus or His Mission

**Only a Perfect Sacrifice Will Do**
Exodus 12: 5a, 46

With the first introduction of the sacrificial lamb, we see the overriding concept of God's sacrifice—only a perfect sacrifice would be accepted. Only the perfect sacrifice could accomplish the purpose of the sacrificial act. Exodus 12:5a describes the lamb as an *unblemished male a year old*. *Male* and *unblemished* (sinless): two identifying characteristics of the sacrifice that easily bring to mind the ultimate sacrifice, the Lamb of God.

Exodus 12:46 then goes on to explain that the Passover lamb would have *no broken bones*, which we have seen in a prior chapter of *The Scarlet Thread*, and that *none of the flesh of the lamb was to be taken outside*. The inquisitive part of my mind asks why—why couldn't the meat be taken outside? It could of course be simply a test of obedience or it could be that the time that God would destroy the firstborn of the Egyptians was near and He did not want any of His people to be outside where they could be caught up in the destruction of lives.

I always find *why* questions in the Scripture interesting because God clearly tells us the *why* when it is important, but when a *why* really has no definitive importance to the matter at hand, I sometimes feel like He sits back and laughs with us as we play around at trying to step, for even a few moments, into His mind.

This is such a circumstance; God doesn't tell us why, but it does make for an interesting experience to consider some possibilities. I think of the contrast of *inside* verses *outside* and I wonder if staying *inside* the house in some way marked the people spiritually, much like putting the blood of the lamb on the door posts marked the houses physically. *Outside* often carries connotations of *being on the outside looking in*, carrying the image that one is wishfully looking inside and wishing to be a part of what is there. Outside also suggests that one is being left out of something that is important. On the other hand, *inside* brings images of being a part of the inner circle of a group, belonging. *Inside* seems to suggest being cherished, while being on the *outside* suggests being unwanted or unwelcome. Perhaps it is too much of a stretch of the terms, but a part of me feels that by telling the Jews to stay inside, God was reminding them that they were His chosen people, and by obeying His instructions, they were, at least for the moment, living up to that choice position.

## Personal Responsibility for Sin
II Kings 14:6; Deuteronomy 24:15

In Peter's sermon on the Day of Pentecost, we find a very important concept that is illustrated in the New Testament and rooted in the Old. Peter says, "Repent, and each of you be baptized in the name of Jesus Christ for the forgiveness of your sins" (Acts 2:38). In Peter's statement we realize the personal nature of the promise—each person must repent of his or her own sins and each person must make that choice to be baptized for the forgiveness of those sins. It has been said that God has no grandchildren! No one can receive the gift of salvation through the choice of another person! It is a personal act that brings each person to the foot of the cross, through the waters of baptism, and then through the gates of heaven.

II Kings 14:6 explains the reality of that concept. The law of God said, "but the sons of the slayers he did not put to death, according to what is written in the book of the Law of Moses, as the LORD commanded, saying, 'The fathers shall not be put to death for the sons, nor the sons be put to death for the fathers; but each shall be put to death for his own sin." With those words, God clearly laid the blame for evil acts at the feet of those who committed them. He purposely let mankind know that every person is responsible for his or her own choices and for the consequences of his or her own sin. Thus, when the time came that God executed His plan for the debt of sin to be paid, it was clearly understood that each person would have to decide whether or not to accept His gift of canceled debt and eternal life.

## Possibility of Immortality
Proverbs 12:28; Ecclesiastes 3:11

Of all the desires of mankind, the search for immortality probably ranks highest of all. Drama, music, and literary works of all types describe the quests, the dreams, or the scientific studies or experiments of those who seek to cheat death, or the diabolical schemes of those who seek to profit from others who attempt to do so. It seems to be built into man to be unsatisfied with this one existence, searching instead for some proof or assurance that something beyond this life exists to make this life worth living.

Some people are drawn to legendary promises of a fountain of youth or a miracle drug that will slow down or stop the aging process. Some are content to strive for some kind of honor or legacy that will live on after they succumb to the end of their appointed days. Still others understand that immortality is not only a possibility; it is a certainty, as we are reminded in Hebrews 9:27, "And inasmuch as it is appointed for men to die once and after this comes judgment."

The reality of immortality, which is clearly seen in the New Testament, is rooted in the pages penned long before the time of Jesus' ministry here on earth. King Solomon, writing in Proverbs 12:28, gives us a glimpse of the reality of the distinction between physical and spiritual death, saying, "In the way of righteousness is life, and in its pathway there is no death."

It is in Ecclesiastes 3:11, another work from the heart of Solomon, that I find myself pausing to wonder at the deep reality that God not only understands that we seek to know what is beyond the veil of the physical world, but He planted that longing in our hearts. "He has also set eternity in their heart," Solomon writes. As I linger over this verse I struggle to put into words the magnitude of how this phrase sometimes affects me. There are times that it merely reminds me that in breathing life into man, God shared a part of Himself and that part longs to return to the Creator; but at other times, I can almost touch the timelessness that is wrapped up in the concept.

*Eternity in my heart* is that glorious promise that I will never die—that spiritual immortality is a guarantee. It is the understanding that all that was, all that is, and all that will be was securely wrapped together by the Creator of the universe and has been set into my heart, so that while I am stranded in this frail, imperfect world, my heart can look ahead to the wondrous, perfect world to come.

Even so, the end of Ecclesiastes 3:11 reminds me, "yet so that man will not find out the work which God has done from the beginning even to the end." The NIV translation says, "yet, no one can fathom what God has done from beginning to end." The Holman Christian Standard Bible translates the phrase as, "but man cannot discover the work God has done from beginning to end." Pondering the reality that as much as I know of my Lord and all that He has shown me in His book and by His Spirit only makes me realize how little I know. Once again I am reminded of Paul's words in I Corinthians 13:12, "For now we see in a mirror dimly, but then face to face; now I know in part, but then I will know fully just as I also have been fully known." This, I think, is the reason for His setting eternity in my heart—that my heart will know that immortality waits and that I will ever long for more, until that time when I will truly know Him fully.

### Promise of Pardon
Isaiah 55:7; Jeremiah 33:8, 50:20

Within the context of any spiritual conversation, the words *forgiveness* and *redemption* can hardly roll off our tongues without the momentary flash of the image of a cross. After all, the whole point of Christ's coming to earth was to bring redemption, restoration, and forgiveness of our sins. Through this journey I have paused at many verses in the Old Testament about these truths, and the verses of this section might easily fit into those same sections. However, as I look deeper into these particular verses, I begin to see the raw edge of a legal concept that, while it is clearly demonstrated in the New Testament, the depth of its meaning could easily be missed.

Isaiah 55:7 says, "Let the wicked forsake his way and the unrighteous man his thoughts; and let him return to the LORD, and He will have compassion on him, and to our God, for He will abundantly pardon." Jeremiah 33:8 prophesies, "I will cleanse them from all their iniquity by which they have sinned against Me, and I will pardon all their iniquities by which they have sinned against Me and by which they have transgressed against Me."

Perhaps the clearest of God's promises of pardon is seen in Jeremiah 50:20, which says, "In those days and at that time, declares the LORD, search will be made for the iniquity of Israel, but there will be none; and for the sins of Judah, but they will not be found; for I will pardon those whom I leave as a remnant." We understand, of course, that the sins and iniquities will not be found because Jesus had covered them with His own blood, thereby making the situation as though they had never been done.

This is the basic concept of forgiveness and redemption that we find prophesied throughout the Old Testament and demonstrated in the New Testament, but it is also the concept of pardon. Compared to words like *redeem* and *forgive*, the word *pardon* is rarely found in the Scriptures; so I pause a bit longer on these verses, wondering what, if anything, is the significance of using the word *pardon*. To me, pardon seems a stronger word; it rings with the sound of a courtroom gavel. It forces the reader to understand that this is more than just a slap on the hand. It is more than just waving off the sins as though they didn't matter. In the use of *pardon*, Isaiah and Jeremiah remind us that the exchange that is being made—from sin to forgiveness, from lives filled with iniquity to lives washed clean by the Savior's blood—this exchange was not just made by the passing of legal briefs from party to party; it was not simply erasing the sin.

Sometimes we tend to throw the words *forgiveness* and *mercy* around like they are everyday things, but *pardon* emphasizes that a serious legal offence has been committed and the consequences of those actions will not go away—sin must be paid by death. The fact that we, the offender got off scot free does not mean that the legal consequences were just wiped away.

As I look at these verses from Isaiah and Jeremiah, I get a glimpse of that final judgment, when all those who refused to accept the Savior must answer for their actions, their failures, and their choices. In that scene I recognize the judge—the humble

Shepherd of Israel, the Lamb of God. I see Him staring down at the offenders, with sadness in His eyes. There will be no joy in that moment; He is "not willing for any to perish but for all to come to repentance" (II Peter 3:9). Nevertheless, there will be many who do perish because they did not repent and claim the pardon of Christ.

## Sin Is Paid for by Blood

Genesis 3:21; Exodus 12:7; Leviticus 17:11 (Also: Exodus 30:10, Leviticus 6:30, 8:15, 12:6-7, 16:18, 16:27; Ezekiel 43:20)

On several occasions Jesus told His disciples that it would be necessary that He suffer, but it was not until His crucifixion that they understood that He actually had to die—that His blood would physically be shed for the sins of the world. It was some time later that the author of Hebrews reminded readers the reason Jesus had to die on the cross, saying, "And according to the Law, one may almost say, all things are cleansed with blood, and without shedding of blood there is no forgiveness" (Hebrews 9:22).

The concept of blood *paying for sin and purchasing forgiveness* is probably first seen in the Garden of Eden, for Genesis 3:21 reveals that "the LORD God made garments of skin for Adam and his wife, and clothed them." Death, of an innocent animal, was required in order to take care of the physical consequences of man's sin. Sin was not paid for, for no animal, innocent or not, could pay that debt. Still, as God personally provided the physical covering for Adam and Eve, He silently set in motion the plan that would truly atone for sin and provide absolute forgiveness and restoration.

Pausing frequently throughout the books of Moses, it is easy to see that the concept that blood was required to pay for sin was implied before the Jews were freed from Egypt and then clearly taught as a part of the sacrificial system. Moses' instructions during the first Passover noted that it was the *blood* that would be placed on the doorposts that would secure the passing of the angel of death and thus the saving of the Jews. Exodus 12:7 records, "Moreover, they shall take some of the blood and put it on the two doorposts and on the lintel of the houses in which they eat it." Later, Leviticus 17:11 emphatically spells out the connection between the sacrificial blood and the future full atonement of mankind: "For the life of the flesh is in the blood, and I have given it to you on the altar to make atonement for your souls; for it is the blood by reason of the life that makes atonement." (Exodus 30:10; Leviticus 6:30, 8:15, 12:6-7, 16:18, 16:27; Ezekiel 43:20 also link *blood* and *atonement*).

# The Scarlet Thread

# IX. Potpourri of Additional Topics

## Defining the category

As I began the recording of my journey through the pages of the Old Testament, I discovered that many of the verses that resonated in my mind with a connection to Jesus did not actually fit nicely into any particular section. Thus, as we approach the end of my journey, I find that a *Potpourri, Miscellaneous, or Other* section is needed. To be truthful, this need did not come as a surprise, for after all I've always known that my God would never fit nicely into little boxes—though the world in general often attempts to put Him there.

Therefore, it is with great joy, that I lay before my Lord, this last chapter of *The Scarlet Thread* to hold those extra moments that relates categories that did not fit well anywhere else or verses that stand as solitary sentinels calling me to meet with Jesus for one more encounter.

With this chapter, I end my first official journey to encounter Jesus in the Old Testament, even as I am aware that the journey will never truly end until the day that I step through that veil that separates His eternal realm from my temporal one.

## Specific Examples—Stops along my journey

### New Testament Scriptures Brought to Mind

Stone rolled away
Genesis 29:8

When I first encountered this verse, I wondered why I hesitated to move on. Was it the image of a stone that needed to be rolled away to reveal an unmistakable source of life or was it the primary character in the story that struck a chord in my mind? On the surface this verse fits snuggly into a narrative that introduces Jacob to the family that was already kin (through his mother Rebecca) and would soon be closer still (through his marriages to Leah and Rachel). At this point, Jacob saw the stone covering the well, recognized Rachel as his mother's brother's daughter, and took it on himself to uncover the water for the sheep. In that moment, perhaps unknowingly, Jacob placed himself into the drama as its hero, the one who would provide life-giving water to the flock. He was a stranger in the land, so he really had no reason to aid the shepherds in that manner, yet he did. Perhaps that was what caught my attention. It was as though a heavenly light illuminated the scene. As I think on the words, I realize that I am witness to the prelude to the great story of redemption. While I listen in on Jacob's words, I already know that he will be the *father of David*, the *father* to the royal line from which the Messiah would come. I already know that many centuries after this scene Jacob's descendant would lay in a cold, dark cave sealed by a great stone and that the world would *hold its breath* until that stone was rolled away to reveal not life-giving water but the reality that the true living water had risen from the grave, just as He said He would.

Treasured memories
Genesis 37:11

As I read Genesis 37:11, about Jacob keeping these memories in his mind, I am reminded that Scripture also tells us "Mary treasured up all these things and pondered them in her heart (Luke 2:19). I have often wondered if Joseph, too, pondered the circumstances of those early days with Mary and the strange birth of the child he called "son," though He was not his son, at all.

Scripture never tells us much of Joseph, but somehow I feel that he, like Jacob, would not have easily forgotten. For many days after Joseph's dreams, and probably frequently in the years that followed, Jacob probably wondered just what part that dream would play in the future that lay ahead. Likewise, I believe Joseph, in whatever number of years he served as *father* to the holy child, frequently thought back on that miraculous night in

Bethlehem, and wondered what part that child in the manger would play in the future of Israel, or the future of all mankind.

## The veil of the tabernacle
Exodus 26:31

The veil of the tabernacle (and of the temple, as well) marked the entrance to the Holy of Holies. Behind that curtain, the presence of God resided. There was no access to that holy place, except as ordained by God—once a year, by the High Priest alone. When I read of the creation of that veil, I can't help think of that moment when it split, from the top to the bottom.

The veil was designed by God. Its beauty testified to the grandness and magnificence of Almighty God and the strength of the twisted fibers intricately woven together testified to His power and might. These thick, heavy curtains guarded that hallowed part of the tabernacle, and later the temple, and reminded everyone that no one was worthy to come into the presence of Yahweh. Then, by the power of the resurrection—the power of God alone—that curtain tore, not by the hands of man but by the hand of God. In that dramatic display, the God of the universe announced that access to Him was no longer restricted. No longer did he choose to reside in the Holy of Holies; instead He would reside in the hearts of His people.

## Laws of warfare
Deuteronomy 20:5-9

In Deuteronomy 20, God lays out the laws of warfare. He begins by reminding them that He is on their side and that they have no reason to be afraid. Then, in verses 5-9, He essentially offers the people several ways to get out of serving.

I can't help but wonder why such a choice is offered. Perhaps the intent was to weed out the number so they would always understand that victory was won by His power rather than their number, or perhaps He was merely eliminating all those whose heart and mind would be more on self than on the battle.

# The Scarlet Thread

Whatever the case, I found as I read the passage that I heard a faint echo from Jesus' parable in Luke 14:16-24 seeping into my mind. In that parable, Jesus said that a man was giving a banquet and had invited many, but instead of notes of thanks for the great invitation, the man received excuses—some of which sound much like the ones permitted in Deuteronomy—"I bought land and have to check on it; I got married and must be with my wife." I find myself wondering if there was any connection between the two pictures. Perhaps God allowed the excuses that enabled soldiers to get out of battle because He already knew that when given the choice to stand with Him or to go their own way, mankind as a whole would choose self over Him, just as Jesus described in His parable.

## Always there
Deuteronomy 31:8; Joshua 1:5

As I read these words of Deuteronomy 31:8 and Joshua 1:5, I hear the words of Jesus echo in my mind: "And surely I am with you always, to the very end of the age. (Matthew 28:20b)" and "Do not let your hearts be troubled and do not be afraid" (John 14:27b).

## Raising up judges
Judges 2:16

As I read the words of Judges 2:16, I think of the final judge—the judge who will one day sit in judgment over all mankind, this same judge who came to us first as Savior, that as many as would heed His call would be saved from the final judgment. I remember that He was indeed *raised up* and He did indeed *deliver all who came to Him* from the hands of the evil one who seeks only their destruction.

## Feeding the multitude
I Samuel 21:3

Reading I Samuel 21:3 immediately sent my thoughts into the gospels to recall Jesus' feeding of the multitudes with only five loaves of bread and two fish.

# Potpourri of Additional Topics

## Return a different way
I Kings 13:10

The circumstances of I King 13 certainly did not mirror those of the magi. Even so, God told the prophet not to "*return by the way which he came to Bethel*," just as He warned the magi to return to their home by a different way (Matthew 2:12). I can't help but wonder how either circumstance would have been it they had not listened to God's command to return a different way.

For just a moment I also contemplate some of the major choices of my life—those which followed the whispered instructions from my Lord and those which were made mostly (if not entirely) from my own selfish desires. I wonder: how would my life be different if those choices had been different?

## Surplus
II Kings 4:43-44

As I read the story of the miraculous feeding of a hundred men with only twenty loaves of barley, and that there was food left over, I found myself laughing. It was like sharing a private joke with a dear, old friend. Knowing that God has always been a God of miracles, I find it odd to realize that I rarely actually think of this kind of miracle outside the New Testament. Thus, when I encountered this section in my journey to find Jesus in the Old Testament, I could almost hear my Lord chuckle as He filled my mind with the memories of His feeding the five thousand, as told by John in 6:1-12.

## Greater is He
II Kings 6:16

Reading II Kings 6:16 brings to mind I John 4:4b: "because greater is He who is in you than he who is in the world."

# The Scarlet Thread

## Power in numbers
I Chronicles 21:1

It is interesting that Scripture immediately explains that Satan is at the root of this new sin that is about to latch onto David. It seems a trifling matter that David wants to count his men—that he wants to know how many fighters he has. Yet we immediately see that Joab recognizes the command for what it is: a lack of faith, the need to rely on the number of fighters rather than God. Verse 6 even goes so far as to tell us that Joab did not count the tribes of Levi or Benjamin because he found the command so abhorrent.

But David let Satan fill his heart. He listened to the whisper that caused him to sin against God, and the rest of the chapter describes the result of that sin. As I read that account, it occurred to me that when David was moved to number (take a census of) the people of Israel, he allowed Satan to interfere in the plans God had for His people. Then I recalled that it was another census that figured prominently in the lives of the people of Israel, a census that brought Joseph and Mary to Bethlehem. I wonder if Satan had a part in that as well. Did he think that by having Caesar Augustus take a census of Israel he was in some way mocking the God of Israel? If so, did he realize, before that miraculous night, that he was actually playing into the plan of God? Did he perhaps realize too late that he had helped to set in motion the very plan he had hoped would never be executed?

## Each to his own city
Ezra 2:1

In Ezra 2:1 it was the simple phrase "each to his city" that caught my attention and thrust my mind into Bethlehem, where centuries after the Jews returned to Israel, Luke recorded, "And everyone was on his way to register for the census, each to his own city" (Luke 2:3).

186

# Potpourri of Additional Topics

## Setting up stumbling blocks
Ezekiel 14:3-4, 7; 18:30; 44:12; Jeremiah 6:21

It is undoubtedly the *stumbling block* image that calls out to me from this verse. Most often, the stumbling block is seen at face value. It is that item (or concept) in the lives of people that causes them to stumble in the path they walk. Thus we find references in the New Testament (Matthew 18:7; Luke 17:1; Romans 14:13; Revelation 2:14) that caution against becoming *one who puts stumbling blocks in the paths of others* that cause them to fall.

Still, the image of the stumbling block speaks to me of Christ, as well. We easily see Christ as the cornerstone—a rock that suggests the principle part of the building or the stone that guides the placement of all others. In that picture we see that Christ is the principle part of our lives and guides all our choices. But in Ezekiel's image in 14:3-4, (also found in Jeremiah 6:21, Ezekiel 14: 3 and 7, Ezekiel 18:30 and Ezekiel 44:12), we can almost see the flip side of that concept: we see the *Chief Cornerstone* as a *stumbling block*. Jeremiah 6:21 goes so far as to tell us that the Lord said, "Behold, I am laying stumbling blocks before this people. And they will stumble against them." What stumbling block would God set before His people; why would He do so? My heart tells me that the words speak not of stones but of choices, and ultimately the chief choice that was set before the Jews—and all mankind—was this: *What will you do with Jesus?*

As I read the words of Ezekiel 14:3-4, I get a picture of a heart cluttered with idols. I see Christ standing to the side and I realize that the heart is closed to Him because it is so filled with the poor choices the person has made. I hear a whisper from Revelation 3:20, "Behold, I stand at the door and knock." For just a moment I feel sorrow for the one whose hardened heart has refused to open to the one who loved so much that He chose the path of the cross to provide forgiveness and restoration. But the sorrow lasts for only a moment before it is replaced by the stinging pain of conviction and guilt, as I realize that the heart upon which I am looking is mine and I understand that the stumbling blocks that we must face is not just *What will you do with Jesus?* Rather, the question is: *What will you continue to do with Jesus every moment of every day?*

At this stop in my journey, I am reminded that no matter how far along life's journey with Christ we may have come, we are never far from the stumbling blocks that threaten to become idols in our hearts and never far from the question: *What will you do with Jesus?*

### The vine dries up
Joel 1:12

The first chapter of Joel is a prophecy of devastation, of coming plagues of locust and drought, and the starvation that will follow. On the surface, this chapter does not appear to be a place that I would stop to meet with Jesus. Nevertheless, verse 12 causes me to pause.

Joel says "*the vine dries up and the fig tree fails,*" and there is something in the words that remind me of Jesus. To be sure, Jesus spoke much of vines, of vineyards, of figs, and such, but as I turned to the pages of the New Testament, I discovered in Luke 13 the memory that had stood just outside my thoughts as I read the words of Joel. In Luke 13:6-9, Jesus told a parable about a man who had a fig tree that had failed to produce fruit for three years. The man was ready to destroy it, but the vine-keeper asked him to give it one more year. He said, "Let it alone, sir, for this year too, until I dig around it and put in fertilizer; and if it bears fruit next year, fine; but if not, cut it down."

One more chance: that's what I find in Luke. That's what was missing in Joel. Joel said that "Indeed, rejoicing dries up from the sons of men." Nevertheless, I know the end of the story; I know that rejoicing did not dry up completely, for the God of creation provided *one more chance.*

# Potpourri of Additional Topics

<u>Inherit the land</u>
Psalm 37:11

Psalm 37:11 reminds me of the Beatitudes, especially Matthew 5:5: "Blessed are the gentle [the meek], for they shall inherit the earth."

<u>Calming the sea</u>
Psalms 65:7, Nahum 1:4

Looking back to begin the sentence in verse 5 of Psalm 65, I read that the psalmist is praising the awesome deeds of God, pointing out that it is God who established the mountains by His strength and stills the roaring waves of the sea. Nahum 1:4 makes a similar declaration, acknowledging that He (God) has the power to rebuke the sea.

As I pause at these passages, I visualize a darkness that has come upon the sea, as dark clouds hide the sun and mighty winds lift the waves to send them pounding upon the decks of small vessels caught up in the tempest. Then in my mind I see the calm face of the Master. I see Him face the storm, lift his arm, and whisper, "Be still." Instantaneously, the wind dies, the waves calm to a ripple and the clouds roll back to reveal the sun. No force of nature dares to disobey the word of its Maker.

My heart rejoices in the remembrance of the gospel accounts of Jesus on the Sea of Galilee—when He calmed the storms (from Mark 4:39 and Matthew 8:26) and when He walked across the waters (Matthew 14:26). Those stories bring me peace and comfort in my own stormy times. The stories also cause me to ponder the foolishness of man—for he, alone of God's creation, dares to ever deny the power of the Creator or attempts to stand against Him. I wonder how we can be so foolish—and how our Lord can be so patient when we are.

# The Scarlet Thread

## Ascending into heaven
Proverbs 30:4

In Proverbs 30:4 the writer was contemplating man's inability to understand the infinite God. As I read Solomon's question, "What is His name or His son's name?" and then hear his own response, "Surely you know," my heart automatically responds, *Of course we know; only the Messiah, God incarnate—only He has ascended into heaven and descended, only He has gathered the wind in His fists, only He is the infinite, Almighty God.*

## No one else
Isaiah 45:22-23

As I read Isaiah 45:22-23, I hear my Lord say in John 14:6, "no one comes to the Father but through Me." I hear Paul's reminder in Romans 14:11, "For it is written, every knee shall bow to Me, and every tongue shall give praise to God." And, I am reminded that Paul wrote that God has highly exalted the Son and has bestowed on him the name above every name, the name at which every knee will bow (from Philippians 2:9-10).

## Live by faith
Habakkuk 2:4

"The righteous will live by faith." These words echo over and over in the New Testament: Romans 1:17; Galatians 3:11; Hebrews 10:38. Reading them in the Old Testament is like discovering the ancient anchor to which the lifelines of mankind are tethered. Indeed, we must live by faith, if we are to live at all. Hebrews 11:6 reminds us that *without* faith, it is impossible to please Him.

## Son of man
Ezekiel 2:1

Throughout the second chapter of Ezekiel the term *Son of man* is used, describing the calling of the prophet. The Lord refers to Ezekiel as Son of man and is told that he is being sent to the rebellious people who have rebelled against Him. Each time the name is used, I remember that *son of man* was a title that Jesus frequently used of Himself. Thus, I see in Ezekiel a clear connection, a picture of the one who would come to those same rebellious people.

Measured with your own measure
Obadiah 1:15

In the words of Obadiah 1:15, I hear the voice of Jesus warning that by the standard of measure we use, so will the measure be returned to us (Mark 4:24: Luke 6:38). There is a valuable lesson of honesty and fairness that is seen in these verses.

The feet that bring good news
Nahum 1:15; Isaiah 52:7

As I encounter the words of Nahum 1:15 and Isaiah 52:7, in my journey through the Old Testament, I am struck by a new understanding. I remember that these words were repeated by Paul in Romans 10:15, but Paul obviously quoted from Isaiah 52:7, rather than Nahum 1:15.

Unlike Isaiah (and Paul's) words that bring images of thankfulness and appreciation for those who care enough to bring mankind the message of hope, Nahum set his prophetic words among others that declared of the destruction that would come. He prophesied that Nineveh would be completely cut off. Somehow, in Nineveh's refusal to respond to the message of the prophets and its subsequent destruction, I see the depth of the condemnation. Nineveh was given many opportunities to hear the word of the Lord. The bringer of good news was there on the mountain, in their presence, but the people of Nineveh chose to turn a deaf ear.
As I look at the two references, which are so nearly alike and yet so different, I feel a chill run through me. I look around me at a world that grows continually more corrupt and I seem to see my Lord standing on a mountain, shaking His head. I hear an echo of words that cut like a knife. *The message is clear; they just won't listen.*

The Scarlet Thread

<u>Slow to anger</u>
Nahum 1:3a

In Nahum's words (Nahum 1:3a), only a few verses before the declaration of destruction that was just mentioned, I am reminded of the patience of the Lord. I think of Peter's words, through the power of the Spirit (II Peter 3:9), "The Lord is not slow about His promise, as some count slowness, but is patient toward you, not wishing for any to perish but for all to come to repentance." While Nahum reminds his readers that the Lord will not leave the guilty unpunished, he does so by first reminding them that the Lord is slow to anger, that He is patient, searching for any evidence that the people are penitent and want to be forgiven.

**Foreshadowing Descriptions**

<u>The offering of the poor</u>
Leviticus 12:8

Reading Leviticus 12:8, I am reminded that when Mary and Joseph took their young child to the temple that first time, two turtledoves were the only offering they could afford to bring. (Luke 2:22-24)

<u>The one who presents the sacrifice</u>
Leviticus 21:21

In Leviticus 21:21, I am reminded that the priest that presents the sacrifice, as well as the sacrifice, must be without blemish. Of course in human terms, only physical defects could be screened out, but in Christ we see that command refers to sin in any form, and of course, only Christ would satisfy the conditions necessary to be able to offer the ultimate sacrifice.
<u>Giving of the Spirit</u>
Numbers 11:29

In Numbers 11:29, we see the first hint that the Lord, who is Spirit, would indeed pour out His Spirit upon His people and that His people would worship Him in spirit and in truth, as described in John 4:23.

# Potpourri of Additional Topics

## Cursed is the one who hangs on a tree
Deuteronomy 21:23

Deuteronomy says that one who is hanged is accursed. How then can it be that Jesus was hanged on the cross, but is not accursed? This passage has sometimes been used, as far back as the crucifixion, to prove that Jesus could not be the Messiah. However, in Galatians 3:13-14, Paul, who was probably one of the most knowledgeable of the Jews at that time in history, explained that Christ was indeed the Messiah because He redeemed us from the curse of the law by becoming a curse for us.

## The Word is near
Deuteronomy 30:14

Deuteronomy 30:14 is emphasizing the need to learn and live the Word of God. Repeatedly Moses says that it is to be spoken of, thought about, and followed. Every effort was to be made to make the Word of the Lord a part of the person's everyday life. But when the comment is made that the Word is very near you, the images take on a more personal feel. Those of us who realize that Jesus is the Living Word, also understand that the Word is indeed near to us, for Jesus is always by our side and is living in us through the Holy Spirit.

Thus when John later records that the Word *was* in the beginning and that the Word *became* flesh, we understand the divinity of Christ a little better.

## The one and only child
Judges 11:34

It was undoubtedly the *one and only child* reference that caught my attention in this verse. Circumstances, even the gender of the child, would have no direct connection to the image that the words brought to my mind. Nonetheless, I paused at this moment merely to rejoice in the sweetness of those words as John used them so many years later, "For God so loved the world that he gave his one and only Son, that whoever believes in him shall not perish by have eternal life" (NIV).

193

# The Scarlet Thread

The foundation of the temple
Ezra 3:6

Ezra 3:6 communicated a simple fact. Upon their return from exile in Babylon, the people of Israel set about getting back to the worship of their Lord, in the manner He had prescribed. They prepared the altar and all the items necessary to begin making sacrifices to the Lord—even before the rebuilding of the temple was begun. In Ezra's words I see the simple desire of the people to come before the Lord and I see the physical realities that they had to overcome to do so.

Being aware of the struggle of the Jews to rebuild the temple and the city of Jerusalem after the Babylonian Captivity, I applaud their efforts. As Ezra records that the sacrifices were begun, even before the foundation was laid for the temple, I smile. For while I see their hearts longing for the physical blocks of the temple to be laid, I look beyond that second temple to the third (the one that will be built during the Tribulation period) and to the fourth (the magnificent one that will be built in Jerusalem during the millennial reign of Christ). Even greater, I look beyond that second temple to see the true temple—the person of Jesus. While the foundation of the physical temples had not been laid, I am reminded that Jesus, the *true foundation*, was and is and always will be.

Sending deliverers
Nehemiah 9:27

At the words of Nehemiah 9:27, I am reminded of all the judges that God sent to deliver His people and of the prophets that He sent to warn them and show them their need to repent. I am reminded, too, that He has sent the Church into the world to point the way back to Him. Mostly, I am reminded that He sent Jesus, the Messiah, to deliver mankind from the oppression of sin and to restore them to the precious relationship with Almighty God that was intended from the very first moment that creation began.

# Potpourri of Additional Topics

## What is man?
Job 15:14

The words of Eliphaz are meant to chastise Job, to perhaps convince him that he is not as wise, or as innocent, as he thinks himself to be. Nevertheless, his question incites in me a desire to answer him; for I believe I know the answer, as all who know Christ do.

"What is man, that he should be pure?"—mankind, covered and entwined with the sins of a lifetime cannot be pure, but the Son of Man was, and is, pure and sinless. "Who is he who is born of a woman, that he should be righteous?"—Jesus, born of Mary, born of the power of the Holy Spirit, born as God incarnate—He is the one who could be born of woman, and yet be righteous.

## Ox in a manger
Job 39:9

I wonder as I read Job 39. God is speaking to Job, describing the creatures of nature, pointing out the very limited understanding that Job has of the creatures. I don't believe that Job 39:9 is in any way related to that manger in Bethlehem so many centuries later. In fact, the ox has never been named as a possible attendee in that great drama. Even so, I pause here for a moment, merely because the mention of a manger cannot be made without bringing vivid images of Jesus as a child lying on the hay.

## Desiring to go into His presence
Job 23:3

Job yearns to find Him—the Lord—and to come to His mercy seat, but of course only through Christ is that truly possible. Only after accepting His forgiveness, can we boldly come into His presence.

## Covering of sin
Psalms 32:1

"How blessed is he whose transgression is forgiven, whose sin is covered!" We are blessed indeed! The covering of sin and the forgiveness of transgression are only made possible through the power of the cross. Jesus' blood was shed for us, and that blood covered the sins of all who choose to accept it.

## Promises

Some of the verses found in this section have already been mentioned in other chapters of *The Scarlet Thread*, yet they appear here as well as I contemplate three great promises that God gave to Israel and to mankind in general. As I pause once more to briefly look at these promises, I realize that hidden within each is a great deal more than those who first received them ever dared to dream. Simple words cannot convey the magnitude and importance of a promise given by the mouth of Jehovah, but since simple words are the only tools I have, I pray that our Holy God will touch your hearts to allow you to hear His words rather than mine.

The promise of a great nation
Genesis 35:11; II Samuel 23:5; Joel 2:32; Obadiah 1:17

In the verses above, and many more we have already looked at, we see God's promise of a future. At the beginning of creation, God already knew that the time would come to select a people, a tribe, and then a family to use as the tools to bring salvation to the earth. He chose Abraham, then Judah, and then the line of David. The reality is that He could have chosen any person upon the face of the earth to begin building His chosen nation. He could have chosen any among the sons of Jacob to become the line of kings. He could have chosen any simple shepherd to become the warrior king that would lead His people and stand as the picture of the King of Kings who would come.

He could have bypassed it all and simply stepped down from heaven, fully-grown and ready to face the cross. *But, He didn't.* Instead He chose the nation of Israel, the line of David, the humble young virgin named Mary. I can't begin to guess why, except that perhaps He knew that man—in his stubbornness, pride, fear, uncertainties, and desperate need to at least try to understand—would need a Savior that could be found in the very seeds of creation, a Savior who could identify with all the frail conditions of man, without succumbing to the sin of man. God knew the needs of man, so He gave them a promise—a promise that not only would the wandering travelers become a prominent nation one day, but that nation would open the doors of heaven to the whole race of man.

In Genesis 35:11 (and many other verses), God promised Abraham that a nation and a company of nations would come from him, and even that kings would come from him. In II Samuel 23:5, David recalls that God made an everlasting covenant with him. (A covenant is an agreement in which two parties promise to fulfill certain conditions. Are there really any words that can describe the significance of a covenant in which the primary party is Almighty God, the maker of the universe? When He said "everlasting," He really meant *everlasting!*) Joel 2:32 and Obadiah 1:17 (and many, many other verses) describe the promise that a remnant of Israel would always survive—after all, He had already given His word that the covenant would be continued forever!

## The promise to dwell with mankind
Exodus 29:45; Zechariah 2:10

Almighty God gave another promise to Moses, to David, to the prophets, and to us. God said in Exodus 29:45, "I will dwell among the sons of Israel" and in Zechariah 2:10, "I will dwell in your midst." Solomon questioned (in II Kings 8:27), "But will God indeed dwell with mankind on the earth? Behold, heaven and the highest heaven cannot contain You; how much less this house which I have built." There is an understood certainty that though we cannot understand it, God does indeed dwell here on earth with us—and He did so physically, in the person of Jesus Christ.

## The promise to be our guide
Exodus 23:20; Malachi 3:1

A third promise that I find in Exodus 23:20 and Malachi 3:1 is more personal. God told Moses He would send an angel before him to protect him. He told Malachi to tell the people that a messenger would be sent to clear the way for the Promised One to come. In all His dealings with His people God let us know that He does not sit back and wait for us to fail and get up and fail again and become frightened and discouraged before He finally steps in. No, He promised that He would lead the way. He would protect us as we walk along beside Him, and He would never leave us. Some of the most beautiful words in Scripture are heard from the mouth of the Savior, "I am with you always, even to the end of the age" (Matthew 28:20b). Being with us, beside us, within us, is a promise that God began making right from the beginning. He was with Adam in the Garden of Eden. He led the way as the Israelites slowly wandered through the wilderness. He was even right there with them in battle, in defeat, and in captivity.

How precious is the thought that Satan's great weapons of fear and despair are crippled by a promise that God made His people at the very beginning of the world—He is here, with us, by us, in us. And greater still, the fear of uncertainty is broken when we remember that God Himself has prepared the way; every step we take is guarded by the one who has already passed that way before.

## Many Terms of Redemption
*Forgive, Forgiven, Forgiveness*: Ezekiel 16:63
*Ransom, Ransomed, Redeem*: Jeremiah 31:11; Hosea 13:14, Nehemiah 1:10; Job 19:25; Psalm 49:7-9, 55:18; Jeremiah 50:34; Lamentations 3:58,
*Restore, Restored*: Lamentations 5:21
*Save, Saved, Atoned, Savior, Salvation*: Psalms 57:3, Proverbs 16:6, Isaiah 45:17,49:8; Hosea 13:4; Habakkuk 3:13

The verses listed above, while using different terms (forgive, ransom, redeem, restore, save, atone, etc.) all speak the same message—God promised that redemption was already guaranteed. I separated the above list, grouping various types of words together, just to make them a little easier to study.

I love how the prophets string together words that create a simple, poignant statement of fact—a fact that whether it is recorded as though it will happen or as though it has already been done, carries the absolute assurance of God that the outcome is already sealed, even though its actual fulfillment may be centuries away.

As I stop to consider these verses, I am reminded of the reality of Christ's actions. He will, He did, redeem His people. He did create the pathway to save them. He became the ransom for anyone who would accept His gift of salvation. In these prophetic verses the Old Testament writers looked ahead to the fulfillment of a promise. As I take the time to gaze upon their words I am reminded not only that my gentle, loving Savior kept those promises, but that He will keep the ones that yet remain—He will return.

Though most of the verses above produce a simple moment of wonder and gratitude as I think upon my Lord, one passage brought special thoughts that I want to share:

<u>Redemption is not ours to give</u>
Psalm 49:7-9

Psalms 49:7-9 explains that man can't "redeem his brother, or give God a ransom for him" and then goes on the say that he "should cease trying forever—that he should live on eternally, that he should not undergo decay." I pondered on this statement for a while, wondering at its meaning. One of my study Bibles suggests that it is merely telling us that we cannot purchase days to extend our lives, but I wonder if maybe more than that the psalmist is reminding us that we don't have the power to bring about the redemption of another—that task is beyond what little power we possess. Only God can redeem. Our part in the plan is to stop trying—stop trying to gain redemption for ourselves or another person—just accept the eternal life that is offered. I remember the peace that filled me when I first realized that another person's salvation isn't my responsibility. All that is asked of me is to tell them about Jesus: I can't redeem another; I can only point them to the *one* who can.

# The Scarlet Thread

## Trinity
Genesis 1:26, 3:22, 11:7; Isaiah 6:8; Deuteronomy 6:4; Isaiah 48:16

There is no doubt in my mind that the *Trinity*, complicated as it may seem, does indeed exist. In the creation process, God, outside of the world that is being created, references a sense of plurality in Himself. Genesis 1:26 relates the words, "Let Us make man in Our image," and Genesis 3:22 records, "Behold, the man has become like one of Us." Use of *our* and *us* clearly indicates that God, speaking of Himself, speaks in what we regard as plural. This identity description is further referenced in Genesis 11:7 (Let us go down) and in Isaiah 6:8 (who will go for Us).

God very clearly communicates in His Word that He is above all, beyond all, and far surpassing all that man can see, feel, and understand. It is therefore not surprising that His very form of being does not fit nicely into a simple definition. In Deuteronomy 6:4, Moses instructs Israel to remember the Lord is One—God emphatically sets Himself apart from the gods of man by continually reminding them that He is One—the One true God. Even so, God calls Himself by many names and He describes His own nature in terms of three that is one—Father, Son, and Spirit. In Isaiah 48, the prophet is prophesying about the promise of deliverance. Through the Spirit, Isaiah conveys the word of the Lord. In verse 16, Isaiah refers to the *Lord GOD, Me* (the Messiah), and *His Spirit*, showing us in a single verse the three parts of the *one* God. Isaiah records, "Come near to Me, listen to this: From the first I have not spoken in secret, from the time it took place, I was there. And now the Lord GOD has sent Me, and His Spirit." "From the first I have not spoken in secret" reminds us that God has never hidden the unique nature of His being. From the beginning He has conveyed the concept that Almighty God is *one*, and that He at the exists as Father, Son, and Holy Spirit.

Wrapped up in the term *Trinity*, which is a man-made word not a God-given one, is all the strands of information that Jehovah has communicated to His people since He first walked with Adam in the garden. The fact that we do not fully understand it and cannot effectively visualize it does not make it any less real. God exists.

God is our heavenly Father. God is our Savior. God's Spirit resides inside us. Jesus is God. Jesus lives inside us through the Holy Spirit.

God is *one*—and yet God approaches us as *three*. Can the three be separated and still be God? Can we experience God in parts? At some point in eternity, when we stand before God, will we be able to identify three parts of God, or will we, even then, see only Jesus—the incarnate God that came to earth in flesh to redeem His people? Jesus said that if we see Him, we have seen the Father (John 14:9).

I don't think that I will ever understand the concept of the Trinity fully; nor do I think that such understanding is necessary. When I lift my prayers to the heavens, God—holy, compassionate Father, loving Son, and comforting Spirit—hears, and whispers to my heart, "*I am here. I am here for you—now and always.*"

## What is Man?
Psalm 8:4-6

Chapter 8 of the book of Psalms is not one that is generally labeled as a Messianic psalm. In fact it does not speak of Christ at all. Even so, I find myself thinking of Jesus as I read it. Perhaps it is the *son of man* phrase that leaps out so quickly. Since Jesus so often referred to Himself as the Son of man, I find myself taking a moment to analyze verses 4 through 6.

In this passage, the psalmist is contemplating the reality of the position that Man was given in creation. As I ponder that very fact, I ask myself: Where is Jesus here? And then I remember Genesis 1:26, "Let us make man in Our image." That explains it—explains where Jesus is in the verse and perhaps, too, why that title, Son of man, was the favorite name He used for Himself.

The psalmist wrote, "You take thought of him, You care for him, and You made him a little lower than God." You is the Creator—God—all of God. In His act as Creator Jesus already loved these frail creatures. He made them ruler over the rest of creation, lower than only God Himself. He gave them value surpassing all other creatures. Perhaps it was His great love for these weak, sin-prone creatures that led Him to identify with them, calling Himself Son of man. Undoubtedly, it was that same great love that led Him to the cross.

## Wounded in the House of a Friend
Zechariah 13:6

Zechariah, in 13:6, asks, "What are these wounds between your arms?" to which the response comes, "Those with which I was wounded in the house of my friends." As I read these words, I wonder: *Of just what wounds is the respondent speaking?* One of the first images that fill my mind would be the scars on Jesus' wrists where the nails held Him to the cross. "Wounded in the house of my friends" could easily be interpreted as the *house of friendship*, thus referring to the betrayal of Judas.

But, then, I seem to be drawn into the deep sadness in the eyes of the humble carpenter from Nazareth. I see in that depth the countless words that have escaped my lips, the almost unending thoughts that have rested too long in my mind, and the vastness of the betrayal that has been a part of my life. I realize that Zechariah could as easily be speaking of me. I realize that as horrible as I see the betrayal of Judas to be, my own is far worse.

Then, as sadness and remorse begins to rise up in me, I realize that amidst the sadness in those eyes, I also see His great love and forgiveness. I draw back from the depths of the sadness in His eyes, far enough to look upon the face of my Master. Then I see that the sadness in His eyes is overshadowed by the smile that reminds me that I am His. I am forgiven, and I will always be welcomed into His presence.

## Song from the King
Song of Solomon 2:4; 2:12, 16; 4:7, 9-10,12; 5:1, 16; 6:1-3; 8:6a

As I began to delve into the Song of Solomon, an image emerged in my mind of the soft, delicate flowers swaying back and forth in the wind, bending first to the right and then to the left. It seems that noted scholars from before the birth of Christ have set forth a wide range of possible interpretations, from various complicated allegorical representations to merely an exquisite song of love.

Song of Solomon was written first as a declaration of love. It is a brilliant example of a literary form of the time and serves as a tribute to Biblical teaching about the marriage commitment. Whether we attempt to force the full song into an allegorical frame or not, Solomon's tribute to his Beloved does at least provide glimpses of the love that God has for His people and His Church. Thus it is not surprising that certain verses or passages do indeed whisper the name of Jesus as I come upon them. Those are the words that are shared in this section of *The Scarlet Thread*.

My Beloved
Song of Solomon 2:4, 16; 6:3

At my first stop, fragments of an old song fill my mind. (*His Banner Over Me*, Carey Landry, early 1970's) One verse began, "There's one way to peace, through the power of His blood; His banner over me is love." The line repeated twice and then finished with "His banner over me is love." Much of the song was drawn from the Song of Solomon, for one verse noted, "He bids me eat at his banqueting table." (Song of Solomon 2:4). Another verse declares, "I'm my Beloved's and He is mine." (Song of Solomon 2:16 and 6:3).

Descriptions of the Lord
Song of Solomon 4:7; 5:16; 8:6

Other verses that cause me to pause described the one the Church waits for, as a bride waits for her groom. Song of Solomon 4:7 says that there is *no blemish* in the beloved. Though the speaker is the one considered in allegorical interpretation to be the Christ figure, the reference none-the-less reminds me that there was no blemish in the Lamb of God.

Song of Solomon 5:16 notes, *This is my beloved* and *this is my friend*. Song of Solomon 8:6a reminds us that *Love (His love) is as strong as death* and *we are sealed by His love*.

# The Scarlet Thread

<u>My sister, my bride</u>
Song of Solomon 4:9, 4:10, 4:12, 5:1

Four times in the Song of Solomon I find the phrase *My sister, my bride* and at each I pause to consider just what it is about those words that wraps around me and fills my soul with joy. I find myself wondering if this is just a case of Solomon expressing a love for his bride that is deeper and more gratifying because the bride is not merely a bride but a friend—a *sister* not in the physical relationship of family but in the soul-bonding relationship that expresses the reality of a relationship that is *closer than a brother (or sister)*.

For just a moment I think back to Abraham, who twice, out of fear, told Pharaoh and Abimelech that Sarah was his sister. When confronted with his words, Abraham admitted his lie, but added in Genesis 20:12, "Besides, she actually is my sister, the daughter of my father, but not the daughter of my mother." As soon as the thought comes to mind, though, I realize that such a custom, while acceptable in ancient times, probably had no bearing on the Song of Solomon's reference to *sister* and *bride*, except that perhaps the closeness that apparently existed in the half-sister/half-brother relationship of Sarai and Abram that may have led to their decision to spend their lives together may serve as an example of that depth of care and companionship that led Solomon to call his bride a sister.

So then, what is it about the concept of *my sister, my bride* that pulls me into Solomon's narrative and whispers the name of Jesus so strongly into my ears? Some scholars have told us that Song of Solomon is to a very large degree an illustration or picture of the relationship between Christ and His Church. As I think on that I realize that the *sister/bride* idea takes on greater significance—for me, in my journey through the Old Testament, and for the Church in general, as we see in the beautiful words of Solomon the depth of Christ's love for us.

All four gospels relate parables describing the relationship between the bride and the bridegroom that are understood to be laying the foundations of the concept of the Church being the bride of Christ. Then in Revelation we read, "Let us rejoice and be glad and give the glory to Him, for the marriage of the Lamb has come and His bride has made herself ready." (19:7) and "Then one of the seven angels who had the seven bowls full of the seven last plaques came and spoke with me, saying, 'Come here, I will show you the bride, the wife of the Lamb'" (21:9).

The concept of the Church as the bride of Christ is one that we find not only comfortable, but comforting. It adds an extra measure of hope and assurance when we, the Church, face the trials of this world. To know that Christ looks upon me first as a *sister*—a child of God, a part of the whole family which includes Jesus, the Son of God—reminds me that there is a personal relationship there that is deeper than just strangers passing by. To know that He looks upon me as a part of *His bride* reminds me that He is waiting anxiously, as anxiously as I am, for the moment when the Church will be ready to be *the wife of the Lamb*.

With such thoughts swirling about in my head, I am no longer unsure of why these verses in Song of Solomon call me to sit at the feet of Jesus for a little while longer. As I read, "You have made my heart beat faster, my sister, my bride" (4:9), I marvel at the truth of His love for all mankind and for me in particular. "How beautiful is your love, my sister, my bride!" (4:10) lets me know that He understands how deeply I love Him, even when my actions fail to demonstrate what my heart feels. In 4:12, Solomon records, "A garden locked is my sister, my bride, a rock garden locked, a spring sealed up," and my mind returns to the perfect Garden of Eden and I rejoice in the guarantee that my love and my relationship with Christ is sealed, unbreakable, and forever.

Then, I consider Song of Solomon 5:1: "I have come into my garden, my sister, my bride; I have gathered my myrrh along with my balsa. I have eaten my honeycomb and my honey; I have drunk my wine and my milk. Eat, friends; Drink and imbibe deeply, O lovers." *I have come, I have eaten, I have drunk*—in all these words I hear my Savior and I picture the marriage supper of the Lamb, where one day the promise will be behind us and it truly will be *I have come*. In that thought, I join with John on

# The Scarlet Thread

Patmos to whisper, "*The Spirit and the bride say, 'Come'*" (Revelation 22:17a).

## The wedding to come
Song of Solomon 2:12; 6:1-2

Song of Solomon 2:12 speaks to me of timing, or perhaps more specifically of a time of waiting. "The flowers have already appeared in the land; the time has arrived for pruning the vines and the voice of the turtle dove have been heard in our land." As I look at this verse, I see a wedding: I see the flowers set in place, I hear the sounds of music and laughter, I watch as the bride stands ready to walk down the aisle. But then I realize the bride is not ready—not really—for there is a shimmering instability in her form. Magnificent as she is, the Bride in not yet complete.

As I ponder the matter, I think, *the flowers have appeared and the dove's voice has sung its tunes* suggests that redemption has already been placed within the grasp of all mankind. *But the pruning of vines has yet to be completed* declares that Heaven must wait for the work of the Church to be completed. Only then can the full, complete Church (the Bride of Christ) stand before the bridegroom. For the moment, there is still work to be done.

When I stop at Song of Solomon 6:1-2, I see that same vision again, but there is a greater urgency in the scene this time. I hear the words attributed to the Friends, "Where has your beloved gone, O most beautiful among women? Where has your beloved turned, that we may seek him with you?" Whether they realize it or not, this is one of the most important questions to touch the lips of the world. *Where has our Beloved gone?* Solomon's bride answers that he has gone to pasture his flock in the gardens and to gather lilies. The Church answers, "He has gone to prepare a place for us—for the Church—for *all* who can be convinced of their need for the redemption He graciously offers.

Standing as the Church, ready to walk down that aisle, I find that the end of the aisle is growing brighter and my heart is drawn forward. My feet are eager to begin the march. I hear the refrain beating within me, "Come now, Lord Jesus."

Even so, my eyes are drawn back to the doorway, where the shadows of unrepentant souls still linger and a different longing rises up within me. I find that my arms reach out to gather in as many as will come, even as my ears listen for the first notes that will call me down the aisle to stand before the bridegroom.

Then my perspective on the scene seems to change. I look upon it as one looking down on an unfolding drama. I desperately long for the scene to move on, for the heavenly wedding march to call the Church down the aisle. But, my eyes continue to glance back to the fading doorway.

As I feel the hesitant touch of a hand grasping for mine, I pray for the strength to set aside my own joy, my own desires. I pray for the strength to pray that heaven will wait just a little longer.

# Final Words about the Journey

Throughout my journey a sense of wonder seemed to fill me. Even after the writing is complete, I find that am repeatedly called back to visit many of the stops again. Each time, from the words that rest upon the pages, memories of my experience with my Lord leap into my heart and touch my very soul.

I pray that this is the same for you. I pray that at some of my stops in this precious journey you, too, found a sense of wonder that touched your soul as you spent moments there with Jesus. I pray that you will return often to those stops, to remember how He first touched your heart and to rest in His presence.

But, my greater prayer is that in the simple words that are recorded in *The Scarlet Thread*, you have caught the inspiration and yearning to embark upon your own journey to share more time with Jesus, digging into the treasure of His ancient word.

# Bible Study Ideas

## Individual Bible Study Recommendations:

(A) <u>Journey through the Old Testament</u>.
Methodically read through the entire Old Testament. Don't be concerned about how long the Journey takes. Whenever you find a verse or passage that makes you pause to think of Jesus, stop. Just sit in His presence. Ask yourself why you see Jesus in this verse or passage. Give the Spirit time to bring to mind knowledge you may already have or new insights into the verse or passage.

Keep a journal to record any special thoughts about the encounter. If the reading has sparked a question or suggested another subject to study, make a note of it and plan to return to that topic at another time.

Remember: there is no *right* or *wrong* way to plan and execute your Journey. Its purpose is merely to provide an opportunity to meet with Jesus and meditate on His Word.

(B) <u>Journey through a particular Old Testament book</u>.
Select book of the Old Testament and follow the instructions in recommendation (A) above.

(C) <u>Use *The Scarlet Thread* as a Guide</u>.
Select specific clusters of verses shared in *The Scarlet Thread* to use as your own Journey stops and proceed as described in (A) and (B) above.

# The Scarlet Thread
## Group Bible Study Recommendations:

**(A)** <u>A Look at Jesus in the Old Testament</u>
(A general small group Bible Study)

*A Look at Jesus in the Old Testament* is a 9-wk Bible Study based on *The Scarlet Thread*. The lessons guide the Bible Study participant through each of the topics of the text, focusing on more universally known passages.

This Bible study relies on a moderate amount of preliminary personal study before the discussions.

It should be noted that, while the text of *The Scarlet Thread* may enhance the readers study, the Bible Study can be conducted even without referring to it. The primary goal of the study is to study the Scripture passages and allow God's Spirt to speak through them.

**(B)** <u>Encountering Jesus in the Old Testament</u>
(A more intensive small group Bible Study)

Like *A Look at Jesus in the Old Testament,* *Encountering Jesus in the Old Testament* is a Bible Study based on *The Scarlet Thread*. This study is intended to be much more intensive than one mentioned above and may like become much longer, as each lesson could possible require two or more sessions to complete.

The meetings following this guide are basically follow-up group discussions, after individual study has been done. Participants select specific examples of each topic and then describe their findings with the group.

# A Look at Jesus in the Old Testament
## (A general small group Bible Study)

The nine lessons in this study guide follow the order of the chapters of *The Scarlet Thread*. Each lesson highlights a sampling of the verses that were mentioned in the related chapter. The group leader may choose to add more of the verses whenever time permits.

The questions for each section are provided to prompt discussions beyond the simple facts that are given in the Scriptures. Ultimately the goal is to step beyond just the facts and recognize how the particular event or circumstance produces a picture of Christ.

While the text of *The Scarlet Thread* may enhance the study by providing extra information or additional points to consider, the Bible Study can be conducted without referring to it. The primary goal of the study is to study the Scripture passages and allow God's Spirt to speak through them.

For Bible Study groups that seek only to use the general breakdown of Old Testament verses that provide images of Christ, rather than the text of *The Scarlet Thread* itself, you are granted permission to make copies of the pages that contain this Bible Study Guide, as needed for your small group study.

# Lesson 1:
## *Pre-incarnate Christ*
(Chapter I, pages 5-18)

By definition, the doctrine of the *pre-incarnate Christ* asserts that Jesus existed before His incarnation and further suggests that in that time before He came to the earth as a baby, He interacted with the world He created. Usually, but not always, passages describing the pre-incarnate Christ refer to *the angel of the LORD,* not to be confused with *an angel of the LORD.*

## *Stops along the Journey—*

What does the term, *pre-incarnate Christ* mean? Do you agree that Jesus sometimes appeared in physical form to people in the Old Testament? Why or why not?

Read the passages listed below and discuss the questions about the encounters that each of the people had with *the angel of the LORD:*

Hagar (Genesis 16:7-14)
Read Genesis 16. Who was Hagar? Why she had run away?

Read Hagar's encounter with *the angel of the Lord* in Genesis 16:7-14. How might she have felt when she realized that the God of Abraham was taking an interest in her? Why might God have chosen to come to her?

What promise did the angel give to Hagar? How is this promise seen as evidence that *the angel of the LORD* is the *pre-incarnate Christ*?

Moses (Exodus 3:2-6)
Read the incident described in Exodus 3:2-6. Why might God have chosen to appear to Moses through fire?

What evidence is given that *the angel of the LORD*, speaking to Moses, was actually the *pre-incarnate Christ*?

Try to put yourself in Moses' shoes. How would it feel to see such an amazing phenomenon? How would it feel to stand in the presence of God?

Gideon (Judges 6:11-27)
Read Judges 6:11-27. Briefly describe the conversation between Gideon and *the angel of the LORD*.

What did the angel say or do to make Gideon realize that he was in the presence of God?

The Scarlet Thread

Do you think we test God in the same manner today? Do you think that He sometimes allows us to do that?

<u>Question to consider</u>

Do you think it is likely that God would ever come to earth again in physical form before Christ's return at the end of the age? Why or why not?

If time permits, discuss some of the other encounters with *the angel of the LORD* that are mentioned in the text of *The Scarlet Thread*.

# Lesson 2:
## *Pictures of Christ in the Lives*
## *of Bible People*
### (Chapter II, pages 19-39)

Throughout the Old Testament, people, objects, or circumstances provide pictures of the one who would one day come to save the world. These passages provided a wide range of descriptions that would help future generations recognize the Messiah and understand that one single theme is woven throughout the entire Bible—the theme of redemption. These pre-Christ descriptions of Jesus also provide greater insight into the how's and why's of some of Jesus' actions. In this lesson, the reader studies descriptions of Jesus found in the lives of Bible people.

## *Stops along the Journey—*

Read the following passages and briefly describe how the person in the passage provides a picture of Jesus. If you choose, study more about the person and include other characteristics or circumstances in the person's life that also reminds you of Jesus.

Abel (Genesis 4:2-4, 8)

Enoch (Genesis 5:21-24)

Noah (Genesis 6:8-9, 22)

# The Scarlet Thread

Melchizedek (Genesis 14:17-24)

Isaac (Genesis 22:6-13)

Jonah (Jonah 1:17, 2:10, 3:1)

Moses
There are many, many characteristics or circumstances in the lives of Moses that remind us of Jesus. List a few of them. (Information about Moses is predominantly found in Exodus.)

David
There are many, many characteristics or circumstance in the lives of David that remind us of Jesus. List a few of them. (Information about David is predominantly found in I and II Samuel.)

Question to consider
If someone were to look at your life, would they find something that would show them a picture of Jesus? Describe one or two examples.

If time permits, discuss any additional Old Testament figures that in some way remind you of Jesus and describe what it is about the person that makes you think of Him.

The Scarlet Thread

# Lesson 3:
## *Pictures of Christ in Specific Objects*
(Chapter III, pages 41-68)

Throughout the Old Testament, people, objects, or circumstances provide pictures of the one who would one day come to save the world. These passages provided a wide range of descriptions that would help future generations recognize the Messiah and understand that one single theme is woven throughout the entire Bible—the theme of redemption. These pre-Christ descriptions of Jesus also provide greater insight into the how's and why's of some of Jesus' actions. In this lesson, the reader studies descriptions of Jesus found in specific objects of events.

## *Stops along the Journey—*

Read the following passages and briefly describe how the object in the passage provides an image of Jesus.

Ark (Noah's) (Genesis 6:18, 7:1, 16)

Bread from Heaven (Exodus 16:4-32; Nehemiah 9:15; Psalms 105:40)

Bronze serpent (Numbers 21:8-9)

218

Cornerstone/Stone (Psalm 118:22, Job 38-4-6, Isaiah 28:16)

Light (Psalms 27:1; 43:3, 118:27; Isaiah 9:2, 49:6, 60:1, 19-20; Daniel 2:20-22)

Rock (Exodus 17: 1-7; Numbers 20:8-12; Psalms 18:2; 31:3, 62:1-2; 95:1, 71:3)

Sacrificial System (Exodus 29:38-42; Numbers 28:1-8)

Scapegoat (Leviticus 16:10)

Living water (Jeremiah 2:13; Jeremiah 17:13; Zechariah 14:8)

# The Scarlet Thread

As we encounter the world around us, there are abundant images that, if we pause to notice, would show us a picture of Jesus. (Snow-covered landscapes illustrate for us how our sins are completely covered by Jesus. Ancient mountains show us the permanence of our Lord.) Can you name a few things you see around you all the time that remind you of the presence of God?

If time permits, discuss some of the other Old Testament objects that in some way remind you of Jesus and describe what it is about the object that describes Him.

# Lesson 4:
## *Pictures of Christ in His Titles*
(Chapter IV, pages 69-88)

Throughout the Old Testament, people, objects, or circumstances provide pictures of the one who would one day come to save the world. These passages provided a wide range of descriptions that would help future generations recognize the Messiah and understand that one single theme is woven throughout the entire Bible—the theme of redemption. These pre-Christ descriptions of Jesus also provide greater insight into the how's and why's of some of Jesus' actions. In this lesson, the reader studies descriptions of Jesus found in specific titles that were found in the Old Testament.

## *Stops along the Journey—*

Read the following passages and briefly describe how the title described in the passage refers to Jesus.

Advocate/Mediator (Job 16:19-20; Job 33:23-24)

First and Last (Isaiah 48:12; Isaiah 44:6)

Horn of My Salvation (II Samuel 22:2-3; Psalm 18:2)

# The Scarlet Thread

King forever (Psalm 10:6; 29:10; 47:2, 7)

Sacrificial Lamb (Isaiah 53:7; Jeremiah 1:19)

Lion of Judah (Hosea 5:14)

Redeemer/Deliverer (Job 19:25; Psalms 19:14; Proverbs 23:11; Isaiah 48:17; Isaiah 49:7; Isaiah 54:5, 8; Isaiah 63:16; Jeremiah 50:34)

Shepherd (Genesis 48: 15; Psalms 23:1; Isaiah 40:11; Ezekiel 34:23, 37:24; Micah 5:4)

<u>Question to consider</u>
Of all the names and titles given to Jesus, which ones have special significance for you? Why?

If time permits discuss some of the other titles that can be applied to Jesus and describe how they apply to Him.

# Lesson 5:
## *Prophecies of Jesus' Birth and Ministry*
(Chapter V, pages 89-110)

Probably the most well-known places that we encounter Jesus in the Old Testament are through the voices of the prophets. Our childhood lessons about the birth, life, death, and resurrection of Jesus are filled with references to passages where the prophets foretold that the Messiah would come.

## *Stops along the Journey—*

The topics for discussion below all pertain to the time from Jesus' birth until just before the crucifixion. They are approached in a prophecy/fulfillment manner, so both Old Testament and New Testament references are given. Read the following passages and briefly describe the detail about Jesus that is prophesied.

Micah 5:2-4 (Matthew 2:1-6, Luke 2: 4-15)

Isaiah 7:14, 9:6-7 (Luke 1:26, 27, 30-35)

Hosea 11:1 (Matthew 2:13-15)

Isaiah 40:3-5; Malachi 3:1 (Matthew 3:3; Matthew 11:10; Mark 1:2-3; Luke 1:76, 3:2-6, 7:27; John 1:23)

# A Look at Jesus in the Old Testament–Bible Study Guide

Zechariah 9:9 (Luke 19:35-37; Matthew 21:8-11)

Isaiah 11:1, 11:10; Jeremiah 23:5, 33:15; Amos 9:11 (Matthew 1:6: Luke 3:31)

Psalm 72:10-11; Isaiah 60:3-6 (Matthew 2:1-2, 7-11)

Question to consider
If you were prophesying in the Old Testament about the birth and life of Jesus, what additional detail might you have wanted to include?

If time permits, discuss details about other prophecies about the birth and life of Jesus that were mentioned in the Old Testament.

# Lesson 6:
## *Prophecies of Jesus' Death and Resurrection*
### (Chapter VI, pages 111-130)

Probably the most well-known places that we encounter Jesus in the Old Testament are through the voices of the prophets. Our childhood lessons about the birth, life, death, and resurrection of Jesus are filled with references to passages where the prophets foretold that the Messiah would come.

## *Stops along the Journey—*

The topics for discussion below all pertain to the time from just before Jesus' crucifixion through the ascension. They are approached in a prophecy/fulfillment manner, so both Old Testament and New Testament references are given. Read the following passages and briefly describe the detail about Jesus that is prophesied.

Zechariah 11:12-13; Psalm 41:9 (Matthew 26:14-16; Luke 22:47-48)

Isaiah 53:7; Jeremiah 11:19 (Acts 8:32)

Psalm 102:10 (John 3:14, 12:32)

# A Look at Jesus in the Old Testament–Bible Study Guide

Zechariah 12:10; Psalm 22:16; Isaiah 53:5 (John 19:34, 37, 20:27)

Psalm 22:18 (Matthew 27:35; Mark 15:24; Luke 23:34; John 19:24)

Psalm 34:20; Exodus 12:46; Numbers 9:12 (John 19:32-36)

Psalm 69:21 (Matthew 27:34, 48; Mark 15:23, 36; John 19:29)

Hosea 6:2 (Matthew 28: 5-7; Luke 24:36-48; John 20:19, 24-29)

Psalm 110:1 (Hebrews 1:3; Acts 2:34-35)

# The Scarlet Thread

Question to consider

If you were prophesying in the Old Testament about the death and resurrection, what additional detail might you have wanted to include?

If time permits discuss additional prophecies about the death and resurrection of Jesus mentioned in the Old Testament.

# Lesson 7:
## *Additional Prophetic Passages*
(Chapter VII, pages 131-160)

In a very real sense, the chapter of *The Scarlet Thread* on which this lesson is based represents a hodge-podge of stops, with little connecting them but the fact they were included in the books of prophecy. Most, but not all of them, refer to the second coming of Christ or to His millennial reign.

## *Stops along the Journey—*

Read the following passages and briefly describe what is learned from this prophecy about Jesus or His coming kingdom.

Woman's Offspring (Genesis 3:15)

David's Crown or Kingdom: Scepter (Genesis 49:10, 24; Numbers 24:17, 19)

David's Crown or Kingdom: Parable of the Branch (Ezekiel 17:22-23)

Day of the Lord/Reckoning: Settling Accounts (Obadiah 1:15)

# The Scarlet Thread

Days Are Coming-Warning (Jeremiah 9:25)

Days Are Coming-Promise: New Covenant (Jeremiah 31:31)

Pour out His Spirit (Isaiah 44:3; Ezekiel 37:14; Joel 2:28)

Messianic Kingdom: Literal Reign (Micah 4:7)

Messianic Kingdom: Picture of Messiah's Land (Isaiah 60:18-20)

The Millennial Reign: Warrior King (Micah 2:12-13)

The Millennial Reign: Peace and Prosperity (Amos 9:13)

The Millennial Reign: Coming True Temple (Haggai 2:9)

Zion, the Place of the Return (Zechariah 14:1-9)

Question to consider
With all the magnificence of the Millennial Kingdom and all the peace and prosperity at the time, it is very hard to understand how anyone would not want to have Christ rule. But Revelation 20-8-9 tells us that a rebellion will occur at the end of the Millennial Reign. Contemplate that for a moment. How do you think such a condition could possibly occur?

If time permits, discuss additional prophecies about the Millennial Kingdom and Reign of Jesus mentioned in the Old Testament.

# Lesson 8:
## *Concepts Relating to Jesus or His Mission*
(Chapter VIII, pages 161-180)

The teachings of Christ and His apostles rest on certain
fundamental premises that were introduced in the Old Testament,
truths and certainties that were woven into creation and the
history of man as surely as threads are woven into an intricate
tapestry.

## *Stops along the Journey—*

Read the following passages and briefly record what you
understand about the concept described in the verses.

Concept of Mercy (Ezra 9:13; Ezekiel 39:25; Jeremiah 33:26;
Isaiah 63:9)




Deliverance Comes at God's Time (Esther 4:13-14)




God Alone Provides Sin's Solution (Genesis 7:16; 22:8;
Deuteronomy 12:5, 14; Psalms 3:8, 37:39, 62:1; Isaiah 43:1;
Jeremiah 3:23b; Jonah 2:9)




No One is Good Enough (Psalms 14:3; Micah 7:2a; II Chronicles
6:36; Ecclesiastes 7:20)

<u>Only a Perfect Sacrifice Will Do</u> (Exodus 12: 5a, 46)




<u>Personal Responsibility for Sin</u> (II Kings 14:6; Deuteronomy 24:15)




<u>Sin Is Paid for by Blood</u> (Genesis 3:21; Exodus 12:7; Leviticus 17:11)




<u>Question to consider</u>
Can you think of any significant concept regarding Jesus' sacrifice and our redemption that does not have its roots in the Old Testament? If so, discuss them with the group.




If time permits, discuss other Old Testament concepts mentioned in *The Scarlet Thread*.

# Lesson 9:
## *Potpourri of Additional Topics*
(Chapter IX, pages 181-208)

Chapter IX of *The Scarlet Thread* includes topics or categories of verses that did not fit well anywhere else in the breakdown of Old Testament verses.

## *Stops along the Journey—*

<u>New Testament Scriptures Brought to Mind</u>
Read the verses listed below. Describe how the verse(s) compare to an equivalent verse(s) in the New Testament.

Joshua 1:5 (Matthew 28:20b; John 14:27b)

II Kings 4:43-44 (John 6:1-12)

II Kings 6:16 (I John 4:4b)

Psalms 37:11 (Matthew 5:5)

Isaiah 45:22-23 (John 14:6; Romans 14:11)

Habakkuk 2:4 (Romans 1:17; Galatians 3:11; Hebrews 10:38)

Foreshadowing Descriptions
Read the verses listed below. Though they are not necessarily
prophetic, they do seem to foreshadow something that will come
about later. Record and discuss the event or circumstance that is
foreshadowed and how it foreshadows a situation or condition in
the New Testament and beyond.

Leviticus 12:8 (Luke 2:22-24)

Numbers 11:29 (John 4:23)

Deuteronomy 21:23 (Galatians 3:13-14)

Promises:
Read the following verses. Describe the promise that is given.

Genesis 35:11; II Samuel 23:5; Joel 2:32; Obadiah 1:17

Exodus 29:45; Zechariah 2:10

Exodus 23:20; Malachi 3:1

# The Scarlet Thread

Trinity:
Read the following verses and discuss the concept of "Trinity" and how God is *one*, but is manifested to us in three different ways—Father, Son, and Holy Spirit. Then briefly describe how you understand the concept of the "Trinity."

Genesis 1:26, Genesis 11:7, Genesis 3:22, Isaiah 6:8, Deuteronomy 6:4; Isaiah 48:16

My Beloved—Christ and the Church:
Read the following verses and briefly describe what you think it will be like in that moment when the Church is called home.

Song of Solomon 2:12, 6:1-2, 8:6a

Question to consider: Has this study brought to mind any specific topic or question about His Word that you want to study more? If so, how and when do you plan to do your study?

If time permits, discuss other topics from Chapter IX of *The Scarlet Thread*.

# Encountering Jesus in the Old Testament

(An intensive small group Bible Study)

This guide may be used for an independent study or it can be used by a small group whose members all seek to delve more deeply into the concept of seeing images of Jesus in the Old Testament. The guide provides only an outline of topics to discuss, so participants will need to keep a notebook or journal for recording thoughts as they study the material.

While this study guide follows the order of the chapters of *The Scarlet Thread*, not every example of Christ's presence that is recorded in *The Scarlet Thread* is included it. Also, it should be noted that this study guide can be used with or without the text of *The Scarlet Thread*. Bible Study groups that seek only to use this guide to prompt their own study, rather than using the text of *The Scarlet Thread* itself, are granted permission to make copies of the pages that contain the study guide, as needed for their study.

To prepare for the discussions, the leader should assign one or more verse clusters or passages listed in the lesson to each participant or to multiple participants if the group is larger than the number of topics provided. Participants, then study the Scripture references on their own, using the Bible and any other resources that may be available to them. Then, at the group meetings, participants report what the Holy Spirit helped them to learn from the passages.

The text of *The Scarlet Thread* can be used as one of the resources, but participants should never lose sight of the fact that the purpose of this study is to guide the group members to follow their own personal journeys to encounter Jesus in the Old Testament.

The Scarlet Thread
# Lesson 1:
## *Pre-incarnate Christ*
(Chapter II, pages 5-18)

By definition, *pre-incarnate* asserts that Jesus existed before His conception and further suggests that in that time before He came to the earth as a baby, He interacted with the world He created. Usually, but not always, passages describing the pre-incarnate Christ refer to *the angel of the LORD*, not to be confused with *an angel of the LORD*.

## *Stops along the Journey—*

The angel of the Lord appeared to:

Hagar (Genesis 16:7-14, 21:17)
Abraham and Isaac (Genesis 22:11-18)
Moses (Exodus 3:2-6)
Balaam (Numbers 22:22-35)
Gideon (Judges 6:11-27)
Samson's parents (Judges 13:2-23)

# Lesson 2:
## *Pictures of Christ in the Lives of Bible People*
(Chapter II, pages 19-39)

Throughout the Old Testament, people, objects, or circumstances provide pictures of the one who would one day come to save the world. These passages provided a wide range of descriptions that would help future generations recognize the Messiah and understand that one single theme is woven throughout the entire Bible—the theme of redemption. These pre-Christ descriptions of Jesus also provide greater insight into the how's and why's of some of Jesus' actions. In this lesson, the reader studies descriptions of Jesus found in the lives of Bible characters.

## *Stops along the Journey—*

Many of the people listed below are mentioned frequently in the Scriptures, but only a few specific references are listed here. (Feel free to add additional names to the list, as well.)

1.  Abel (Genesis 4:2-8)
2.  Enoch (Genesis 5:21-24)
3.  Noah (Genesis 6-9)
4.  Job (Job 1:1-8)
5.  Melchizedek (Genesis 14:7-24)
6.  Isaac (Genesis 22:6-13)
7.  Moses (Exodus 3:2-8; 20:18-21)
8.  Boaz (Ruth 4:3-6)
9.  David (I Samuel 16:12-13; 17:32-49; II Samuel 9:1-13)
10  Jeremiah (Jeremiah 20:2; 26:7-8; 32:2; 37:15-16; 38:6)
11. Jonah (Jonah 1:4-9, 12-17; 2:10; 3:1)

# Lesson 3:
# *Pictures of Christ in Specific Objects*
### (Chapter III, pages 41-68)

In this lesson, the reader studies descriptions of Jesus found in specific objects of events.

## *Stops along the Journey—*

1.  Ark (Noah's) (Genesis 6:18, 7:1, 16)
2.  Ark of the Covenant (Exodus 25:10-22)
3.  Bread from Heaven (Exodus 16:4-32; Nehemiah 9:15; Psalm 105:40)
4.  Unleavened Bread (Exodus 12:8; Ezekiel 45:2)
5.  Bronze serpent (Numbers 21:8-9)

6. Cities of Refuge (Numbers 35: 1-15, 22-28; Joshua 20:1-9, I Chronicles 6:57, 67)
7. Chief Cornerstone (Psalm 118:22)
8. Foundation Stone (Job 38-4-6; Isaiah 28:16)
9. Light and Salvation (Psalms 27:1; 43:3, 118:27; Isaiah 9:2)
10. Ransom (Psalms 31:5, 69:18; Jeremiah 31:11; Hosea 13:14; Micah 6:4)
11. Rock that Was Struck (Exodus 17: 1-7; Numbers 20:8-12)
12. Rock and Salvation (II Samuel 2:2-3, 33, 47; Isaiah 17:10, 26:4; Psalm:2; 19:14))
13. Sacrificial System (Multiple chapters of Leviticus; Exodus 29:38-42; Numbers 28:1-8)
14. Scapegoat (Leviticus 16:10)
15. Vine (Jeremiah 2:21)
16. Fountain of Living Waters (Jeremiah 2:13, 17:13; Zechariah 13:1)
17. Deliverance through Water (Genesis 6-9; II Kings 5:10-14, Exodus 14:13-30)

# Lesson 4:
## *Pictures of Christ in His Titles*
### (Chapter IV, pages 69-88)

In this lesson, the reader studies descriptions of Jesus found in specific titles that were later applied to Christ.

## *Stops along the Journey—*

1. Advocate/Mediator (Job 16:19-20; 33:23-24)
2. Anointed One (Psalms 2:2)
3. First and Last (Isaiah 48:12, 44:6)
4. Hope of Israel/My Hope (Jeremiah 14:8, 17:13; Psalm 39:7, 71:5; Ezekiel 37:11-14)
5. Horn of my salvation/Horn (II Samuel 22:2-3; Psalms 18:2)
6. King Forever (Psalm 10:16; 29:10; 47:2, 7; Jeremiah 10:10; Zechariah 14:9)
7. The Passover Lamb (Exodus 12:5, 21)

8. Lily of the Valley/Rose of Sharon (Song of Solomon 2:1; Isaiah 35:1-2; Hosea 14:5)
9. Lion of Judah (Hosea 5:14)
10. Redeemer/Deliverer (Job 19:25; Psalms 19:14; Proverbs 23:11; Isaiah 48:17, 49:7, 54:5, 8, 63:16; Jeremiah 50:34)
11. Shepherd (Genesis 48: 15; Psalms 23:1; Isaiah 40:11; Ezekiel 34:23, 37:24; Micah 5:4)

# Lesson 5:
## *Prophecies of Jesus' Birth and Ministry*
(Chapter V, pages 89-110)

Probably the most well-known places that we encounter Jesus in the Old Testament are through the voices of the prophets. Our childhood lessons about the birth, life, death, and resurrection of Jesus are filled with references to passages where the prophets foretold that the Messiah would come.

The topics for discussion below all pertain to the time from Jesus' birth until just before the crucifixion. They are approached in a prophecy/fulfillment manner, so both Old Testament and New Testament references are given.

## *Stops along the Journey—*

1. Born in Bethlehem Micah 5:2-4 (Matthew 2:1-6, Luke 2:4-15)
2. Born of a Virgin Isaiah 7:14, 9:6-7 (Luke 1:26, 27, 30-35)
3. Called Out of Egypt Hosea 11:1 (Matthew 2:13-15)
4. Great Weeping in Ramah Jeremiah 31:15 (Matthew 2:16-18)
5. People in Darkness See the Light Isaiah 9:1-2, 10:17 (Matthew 4:12-17)
6. Messenger Sent to Prepare the Way Isaiah 40:3-5; Malachi 3:1 (Matthew 3:3, 11:10, Mark 1:2-3; Luke 1:76, 3:2-6, 7:27; John 1:23)
7. Enter Jerusalem on a Donkey Zechariah 9:9 (Luke 19:35-37, Matthew 21:8-11)

8. Lord's House Called a Den of Robbers Jeremiah 7:11 (Matthew 21:13; Mark 11:17; Luke 19:46)
9. Rejected by His Own Isaiah 53:3, Psalm 118:22 (John 1:11)
10. From the Line of David Isaiah 11:1, 10, Jeremiah 23:5, 33:15 (Matthew 1:6; Luke 3:31) (Isaiah 4:2, 53:2; Zechariah 3:8, Zechariah 6:12
11. Called a Nazarene Matthew 2:23 (Isaiah 11:1,10; Amos 9:11)
12. Visited by Wise Men from the East Isaiah 60:3; Psalm 72:10-11; Isaiah 60:4-6 (Matthew 2:1-2, 7-11)

# Lesson 6:
## *Prophecies of Jesus' Death and Resurrection*
### (Chapter VI, pages 111-130)

Probably the most well-known places that we encounter Jesus in the Old Testament are through the voices of the prophets. Our childhood lessons about the birth, life, death, and resurrection of Jesus are filled with references to passages where the prophets foretold that the Messiah would come.

The topics for discussion below all pertain to the time from just prior to the crucifixion through the resurrection of Jesus. They are approached in a prophecy/fulfillment manner, so both Old Testament and New Testament references are given.

## *Stops along the Journey—*

1. Betrayed by a Friend for 30 Pieces of Silver. Zechariah 11:12-13, Psalm 41:9 (Matthew 26:14-16, Luke 22:47-48)
2. Led like a Lamb to the Slaughter Isaiah 53:7; Jeremiah 11:19 (Acts 8:32)
3. Not Open His Mouth to Defend Himself Psalm 38:13-14; Isaiah 53:7 (Matthew 26:63, 27:12-14; Mark 14:61; Acts 8:32)
4. Convicted on the Word of False Witnesses Psalm 35:11 (Mark 14:57-62; Luke 23:8-10)
5. Struck by Authorities Zechariah 13:6-7 (Mark 14:27; Matthew 26:31)
6. Lifted Up  Psalm 102:10 (John 3:14, 12:32)

7. <u>Pierced</u> Zechariah 12:10; Psalm 22:16; Isaiah 53:5, 49:16 (John 19:34, 37, 20:27)

8. <u>Lots Cast for His Garments</u> Psalm 22:18 (Matthew 27:35; Mark 15:24; Luke 23:34; John 19:24)

9. <u>No Bones Broken</u> Psalm 34:20; Exodus 12:46; Numbers 9:12 (John 19:32-36)

10. <u>Offered Vinegar to Drink</u> Psalm 69:21 (Matthew 27:34, 48; Mark 15:23, 36; John 19:29)

11. <u>Scorned and Laughed at by the Crowd</u> Psalm 22:6-7, 109:25 (Matthew 27:39-40; Mark 15:29-32)

12. <u>Sun Will go Down at Noon</u> Amos 8:9 (Matthew 27:45)

13. <u>Grave with the Wicked, with the Rich in Death</u> Isaiah 53:9 (Matthew 27:57-60)

14. <u>Raised on the Third Day</u> Hosea 6:2 (Matthew 28: 5-7; Luke 24:36-48; John 20:19, 24-29)

15. <u>Ascent to Sit at the Right Hand of the Father</u> Psalm 110:1 (Hebrews 1:3; Acts 2:34-35)

# Lesson 7:
## *Additional Prophetic Passages*
### (Chapter VII, pages 131-160)

In a very real sense, the chapter of *The Scarlet Thread* on which this lesson is based represents a hodge-podge of stops, with little connecting them but the fact they were included in the books of prophecy. Most, but not all of them, refer to the second coming of Christ or to His millennial reign.

## *Stops along the Journey—*

1. <u>Woman's Offspring</u> (Genesis 3:15)

2. <u>David's Crown or Kingdom: Scepter</u> (Genesis 49: 10; 49:24; Numbers 24:17, 19)

3 . <u>David's Crown or Kingdom: Parable of the Branch</u> (Ezekiel 17:22-23)

4. <u>Day of the Lord/Reckoning</u> (Amos 5:18, 20; Obadiah 1:15; Zephaniah 1:7, 14-18; Malachi 4:5)

5. Days Are Coming-Warning (Jeremiah 9:25)
6. Days Are Coming-Promise (Jeremiah 33:14, 31:31, 38; Amos 8:11)
7. Pour out His Spirit (Isaiah 44:3; Ezekiel 37:14; Joel 2:28)
8. Messianic Kingdom (Micah 4:7; Zechariah 8:3; 14:4; Jeremiah 23:3; Isaiah 60:18-20, Daniel 2:44, 7:9)
9. The Millennial Reign (Micah 2:12-13, 4:1-7, 5:4-5; Joel 3:18; Amos 9:13; Habakkuk 2:14; Haggai 2:9)
10. Zion, the Place of the Return (Zechariah 14:1-9)

# Lesson 8:
## *Concepts Relating to Jesus or His Mission*
### (Chapter VIII, pages 161-180)

The teachings of Christ and His apostles rest on certain fundamental premises that were introduced in the Old Testament, truths and certainties that were woven into creation and the history of man as surely as threads are woven into an intricate tapestry.

## *Stops along the Journey—*

1. Atonement for Sin (Leviticus 1:4-5, Chapter 8, 16:10)
2. Concept of Mercy (Ezra 9:13; Ezekiel 39:25; Jeremiah 33:26; Isaiah 63:9)
3. Deliverance Comes at God's Time (Esther 4:13-14)
4. Firstborn Is Owed to God (Exodus 13:1-2; Deuteronomy 15:19, Numbers 3:13, 41, 8:16-18)
5. God Alone Provides Sin's Solution (Genesis 7:16; 22:8; Deuteronomy 12:5, 14; Psalms 3:8, 37:39, 62:1; Isaiah 43:1; Jeremiah 3:23b; Jonah 2:9)
6. Life after Bondage (Ezra 9:9)
7. No One is Good Enough (Psalms 14:3; Micah 7:2a; II Chronicles 6:36; Ecclesiastes 7:20)
8. Only a Perfect Sacrifice Will Do (Exodus 12: 5a, 46)
9. Personal Responsibility for Sin (II Kings 14:6, Deuteronomy 24:15)

10. <u>Possibility of Immortality</u> (Proverbs 12:28; Ecclesiastes 3:11)
11. <u>Promise of Pardon</u> (Isaiah 55:7, Jeremiah 33:8, 50:20)
12. <u>Sin Is Paid for by Blood</u> (Genesis 3:21; Exodus 12:7; Leviticus 17:11)

# Lesson 9:
## *Potpourri of Additional Topics*
### (Chapter IX, pages 181-208)

Chapter IX of *The Scarlet Thread* includes categories that did not fit well anywhere else or verses that stand as solidary guards that called me to meet Him for one more encounter.

## Stops along the Journey—

1. <u>New Testament Scriptures Brought to Mind</u>

Deuteronomy 20:5-9
Joshua 1:5
I Samuel 21:3
I Kings 13:10
II Kings 4:43-44
II Kings 6:16
Ezekiel 14:4

Nehemiah 7:64
Psalms 65:7, Nahum 1:4
Isaiah 45:22-23
Habakkuk 2:4
Obadiah 1:15
Nahum 1:3

2. <u>Foreshadowing Descriptions</u>

Leviticus 12:8
Numbers 11:29
Deuteronomy 21:23
Deuteronomy 30:14

Nehemiah 9:27
Psalms 32:1

3. <u>Promises</u>
a. Genesis 35:11; II Samuel 23:5; Joel 2:32; Obadiah 1:17
b. Exodus 29:45; Zechariah 2:10
c. Exodus 23:20; Malachi 3:1

4. Trinity (Genesis 1:26, 11:7, 3:22; Isaiah 6:8; Deuteronomy 6:4; Isaiah 48:16)

5. Wounded in the House of a Friend (Zechariah 13:6)

6. Love Song of the King (Song of Solomon 2:4; 2:12, 16; 4:7, 9-10,12; 5:1, 16; 6:1-3; 8:6a)

# Scarlet Thread Verses

| | | |
|---|---|---|
| Genesis 1:26 | Exodus 14: 21-22 | Numbers 35:22-28 |
| Genesis 11:5 | Exodus 16:4-32 | Numbers 8:16-18 |
| Genesis 11:7 | Exodus 17: 1-7 | Numbers 9:12 |
| Genesis 14:18 | Exodus 17:6 | Deuteronomy 12:5 |
| Genesis 16:7-14 | Exodus 18:13-16 | Deut. 12:14 |
| Genesis 22:11-18 | Exodus 19:20 | Deut. 15:19 |
| Genesis 22:6-13 | Exodus 20:19 | Deut. 20:5-9 |
| Genesis 22:7-8 | Exodus 23:20 | Deut. 21:23 |
| Genesis 22:8 | Exodus 23:23 | Deut. 24:16 |
| Genesis 29:8 | Exodus 25:10-22 | Deut. 30:14 |
| Genesis 3:15 | Exodus 25:30 | Deuteronomy 31:8 |
| Genesis 3:21 | Exodus 26:31 | Deuteronomy 6:4 |
| Genesis 3:22 | Exodus 29:38-42 | Deuteronomy 8:3 |
| Genesis 35:11 | Exodus 29:45 | Joshua 1:5 |
| Genesis 37:11 | Exodus 3:2-8 | Joshua 20:1-9 |
| Genesis 4:2-4 | Exodus 3:2-6 | Judges 11:34 |
| Genesis 4:8 | Exodus 32:34 | Judges 13:2-23 |
| Genesis 48:15 | Leviticus 1:4-5 | Judges 2:1-5 |
| Genesis 49:10 | Leviticus 12:8 | Judges 2:16 |
| Genesis 49:24 | Leviticus 16:10 | Judges 5:23 |
| Genesis 5:21-24 | Leviticus 17:11 | Judges 6:11-27 |
| Genesis 6:18 | Leviticus 21:21 | Ruth 2:12 |
| Genesis 6:8-9 | Numbers 11:29 | Ruth 4:3-6 |
| Genesis 6:22 | Numbers 20:8 | I Samuel 16: 12-13 |
| Genesis 7:1 | Numbers 20:10 | I Samuel 17:32-49 |
| Genesis 7:16 | Numbers 20:8-12 | I Samuel 2:35 |
| Exodus 12: 5a | Numbers 21:11 | I Samuel 21:3 |
| Exodus 12:21 | Numbers 22:22-35 | II Samuel 22:33 |
| Exodus 12:3 | Numbers 24:17 | II Samuel 22:47 |
| Exodus 12:46 | Numbers 24:19 | II Samuel 22:2-3 |
| Exodus 12:5 | Numbers 28:1-8 | II Samuel 22:3 |
| Exodus 12:7 | Numbers 3:13 | II Samuel 22:31 |
| Exodus 12:8 | Numbers 3:41 | II Samuel 23:4 |
| Exodus 13:1-2 | Numbers 35: 1-15 | II Samuel 23:5 |

| | | |
|---|---|---|
| II Samuel 24:15-17 | Esther 4:13-14 | Psalm 18:30 |
| II Samuel 7:1-16 | Job 1:1 | Psalm 19:14 |
| II Samuel 7:16 | Job 1:8 | Psalm 19:14 |
| II Samuel 9:1-13 | Job 15:14 | Psalm 2:12 |
| I Kings 13:10 | Job 16:19-20 | Psalm 2:2 |
| I Kings 19:1-8 | Job 19:25 | Psalm 2:6 |
| I Kings 7:48 | Job 23:3 | Psalm 2:7-12 |
| I Kings 8:25 | Job 24:13 | Psalm 22:1 |
| II Kings 1:1-16 | Job 33:23-24 | Psalm 22:16 |
| II Kings 13:5 | Job 33:23-30 | Psalm 22:18 |
| II Kings 14:6 | Job 38:4-6 | Psalm 22:6-7 |
| II Kings 19:22 | Job 39:9 | Psalm 23:1 |
| II Kings 19:30 | Psalm 10:16 | Psalm 24:7-10 |
| II Kings 4:43-44 | Psalm 102:10 | Psalm 25:20 |
| II Kings 6:16 | Psalm 105:40 | Psalm 27:1 |
| II Kings 8:19 | Psalm 105:41 | Psalm 28:1 |
| I Chronicles 17:12 | Psalm 108:8 | Psalm 28:9 |
| I Chronicles 17: 14 | Psalm 109:25 | Psalm 29:10 |
| I Chronicles 21:1 | Psalm 11:1 | Psalm 3:8 |
| I Chron. 21:15-17 | Psalm 110:1 | Psalm 31:1 |
| I Chronicles 22:10 | Psalm 118:22 | Psalm 31:19 |
| I Chronicles 28:7 | Psalm 118:27 | Psalm 31:3 |
| I Chronicles 6:57 | Psalm 118:8 | Psalm 31:5 |
| I Chronicles 6:67 | Psalm 118:9 | Psalm 32:1 |
| II Chronicles 21:7 | Psalm 132:17-18 | Psalm 34:20 |
| II Chronicles 30:15 | Psalm 14:3 | Psalm 34:22 |
| II Chronicles 35:6 | Psalm 14:6 | Psalm 34:7 |
| II Chronicles 6:36 | Psalm 14:7 | Psalm 34:8 |
| Ezra 2:1 | Psalm 141:8 | Psalm 35:11 |
| Ezra 3:6 | Psalm 142:5 | Psalm 36:7 |
| Ezra 6:20 | Psalm 143:9 | Psalm 37:11 |
| Ezra 9:13 | Psalm 144:2 | Psalm 37:39 |
| Ezra 9:9 | Psalm 148:14 | Psalm 37:40 |
| Nehemiah 1:10 | Psalm 16:1 | Psalm 38:13-14 |
| Nehemiah 9:15 | Psalm 16:10 | Psalm 39:7 |
| Nehemiah 9:20 | Psalm 17:7 | Psalm 41:9 |
| Nehemiah 9:27 | Psalm 18:2 | Psalm 43:3 |

| | | |
|---|---|---|
| Psalm 46:1 | Psalm 80:1 | Isaiah 12:6 |
| Psalm 47: 2 | Psalm 80:15 | Isaiah 14:32 |
| Psalm 47: 7 | Psalm 89:18 | Isaiah 16:1 |
| Psalm 49:7-9 | Psalm 89:27-29 | Isaiah 17:10 |
| Psalm 5:11 | Psalm 91:2 | Isaiah 17:7 |
| Psalm 52:7 | Psalm 91:4 | Isaiah 2:12 |
| Psalm 53:6 | Psalm 91:9 | Isaiah 22:22 |
| Psalm 55:18 | Psalm 94:22 | Isaiah 25:4 |
| Psalm 55:8 | Psalm 95:1 | Isaiah 26:4 |
| Psalm 57:1 | Proverbs 12:28 | Isaiah 28:16 |
| Psalm 57:3 | Proverbs 14:32 | Isaiah 29:19 |
| Psalm 59:16 | Proverbs 14:26 | Isaiah 30:11-12 |
| Psalm 61:3 | Proverbs 16:6 | Isaiah 30:15 |
| Psalm 61:4 | Proverbs 23:11 | Isaiah 31:1 |
| Psalm 62:1 | Proverbs 30:4 | Isaiah 32:2 |
| Psalm 62:1-2 | Proverbs 30:5 | Isaiah 35:1-2 |
| Psalm 62:5 | Ecclesiastes 3:11 | Isaiah 37:23 |
| Psalm 62:6-7 | Ecclesiastes 7:20 | Isaiah 37:36 |
| Psalm 62:8 | SS 2:1 | Isaiah 4:2 |
| Psalm 64:10 | SS 2:12 | Isaiah 4:6 |
| Psalm 65:7 | SS 2:16 | Isaiah 40:11 |
| Psalm 69:18 | SS 2:4 | Isaiah 40:3-5 |
| Psalm 69:21 | SS 4:12 | Isaiah 41:14 |
| Psalm 7:1 | SS 4:7 | Isaiah 41:16 |
| Psalm 71:1 | SS 4:9-10 | Isaiah 41:20 |
| Psalm 71:22 | SS 5:1 | Isaiah 42:1 |
| Psalm 71:3 | SS 5:16 | Isaiah 43:1 |
| Psalm 71:5 | SS 6:1-3 | Isaiah 43:14 |
| Psalm 71:7 | SS 8:6a | Isaiah 43:14-15 |
| Psalm 72:10-11 | Isaiah 1:11 | Isaiah 43:3 |
| Psalm 73:28 | Isaiah 1:4 | Isaiah 44:24 |
| Psalm 78:20 | Isaiah 10: 31-32 | Isaiah 44:6 |
| Psalm 78:2-4 | Isaiah 10:17 | Isaiah 45:11 |
| Psalm 78:35 | Isaiah 10:20 | Isaiah 45:17 |
| Psalm 78:41 | Isaiah 11:1 | Isaiah 45:22-23 |
| Psalm 8:4-6 | Isaiah 11:10 | Isaiah 47:4 |

| | | |
|---|---|---|
| Isaiah 48:12 | Isaiah 9:1-2 | Jeremiah 7:11 |
| Isaiah 48:16 | Isaiah 9:2 | Jeremiah 9:25 |
| Isaiah 48:17 | Isaiah 9:6-7 | Jeremiah 26:7-8 |
| Isaiah 48:21 | Jeremiah 10:10 | Jeremiah 37:15-16 |
| Isaiah 49:16 | Jeremiah 11:19 | Lam. 2:3 (KJV) |
| Isaiah 49:6 | Jeremiah 14:8 | Lam. 3:20-22 |
| Isaiah 49:7 | Jeremiah 16:14-15 | Lam. 3:58 |
| Isaiah 49:26 | Jeremiah 16:19 | Lam. 5:21 |
| Isaiah 49:8 | Jeremiah 17:13 | Ezekiel 14:3-4, 7 |
| Isaiah 5:19 | Jeremiah 17:17 | Ezekiel 16:63 |
| Isaiah 5:24 | Jeremiah 2:13 | Ezekiel 17:2 |
| Isaiah 52:7 | Jeremiah 2:21 | Ezekiel 17:22-23 |
| Isaiah 53:2 | Jeremiah 20:2 | Ezekiel 18:30 |
| Isaiah 53:3 | Jeremiah 23:3 | Ezekiel 2:1 |
| Isaiah 53:5 | Jeremiah 23:5 | Ezekiel 9:2-4 |
| Isaiah 53:7 | Jeremiah 23:6 | Ezekiel 20:49 |
| Isaiah 53:9 | Jeremiah 23:7 | Ezekiel 29:21 |
| Isaiah 54:5 | Jeremiah 3:15-18 | Ezekiel 34:23 |
| Isaiah 54:8 | Jeremiah 3:23b | Ezekiel 37:11-14 |
| Isaiah 55:5 | Jeremiah 30:3 | Ezekiel 37:24 |
| Isaiah 55:7 | Jeremiah 30:9 | Ezekiel 37:25-26 |
| Isaiah 57:13 | Jeremiah 31:11 | Ezekiel 39:25 |
| Isaiah 59:20 | Jeremiah 31:15 | Ezekiel 39:7 |
| Isaiah 6:8 | Jeremiah 31:31 | Ezekiel 40:3 |
| Isaiah 60:1 | Jeremiah 31:38 | Ezekiel 44:12 |
| Isaiah 60:3 | Jeremiah 32:2 | Ezekiel 45:21 |
| Isaiah 60:4-10 | Jeremiah 33:14 | Ezekiel 46:6 |
| Isaiah 60: 19-20 | Jeremiah 33:14-18 | Daniel 2:20-22 |
| Isaiah 60:14 | Jeremiah 33:15 | Daniel 2:44-45 |
| Isaiah 60:16 | Jeremiah 33:26 | Daniel 7:13-14 |
| Isaiah 60:18-20 | Jeremiah 33:8 | Daniel 7:9 |
| Isaiah 60:9 | Jeremiah 38:6 | Daniel 9:25-26 |
| Isaiah 61:1-4 | Jeremiah 50:20 | Daniel 10:5, 16-19 |
| Isaiah 63:16 | Jeremiah 50:29 | Daniel 12:7 |
| Isaiah 63:9 | Jeremiah 50:34 | Hosea 11:1 |
| Isaiah 7:14 | Jeremiah 51:5 | Hosea 12:4-5 |
| Isaiah 8:14 | Jeremiah 6:21 | Hosea 13:14 |

Hosea 13:14
Hosea 13:4
Hosea 14:5
Hosea 5:14
Hosea 6:2
Joel 1:12
Joel 2:32
Joel 3:16
Joel 3:18
Amos 5:18
Amos 5:20
Amos 8:11
Amos 8:9
Amos 9:11
Amos 9:13
Obadiah 1:15
Obadiah 1:17
Jonah 1:17
Jonah 1:4-9
Jonah 12-16
Jonah 2:9-10
Jonah 3:1
Micah 2:12-13
Micah 4:1-7
Micah 5:2-4
Micah 5:4-5
Micah 6:4
Micah 7:2a
Micah 7:7-9
Nahum 1:15
Nahum 1:3a
Nahum 1:4
Nahum 1:7
Nahum 2:2
Habakkuk 2:14
Habakkuk 2:3

Habakkuk 2:4
Habakkuk 3:13
Zephaniah 1:7
Zephaniah 3:12
Zephaniah 3:15
Haggai 2:20-23
Haggai 2:6-7
Haggai 2:9
Zechariah 1:7-14
Zechariah 10:3-4
Zechariah 11:12-13
Zechariah 12:10
Zechariah 12:3
Zechariah 12:8
Zechariah 13:1
Zechariah 13:6-7
Zechariah 14:1-9
Zechariah 14:4
Zechariah 14:8
Zechariah 14:9
Zechariah 2:10
Zechariah 3:1-7
Zechariah 3:8
Zechariah 6:12
Zechariah 8:3
Zechariah 9:9
Malachi 3:1
Malachi 4:5

# Identification of Scarlet Thread Categories, by Book

| BOOK | Pre-incarnate | Typology | Prophecy | Concept | Potpourri |
|------|-----------|----------|----------|---------|-----------|
| Genesis | X | X | X | X | X |
| Exodus | X | X | X | X | X |
| Leviticus | | X | | X | X |
| Numbers | X | X | X | X | X |
| Deuteronomy | | X | | X | X |
| Joshua | | X | | | X |
| Judges | X | X | | | X |
| Ruth | | X | | | |
| I Samuel | | X | X | | X |
| II Samuel | X | X | X | | X |
| I Kings | X | X | X | | X |
| II Kings | X | X | X | X | X |
| I Chronicles | X | X | X | | X |
| II Chronicles | | X | X | X | |
| Ezra | | X | | X | X |
| Nehemiah | | X | | | X |
| Esther | | X | | X | |
| Job | | X | | | X |
| Psalms | X | X | X | X | X |
| Proverbs | | X | | X | X |
| Ecclesiastes | | X | | X | |
| S.S. | | X | | | X |
| Isaiah | X | X | X | X | X |
| Jeremiah | | X | X | X | X |
| Lamentations | | X | | | X |
| Ezekiel | | X | X | X | X |
| Daniel | | X | X | | |
| Hosea | X | X | X | | X |
| Joel | | X | X | | X |
| Amos | | X | X | | |

# Reference Information

| BOOK | Pre-incarnate | Typology | Prophecy | Concept | Potpourri |
|------|---------------|----------|----------|---------|-----------|
| Obadiah | | X | X | | X |
| Jonah | | X | | X | |
| Micah | | X | X | X | |
| Nahum | | X | X | | X |
| Habakkuk | | X | X | | X |
| Zephaniah | | X | X | | |
| Haggai | | X | X | | |
| Zechariah | X | X | X | | X |
| Malachi | | X | X | | X |

# The Scarlet Thread

About the Author/Publisher...

Eleanor P. Hamilton is a wife, mother, and grandmother, currently living in Maryland. She accepted Jesus as Savior and Lord of her life at an early age, and has sought since then to serve Him in whatever positions the Spirit has set before her, generally doing so in children's or women's ministries.

Eleanor is writer and publisher of Children's Ministry curriculum and resources. In 2004, she began Autumn Light Publications for the purpose of making materials that she has used repeatedly in her own classes available to others who teach and lead children.

*The Scarlet Thread*, though not directly a Children's Ministry resource, is included in the Autumn Light lineup as one more tool to "build up" the Children's Ministry leader, or any other Christian adult, through the study of God's Word.

CPSIA information can be obtained
at www.ICGtesting.com
Printed in the USA
BVHW01s0844230118
506061BV00021B/347/P